taste of home
almost
HOMEMADE

EDITORIAL
Editor-in-Chief Catherine Cassidy

Executive Editor/Print & Digital Books Stephen C. George
Creative Director Howard Greenberg
Editorial Services Manager Kerri Balliet

Senior Editor/Print & Digital Books Mark Hagen
Editor Krista Lanphier
Associate Creative Director Edwin Robles Jr.
Art Director Raeann Sundholm
Content Production Manager Julie Wagner
Contributing Layout Designer Matt Fukuda
Copy Chief Deb Warlaumont Mulvey
Copy Editor Mary C. Hanson
Recipe Editor Mary King
Recipe Content Manager Colleen King
Assistant Photo Coordinator Mary Ann Koebernik
Recipe Testing Taste of Home Test Kitchen
Food Photography Taste of Home Photo Studio
Editorial Assistant Marilyn Iczkowski

BUSINESS
Vice President, Publisher Jan Studin, jan_studin@rd.com
Regional Account Director Donna Lindskog, donna_lindskog@rd.com
Eastern Account Director Joanne Carrara
Eastern Account Manager Kari Nestor
Account Manager Gina Minerbi
Midwest & Western Account Director Jackie Fallon
Midwest Account Manager Lorna Phillips
Michigan Sales Representative Linda C. Donaldson
Southwestern Account Representative Summer Nilsson

Corporate Digital & Integrated Sales Director, N.A. Steve Sottile
Associate Marketing Director, Integrated Solutions Katie Gaon Wilson
Digital Sales Planner Tim Baarda

General Manager, Taste of Home Cooking Schools Erin Puariea

Direct Response Advertising Katherine Zito, David Geller Associates

Vice President, Creative Director Paul Livornese
Executive Director, Brand Marketing Leah West
Senior Marketing Manager Vanessa Bailey
Associate Marketing Manager Betsy Connors

Vice President, Magazine Marketing Dave Fiegel

READER'S DIGEST NORTH AMERICA
Vice President, Business Development Jonathan Bigham
President, Books and Home Entertaining Harold Clarke
Chief Financial Officer Howard Halligan
Vice President, General Manager, Reader's Digest Media Marilynn Jacobs
Chief Content Officer, Milwaukee Mark Jannot
Chief Marketing Officer Renee Jordan
Vice President, Chief Sales Officer Mark Josephson
General Manager, Milwaukee Frank Quigley
Vice President, Chief Content Officer Liz Vaccariello

THE READER'S DIGEST ASSOCIATION, INC.
President and Chief Executive Officer Robert E. Guth

COVER PHOTOGRAPHY
Photographer Dan Roberts
Food Stylist Sue Draheim
Set Styling Manager Stephanie Marchese

Pictured on the front cover Cheesy Shell Lasagna, p. 161
Pictured on the back cover Maple-Mocha Brownie Torte, p. 194,
Southwest Burgers, p. 222

©2012 Reiman Media Group, LLC
5400 S. 60th St., Greendale WI 53129

International Standard Book Number: 978-1-61765-143-4
International Standard Serial Number: 2154-4662

table of contents

Introduction 4

Snacks & Appetizers 6

Breakfast & Brunch 30

Standout Side Dishes 52

Bountiful Breads 78

Sensational Soups 100

Memorable Main Courses 118

All-in-One Dinners 142

Slow Cooker Cuisine 166

Delectable Desserts 184

Holidays & Parties 212

Indexes 242

homemade *flavor*
WITHOUT
THE WORK!

Short on time? If a tight schedule is what's keeping you from setting hearty meals on the table, then welcome to **Taste of Home Almost Homemade!** This collection of quick and easy recipes makes it a snap to serve comforting favorites by combining packaged or frozen goods with fresh and wholesome ingredients.

Each of the **288 delicious dishes** found here turns a boxed mix, jarred sauce, canned good, frozen veggie or other convenience item into a fuss-free specialty loaded with **from-scratch flavor!** That means less work for you and fewer trips to expensive fast-food joints. Best of all, you'll have ample time to enjoy a **hot and satisfying meal** with your family...even on your busiest nights!

I searched a long time for an easy banana bread recipe. This one takes no time at all because a yellow cake mix streamlines preparation. The fact that the recipe makes two moist, golden loaves is a bonus.
—MARIE DAVIS
PENDLETON, SOUTH CAROLINA

easy shortcuts WITH IMPRESSIVE RESULTS

For on-the-go cooks, it's a cinch to use packaged pantry ingredients to add zing to a recipe or cut down on prep time—and we show you how. Dried stuffing and sauce mixes, jarred mushrooms, canned artichoke hearts or prepared pesto are all efficient, time-saving ingredients to **add pizzazz** to your dishes.

While at the grocery store, stock up on ready-made items such as creamy canned soups, frozen vegetable medleys, rotisserie chicken or frozen phyllo dough, then just add a few ingredients at home for a dish that's both easier and yummier than pricey takeout!

You'll find dozens of **quick-to-fix** recipes here, from finger-lickin' appetizers to scrumptious desserts, and all are as easy on the pocketbook as they are to prepare. Don't worry—we'll keep these amazing shortcuts your secret. Your family won't be able to tell the difference between these dishes and ones that are completely homemade!

reliable recipes from HOME COOKS JUST LIKE YOU!

Most recipes in this cookbook come from real cooks just like you! Every recipe has been tasted, tested and approved by our **Test Kitchen** professionals, so you can be sure that you're serving your family the very best. Plus, you'll find helpful tips and cooking advice throughout the book.

With easy-to-follow directions and beautiful color photographs, *Taste of Home Almost Homemade* will be the most valuable recipe source in your kitchen!

66 These wings are everything you love about chicken—crispy on the outside with a moist and tender center—including Southwestern zip.
—**BLANCHE GIBSON** GORDON, WISCONSIN

snacks & appetizers

Yummy and quick-to-fix, these bites are ready in a flash, leaving you plenty of time to spare for finishing up other tasks or spending time with family and friends.

Chicken, Pear & Gorgonzola Tarts

PREP: 30 MIN. • **COOK:** 5 MIN. • **YIELD:** 2½ DOZEN

I've been experimenting with candied bacon and tried incorporating it into some of my favorite recipes. These little bites are a hit wherever I take them. They're a great way to use up leftover chicken, but you can leave it out entirely if you want. Feel free to get creative with garnishing the tasty bites.

—KATHLEEN BOULANGER
WILLISTON, VERMONT

- 8   bacon strips
- 1½ teaspoons brown sugar
- ¼   teaspoon ground cinnamon
- ¾   cup finely chopped cooked chicken breast
- ⅓   cup pear nectar
- ¼   cup finely chopped dried pears
- 3   tablespoons apricot preserves
- 2   teaspoons butter
- ¼   teaspoon salt
- ¼   teaspoon pepper
- 2   packages (1.9 ounces each) frozen miniature phyllo tart shells
- ⅓   cup crumbled Gorgonzola cheese

1. Place bacon in a 15-in. x 10-in. x 1-in. baking pan; broil 4 in. from the heat for 4-6 minutes on each side or until crisp. Combine brown sugar and cinnamon; sprinkle over bacon. Broil 1 minute longer or until bacon is glazed and bubbly. Drain on paper towels. Cool slightly and crumble.

2. In a small skillet, combine the chicken, pear nectar, pears, preserves, butter, salt and pepper. Bring to a boil; cook, stirring occasionally, for 3-4 minutes or until thickened. Spoon about 1 teaspoonful of filling into each tart shell; place tarts on a baking sheet. Sprinkle with bacon and cheese.

3. Bake at 350° for 5-7 minutes or until heated through. Serve warm.

Cheesy Onion Roll-Ups

These roll-ups are very fast to fix and perfect for taking to parties. You can make them ahead, then keep them wrapped in the refrigerator until you're ready to leave.
—**BARBARA KEITH** FAUCETT, MISSOURI

PREP: 20 MIN. + CHILLING • **YIELD:** ABOUT 5 DOZEN

- 1 cup (8 ounces) sour cream
- 1 package (8 ounces) cream cheese, softened
- ½ cup finely shredded cheddar cheese
- ¾ cup sliced green onions
- 1 tablespoon lime juice
- 1 tablespoon minced seeded jalapeno pepper
- 1 package (10 ounces) flour tortillas (6 inches), warmed
  Picante sauce

1. In a large bowl, combine the first six ingredients. Spread over each tortilla and roll up tightly. Wrap and refrigerate for at least 1 hour. Slice into 1-in. pieces. Serve with picante sauce.

EDITOR'S NOTE: Wear disposable gloves when cutting hot peppers; the oils can burn skin. Avoid touching your face.

No-Bones Chicken Wing Dip

My hot party dip delivers all the great flavor of the chicken wings we love to snack on—no bones about it!
—**SHIRLEY GAWLIK** OAKFIELD, NEW YORK

PREP: 15 MIN. • **BAKE:** 25 MIN. • **YIELD:** 6½ CUPS

- 1 package (8 ounces) cream cheese, softened
- 2 cups (16 ounces) sour cream
- 1 cup blue cheese salad dressing
- ½ cup buffalo wing sauce
- 2½ cups shredded cooked chicken
- 2 cups (8 ounces) provolone cheese
  Baby carrots, celery ribs and crackers

1. In a large bowl, beat the cream cheese, sour cream, salad dressing and buffalo wing sauce until blended. Stir in chicken and provolone cheese.

2. Transfer to a greased 2-qt. baking dish. Cover and bake at 350° for 25-30 minutes or until hot and bubbly. Serve warm with carrots, celery and crackers.

Pineapple and almonds
enhance the creamy
chicken salad in these
cute tartlets made with
convenient refrigerated
pie pastry.
—LOIS HOLDSON
MILLERSVILLE,
MARYLAND

Chicken Salad Cups

PREP: 30 MIN. + CHILLING • **BAKE:** 10 MIN. + COOLING
YIELD: 14 SERVINGS

- 1 **package (15 ounces) refrigerated pie pastry**
- 2 **cups cubed cooked chicken**
- 1 **can (8 ounces) unsweetened crushed pineapple, drained**
- ½ **cup slivered almonds**
- ½ **cup chopped celery**
- ½ **cup shredded cheddar cheese**
- ½ **cup mayonnaise**
- ½ **teaspoon salt**
- ½ **teaspoon paprika**

TOPPING:
- ½ **cup sour cream**
- ¼ **cup mayonnaise**
- ½ **cup shredded cheddar cheese**

1. Cut each sheet of pie pastry into 4½-in. rounds; reroll scraps and cut out additional circles. Press pastry onto the bottom and up the sides of 14 ungreased muffin cups.

2. Bake at 450° for 6-7 minutes or until golden brown. Cool on a wire rack.

3. In a large bowl, combine the chicken, pineapple, almonds, celery, cheese, mayonnaise, salt and paprika; refrigerate until chilled.

4. Just before serving, spoon two rounded tablespoonfuls of chicken salad into each pastry cup. Combine sour cream and mayonnaise; spoon over filling. Sprinkle with cheese.

Feta Pitas

Toasty pitas sprinkled with tasty toppings always get rave reviews. These pizza-like snacks are both fun and filling.
—**TAMMY LYNN SMITH** LIVE OAK, TEXAS

PREP/TOTAL TIME: 20 MIN. • **YIELD:** 6 SERVINGS

- 6 **whole pita breads**
- 1½ **cups (6 ounces) crumbled feta cheese**
- 3 **teaspoons Italian seasoning**
- ¾ **cup thinly sliced red onion**
- 1 **small tomato, thinly sliced**

1. Place pita breads on an ungreased baking sheet. Sprinkle with cheese and Italian seasoning. Top with onion and tomato.

2. Bake at 350° for 10-12 minutes. Cut into wedges if desired. Serve immediately.

Party Meatballs

PREP: 40 MIN. • **BAKE:** 15 MIN. • **YIELD:** ABOUT 5 DOZEN

- ¾ **cup evaporated milk**
- 1 **envelope onion soup mix**
- 1 **tablespoon plus 2 teaspoons Worcestershire sauce, divided**
- 2 **pounds ground beef**
- 2 **cups ketchup**
- 1 **cup packed brown sugar**

1. In a large bowl, combine the milk, soup mix and 2 teaspoons Worcestershire sauce. Crumble beef over mixture and mix well.

2. With wet hands, shape into 1-in. balls. Place meatballs on a greased rack in a shallow baking pan. Bake, uncovered, at 400° for 12 minutes or until meat is no longer pink. Drain on paper towels.

3. Meanwhile, combine the ketchup, brown sugar and remaining Worcestershire sauce in a large saucepan or Dutch oven. Bring to a boil over medium heat. Cook and stir until thickened. Reduce heat; add meatballs. Simmer until heated through, about 15 minutes.

These meatballs in a sweet, tangy sauce can be made a day in advance and reheated. They're terrific for big family gatherings.
—**IRMA SCHNUELLE** MANITOWOC, WISCONSIN

3. Line a 15-in. x 10-in. x 1-in. baking pan with foil and heavily grease the foil. Using a slotted spoon, place wings in pan. Discard marinade. Bake, uncovered, at 375° for 30 minutes, turning once.

4. Meanwhile, in a small saucepan, bring reserved raspberry mixture to a boil. Reduce heat; simmer, uncovered, for 10-15 minutes or until thickened. Brush over wings.

5. Bake 20-25 minutes longer or until chicken juices run clear, turning and basting once.

Pretty Pumpkin Wontons

This versatile and easy recipe is perfect as an appetizer, snack or dessert. The flavors meld beautifully, and everyone loves it! I made it up after having squash ravioli at a restaurant and wanting to put my own twist on the dish.
—**JONI HILTON** ROCKLIN, CALIFORNIA

PREP: 40 MIN. • **COOK:** 15 MIN.
YIELD: 40 WONTONS (1½ CUPS DIP)

- 1 can (15 ounces) solid-pack pumpkin
- 1 cup ricotta cheese
- 1 teaspoon salt
- 40 wonton wrappers
  Oil for deep-fat frying
DIP:
- 1 cup confectioners' sugar
- ½ cup sour cream
- ½ cup apricot preserves
- 1 teaspoon ground cinnamon

1. In a small bowl, combine the pumpkin, cheese and salt. Place 1 tablespoonful in the center of a wonton wrapper. (Keep remaining wrappers covered with a damp paper towel until ready to use.) Moisten edges with water; bring corners to center over filling and press edges together to seal. Repeat.

2. In an electric skillet or deep-fat fryer, heat oil to 375°. Fry wontons in batches for 30-60 seconds on each side or until golden brown. Drain on paper towels.

3. Meanwhile, in a small bowl, combine dip ingredients. Serve with wontons.

These fruity glazed wings are a staple at our house. Not only are they great for entertaining, but they also make a tasty entree with rice.
—**SUE SEYMOUR** VALATIE, NEW YORK

Raspberry Glazed Wings

PREP: 50 MIN. + MARINATING • **BAKE:** 50 MIN.
YIELD: 10-12 SERVINGS

- 1½ cups seedless raspberry jam
- ½ cup cider vinegar
- ½ cup soy sauce
- 6 garlic cloves, minced
- 2 teaspoons pepper
- 16 chicken wings (about 3 pounds)

1. In a large saucepan, combine the jam, vinegar, soy sauce, garlic and pepper. Bring to a boil; boil for 1 minute.

2. Cut chicken wings into three sections; discard wing tips. Place wings in a large bowl; add half of the raspberry mixture and toss to coat. Cover and refrigerate for 4 hours. Cover and refrigerate remaining raspberry mixture.

Hot Spinach Artichoke Dip

PREP/TOTAL TIME: 25 MIN. • **YIELD:** 2 CUPS

- 1 jar (6½ ounces) marinated artichoke hearts, drained and chopped
- 2 tablespoons chopped onion
- 1 tablespoon butter, softened
- 1 package (10 ounces) frozen chopped spinach, thawed and well drained
- ¼ cup grated Parmesan cheese
- 2 cups (8 ounces) shredded Colby/Monterey Jack cheese
- ½ cup milk
- ¾ teaspoon Creole seasoning
  Vegetables, tortilla chips or crackers

1. In a skillet, saute artichokes and onion in butter until onion is tender. Stir in spinach and Parmesan cheese; cook over low heat until spinach is heated through. Add Colby/Monterey Jack cheese, milk and Creole seasoning; heat until cheese is melted. Serve immediately with vegetables, tortilla chips or crackers.

EDITOR'S NOTE: The following spices may be substituted for 1 teaspoon Creole seasoning: ¼ teaspoon each of dried thyme, ground cumin and cayenne pepper.

Makeover Garlic Spinach Balls

These pop-in-your-mouth nibblers not only taste sensational, they're also a great way to get picky eaters to eat their spinach!
—**AMY HORNBUCKLE** PRATTVILLE, ALABAMA

PREP: 25 MIN. • **BAKE:** 15 MIN. • **YIELD:** 2 DOZEN

2	cups crushed seasoned stuffing
1	cup finely chopped onion
¾	cup egg substitute
1	egg, lightly beaten
¼	cup grated Parmesan cheese
¼	cup butter, melted
3	tablespoons reduced-sodium chicken broth or vegetable broth
1	garlic clove, minced
1½	teaspoons dried thyme
¼	teaspoon pepper
⅛	teaspoon salt
2	packages (10 ounces each) frozen chopped spinach, thawed and squeezed dry

1. In a large bowl, combine the first 11 ingredients. Stir in spinach until blended. Roll into 1-in. balls.

2. Place in a 15-in. x 10-in. x 1-in. baking pan coated with cooking spray. Bake at 350° for 15-20 minutes or until golden brown.

Perfect for parties, this quick dip features flavors of the Southwest with chili, guacamole and cheese. It's ideal for movie night, the big game or whenever guests drop in unexpectedly and you need something fast—and tasty.
—**MARTHA BLONDE** LANSING, MICHIGAN

Chili Cheese Dip

PREP/TOTAL TIME: 10 MIN. • **YIELD:** 3 CUPS

1	can (15 ounces) chili without beans
1½	cups (6 ounces) shredded cheddar cheese
1	cup chopped lettuce
1	cup prepared guacamole dip
	Tortilla chips

1. In a large microwave-safe serving bowl, microwave chili on high for 2-3 minutes or until heated through. Top with cheese, lettuce and guacamole. Serve with chips.

EDITOR'S NOTE: This recipe was tested in a 1,100-watt microwave.

Chicken Taco Cups

PREP: 20 MIN. • **BAKE:** 20 MIN. • **YIELD:** 3 DOZEN

- 1 **pound boneless skinless chicken breasts, cut into 1-inch pieces**
- 1 **envelope reduced-sodium taco seasoning**
- 1 **small onion, chopped**
- 1 **jar (16 ounces) salsa, divided**
- 2 **cups (8 ounces) shredded reduced-fat cheddar cheese, divided**
- 36 **wonton wrappers**
  Sour cream, chopped green onions and chopped ripe olives, optional

1. Sprinkle chicken with taco seasoning. In a large skillet coated with cooking spray, cook and stir the chicken over medium heat for 5 minutes or until meat is no longer pink.

2. Transfer chicken to a food processor; cover and process until chopped. In a large bowl, combine the chicken, onion, half of the salsa and 1 cup cheese.

3. Press wonton wrappers into miniature muffin cups coated with cooking spray. Bake at 375° for 5 minutes or until lightly browned.

4. Spoon rounded tablespoonfuls of chicken mixture into cups; top with remaining salsa and cheese. Bake 15 minutes longer or until heated through. Serve warm. Garnish with sour cream, green onions and olives if desired.

Corny Chocolate Crunch

Here's a crispy snack that's easy and appeals to noshers of all ages. Mix up a batch and just watch it disappear!
—**DELORES WARD** DECATUR, INDIANA

PREP/TOTAL TIME: 20 MIN. • **YIELD:** ABOUT 5 QUARTS

- 3 quarts popped popcorn
- 3 cups Corn Chex
- 3 cups broken corn chips
- 1 package (10 to 11 ounces) butterscotch chips
- 12 ounces dark chocolate candy coating, coarsely chopped

1. In a large bowl, combine the popcorn, cereal and corn chips; set aside. In a microwave, melt butterscotch chips and candy coating; stir until smooth.

2. Pour over popcorn mixture and toss to coat. Spread into two greased 15-in. x 10-in. x 1-in. baking pans. When cool enough to handle, break into pieces.

Marshmallow Fruit Dip

Dress up any fresh fruit with a sweet, creamy dip that takes just 10 minutes to blend together. I serve it in a bowl surrounded by fresh strawberries at spring brunches, showers or luncheons.
—**CINDY STEFFEN** CEDARBURG, WISCONSIN

PREP/TOTAL TIME: 10 MIN. • **YIELD:** 5 CUPS

- 1 package (8 ounces) cream cheese, softened
- ¾ cup (6 ounces) cherry yogurt
- 1 carton (8 ounces) frozen whipped topping, thawed
- 1 jar (7 ounces) marshmallow creme
  Assorted fresh fruit

1. In a large bowl, beat cream cheese and yogurt until blended. Fold in whipped topping and marshmallow creme. Serve with fruit.

Crab Spread

PREP/TOTAL TIME: 20 MIN. • **YIELD:** 2 CUPS

- 1 **package (8 ounces) cream cheese, softened**
- 1 **can (6 ounces) crabmeat, drained, flaked and cartilage removed**
- 2 **tablespoons mayonnaise**
- 1 **teaspoon Dijon mustard**
- ½ **teaspoon lemon-pepper seasoning**
- ¼ **teaspoon minced garlic**
  Paprika
  Assorted crackers or vegetables

1. In a small bowl, combine the first six ingredients. To serve chilled, cover and refrigerate until serving. Sprinkle with paprika.

2. To serve warm, spoon into a greased 3-cup baking dish. Bake, uncovered, at 375° for 15 minutes or until heated through. Serve with crackers or vegetables.

faux crabmeat

Imitation crabmeat, most often made with Alaskan pollack, can be substituted for real crab in equal proportions in many recipes. However, keep in mind that the flavor and texture will be different than if you use canned crabmeat.

Chicken Salad In Baskets

PREP: 15 MIN. • **BAKE:** 15 MIN. + CHILLING
YIELD: 20 APPETIZERS

- 1 **cup diced cooked chicken**
- 3 **bacon strips, cooked and crumbled**
- 1/3 **cup chopped mushrooms**
- 2 **tablespoons chopped pecans**
- 2 **tablespoons diced peeled apple**
- 1/4 **cup mayonnaise**
- 1/8 **teaspoon salt**
  Dash pepper
- 20 **slices bread**
- 6 **tablespoons butter, melted**
- 2 **tablespoons minced fresh parsley**

1. In a small bowl, combine the first five ingredients. Combine the mayonnaise, salt and pepper; add to chicken mixture and stir to coat. Cover and refrigerate until serving.

2. Cut each slice of bread with a 3-in. round cookie cutter; brush both sides with butter. Press into ungreased mini muffin cups. Bake at 350° for 11-13 minutes or until golden brown and crisp.

3. Cool for 3 minutes before removing from pans to wire racks to cool completely. Spoon 1 tablespoonful chicken salad into each bread basket. Cover and refrigerate for up to 2 hours. Just before serving, sprinkle with parsley.

Asparagus Snack Squares

PREP: 25 MIN. • **BAKE:** 15 MIN. • **YIELD:** 36 SERVINGS

- 1   **cup chopped sweet onion**
- 3   **tablespoons butter**
- 2   **garlic cloves, minced**
- 1   **pound fresh asparagus, trimmed**
- ¼   **teaspoon pepper**
- 2   **tubes (8 ounces each) refrigerated crescent rolls**
- 1   **cup (4 ounces) shredded part-skim mozzarella cheese**
- 1   **cup (4 ounces) shredded Swiss cheese**

1. In a large skillet, saute onion in butter until tender. Add garlic; cook 1 minute longer.

2. Cut asparagus into 1-in. pieces; set the tips aside. Add remaining asparagus to skillet; saute until crisp-tender. Add asparagus tips and pepper; saute 1-2 minutes longer or until asparagus is tender.

3. Press dough into an ungreased 15-in. x 10-in. x 1-in. baking pan; seal seams and perforations. Bake at 375° for 6-8 minutes or until lightly browned.

4. Top with asparagus mixture; sprinkle with cheeses. Bake 6-8 minutes longer or until cheese is melted. Cut into squares.

Horseradish Ham Cubes

Looking for a zesty twist on the same old ham roll-ups? See what a hefty dash of horseradish brings to the party!
—**CONNIE TOLLEY** OAK HILL, WEST VIRGINIA

PREP: 15 MIN. + CHILLING • **YIELD:** ABOUT 5 DOZEN

- 1 package (8 ounces) cream cheese, softened
- 2 tablespoons prepared horseradish
- 1 teaspoon Worcestershire sauce
- ½ teaspoon seasoned salt
- ⅛ teaspoon pepper
- 10 square slices deli ham

1. In a small bowl, beat the cream cheese, horseradish, Worcestershire sauce, seasoned salt and pepper.

2. Set aside 2 ham slices; spread about 2 tablespoons of cream cheese mixture over each remaining slice. Make two stacks, using four ham slices for each; top each stack with reserved slices. Wrap each stack in plastic wrap and chill for 4 hours. Cut each stack into 1-in. cubes.

Crispy Taco Wings

These wings are everything you love about chicken—crispy on the outside with a moist and tender center—including Southwestern zip.
—**BLANCHE GIBSON** GORDON, WISCONSIN

PREP: 15 MIN. • **BAKE:** 30 MIN. • **YIELD:** 2 DOZEN

- ½ cup all-purpose flour
- 1 envelope taco seasoning
- 2½ pounds chicken wingettes and drummettes
- ½ cup butter, melted
- 1¾ cups crushed corn chips

1. In a large shallow bowl, combine flour and taco seasoning. Add wings, a few at a time, and coat. Place butter and corn chips in separate shallow bowls. Dip wings in butter, then coat with chips.

2. Transfer to a greased 15-in. x 10-in. x 1-in. baking pan. Bake, uncovered, at 350° for 30-40 minutes or until juices run clear.

Apple-Nut Blue Cheese Tartlets

PREP: 25 MIN. • BAKE: 10 MIN. • YIELD: 15 APPETIZERS

- 1 large apple, peeled and finely chopped
- 1 medium onion, finely chopped
- 2 teaspoons butter
- 1 cup (4 ounces) crumbled blue cheese
- 4 tablespoons finely chopped walnuts, toasted, divided
- ½ teaspoon salt
- 1 package (1.9 ounces) frozen miniature phyllo tart shells

1. In a small nonstick skillet, saute apple and onion in butter until tender. Remove from the heat; stir in the blue cheese, 3 tablespoons walnuts and salt. Spoon a rounded tablespoonful into each tart shell.

2. Place on an ungreased baking sheet. Bake at 350° for 5 minutes. Sprinkle with remaining walnuts; bake 2-3 minutes longer or until lightly browned.

Brie in Puff Pastry

My husband was in the Air Force, so we've entertained guests in many parts of the world. I acquired this recipe while in California, and it's still one of my very favorite appetizers.
—**SANDRA TWAIT** TAMPA, FLORIDA

PREP: 15 MIN. • BAKE: 20 MIN. + STANDING
YIELD: 10 SERVINGS

- 1 round (13.2 ounces) Brie cheese
- ½ cup crumbled blue cheese
- 1 sheet frozen puff pastry, thawed
- ¼ cup apricot jam
- ½ cup slivered almonds, toasted
- 1 egg, lightly beaten
  Assorted crackers

1. Slice Brie horizontally in half. Sprinkle one cut side of Brie with blue cheese; top with remaining Brie.

2. On a lightly floured surface, roll out pastry into a 14-in. square. Cut off corners to make a circle. Spread jam to within 1 in. of pastry edge; sprinkle with nuts. Place Brie on top; fold pastry over the cheese and pinch edges to seal.

These blue cheese tarts may look and taste gourmet, but they're easy to make and have loads of flavor. For convenience, make the phyllo shells and filling in advance, then just fill the cups and warm them in the oven before serving.
—**TRISHA KRUSE** EAGLE, IDAHO

3. Place seam side down on an ungreased baking sheet. Brush top and sides of pastry with egg. Bake at 400° for 20 minutes or until golden brown. Immediately remove from the baking sheet. Let stand for 1 hour before serving. Serve with crackers.

1. Unroll crescent dough and press onto the bottom and ½ in. up the sides of an ungreased 13-in. x 9-in. baking dish; seal seams and perforations. Sprinkle with Parmesan cheese. Bake at 375° for 8-10 minutes or until lightly browned.

2. Meanwhile, in a small bowl, beat the cream cheese, sour cream and egg until smooth. Stir in dill and seasoned salt. Spread over crust. Sprinkle with artichokes, green onions and pimientos.

3. Bake 15-20 minutes longer or until edges are golden brown. Cut into squares.

Goat Cheese, Pear & Onion Pizza

Goat cheese and basil take this pizza to a new flavor level. My husband and I developed the recipe several years ago because we love onions. It's always a hit with guests!
—**RADELLE KNAPPENBERGER** OVIEDO, FLORIDA

PREP: 30 MIN. • **BAKE:** 10 MIN. • **YIELD:** 12 SLICES

- 3 **cups thinly sliced red onions**
- 3 **teaspoons olive oil, divided**
- 2 **garlic cloves, minced**
- 1 **prebaked 12-inch thin pizza crust**
- 2 **medium pears, peeled and sliced**
- ¾ **cup shredded part-skim mozzarella cheese**
- ⅓ **cup goat cheese**
- 8 **fresh basil leaves, thinly sliced**
- 1 **teaspoon dried oregano**
- ¼ **teaspoon pepper**

1. In a large nonstick skillet coated with cooking spray, saute onions in 2 teaspoons oil until tender. Add garlic; saute 2-3 minutes longer. Place crust on an ungreased 12-in. pizza pan; spread with onion mixture to within 1 in. of edges.

2. In the same skillet, saute pears in remaining oil until tender. Arrange over onion mixture. Sprinkle with cheeses.

3. Bake at 450° for 10-12 minutes or until the edges are lightly browned. Sprinkle with the basil, oregano and pepper.

My family loves this appetizer— warm or cold. It's great for any occasion!
—**MARY ANN DELL**
PHOENIXVILLE, PENNSYLVANIA

Artichoke Crescent Appetizers

PREP: 20 MIN. • **BAKE:** 15 MIN. • **YIELD:** ABOUT 2 DOZEN

- 1 **tube (8 ounces) refrigerated crescent rolls**
- 2 **tablespoons grated Parmesan cheese**
- 2 **packages (3 ounces each) cream cheese, softened**
- ½ **cup sour cream**
- 1 **egg**
- ½ **teaspoon dill weed**
- ¼ **teaspoon seasoned salt**
- 1 **can (14 ounces) water-packed artichoke hearts, rinsed, drained and chopped**
- ⅓ **cup thinly chopped green onions**
- 1 **jar (2 ounces) diced pimientos, drained**

Guacamole Appetizer Squares

This cold appetizer pizza has been a staple at family functions for many years. I know you'll love it, too.
—LAURIE PESTER COLSTRIP, MONTANA

PREP: 20 MIN. • **BAKE:** 10 MIN. + COOLING
YIELD: ABOUT 3 DOZEN

- 2 tubes (8 ounces each) refrigerated crescent rolls
- 1½ teaspoons taco seasoning
- 1 package (1 pound) sliced bacon, diced
- 1 package (8 ounces) cream cheese, softened
- 1½ cups guacamole
- 3 plum tomatoes, chopped
- 1 can (3.8 ounces) sliced ripe olives, drained

1. Unroll both tubes of crescent dough and pat into an ungreased 15-in. x 10-in. x 1-in. baking pan; seal seams and perforations. Build up edges. Prick dough with a fork; sprinkle with taco seasoning. Bake at 375° for 10-12 minutes or until golden brown. Cool completely on a wire rack.

2. In a large skillet, cook bacon over medium heat until crisp. Using a slotted spoon, remove to paper towels. In a small bowl, beat cream cheese and guacamole until smooth.

3. Spread cream cheese mixture over crust. Sprinkle with bacon, tomatoes and olives. Refrigerate until serving. Cut into squares.

homemade guacamole

If you have a few avocados on hand, you can easily make your own guacamole. Use a fork to mash 3 medium ripe avocados in a bowl. Stir in ¼ cup each of finely chopped onion and minced fresh cilantro, 2 tablespoons lime juice and ⅛ teaspoon salt. This makes two cups of yummy guacamole dip!

1. In a large saucepan, bring ½ in. of water to a boil. Add asparagus; cover and boil for 3 minutes. Drain and set aside.

2. In a small bowl, beat the cream cheese, milk and mayonnaise until smooth. Stir in the pimientos, onion, salt and pepper.

3. Unroll crescent dough and separate into triangles; place on an ungreased baking sheet.

4. Spoon 1 teaspoon of cream cheese mixture into the center of each triangle; top with asparagus. Top each with another teaspoonful of cream cheese mixture. Bring three corners of dough together and twist; pinch edges to seal.

5. Brush with butter; sprinkle with bread crumbs. Bake at 375° for 15-18 minutes or until golden brown.

These cute bundles, stuffed with a savory asparagus-cream cheese mixture, make a tasty addition to any Easter or springtime brunch.
—CYNTHIA LINTHICUM TOWSON, MARYLAND

Asparagus Brunch Pockets

PREP: 20 MIN. • **BAKE:** 15 MIN. • **YIELD:** 8 SERVINGS

- 1 **pound fresh asparagus, trimmed and cut into 1-inch pieces**
- 4 **ounces cream cheese, softened**
- 1 **tablespoon 2% milk**
- 1 **tablespoon mayonnaise**
- 1 **tablespoon diced pimientos**
- 1 **tablespoon finely chopped onion**
- ⅛ **teaspoon salt**
  Pinch pepper
- 1 **tube (8 ounces) refrigerated crescent rolls**
- 2 **teaspoons butter, melted**
- 1 **tablespoon seasoned bread crumbs**

Chicken French Bread Pizza

Fun, delicious and ready in minutes, this recipe is great for casual get-togethers and easy to double for larger parties.
—LAURA MAHAFFEY ANNAPOLIS, MARYLAND

PREP/TOTAL TIME: 20 MIN. • **YIELD:** 4 SERVINGS

- 1 **loaf (1 pound) French bread**
- ½ **cup butter, softened**
- ½ **cup shredded cheddar cheese**
- ⅓ **cup grated Parmesan cheese**
- 1 **garlic clove, minced**
- ¼ **teaspoon Italian seasoning**
- 1 **can (10 ounces) chunk white chicken, drained and flaked**
- 1 **cup (4 ounces) shredded part-skim mozzarella cheese**
- ½ **cup chopped sweet red pepper**
- ½ **cup chopped green onion**

1. Cut bread in half lengthwise, then in half widthwise. In a small bowl, combine the butter, cheeses, garlic and Italian seasoning; spread over bread. Top with the remaining ingredients. Place on a baking sheet.

2. Bake at 350° for 10-12 minutes or until cheese is melted. Cut into smaller pieces if desired.

Barbecue Muncher Mix

Looking for a twist on standard party mix? My family enjoys this barbecue-seasoned snack at Christmas and throughout the year. It also makes a nice addition to a holiday gift basket.
—**MRS. DEAN HOLMES** ALTAMONT, KANSAS

PREP: 10 MIN. • **BAKE:** 1 HOUR • **YIELD:** 14 CUPS

- 4 **cups Corn Chex**
- 4 **cups Wheat Chex**
- 2 **cups cheese-flavored snack crackers**
- 2 **cups pretzel sticks**
- 2 **cups mixed nuts or dry roasted peanuts**
- ½ **cup butter, cubed**
- 4 **to 5 tablespoons barbecue sauce**
- 1 **tablespoon Worcestershire sauce**
- 1 **teaspoon seasoned salt**

1. In a large roasting pan, combine the cereals, crackers, pretzels and nuts; set aside.

2. In a small saucepan, melt the butter; stir in the barbecue sauce, Worcestershire sauce and seasoned salt until blended. Pour over the cereal mixture and stir to coat.

3. Bake, uncovered, at 250° for 1 hour, stirring every 15 minutes. Spread on waxed paper to cool completely. Store in airtight containers.

Gouda Bites

I season refrigerated dough with garlic powder to create these golden cheese-filled cups. What could be easier?
—**PHYLLIS BEHRINGER** DEFIANCE, OHIO

PREP/TOTAL TIME: 25 MIN. • **YIELD:** 2 DOZEN

- 1 **tube (8 ounces) refrigerated reduced-fat crescent rolls**
- ½ **teaspoon garlic powder**
- 5 **ounces Gouda cheese, cut into 24 pieces**

1. Unroll crescent dough into one long rectangle; seal seams and perforations. Sprinkle with garlic powder. Cut into 24 pieces; lightly press onto the bottom and up the sides of ungreased miniature muffin cups.

2. Bake at 375° for 3 minutes. Place a piece of cheese in each cup. Bake 8-10 minutes longer or until golden brown and cheese is melted. Serve warm.

Double Chocolate Fondue

Thick, rich and luscious, this yummy dip doesn't last long. In fact, I sometimes eat spoonfuls right out of the refrigerator! You can also use pretzel sticks as dippers.
—**CINDY STETZER** ALLIANCE, OHIO

PREP/TOTAL TIME: 20 MIN. • **YIELD:** 1⅓ CUPS

- 1 cup sugar
- 2 cans (5 ounces each) evaporated milk, divided
- ½ cup baking cocoa
- 4 ounces unsweetened chocolate, chopped
- 2 tablespoons butter
- 1 teaspoon vanilla extract
  Cubed pound cake and assorted fresh fruit

1. In a small saucepan, combine sugar and 1 can milk. Cook over low heat, stirring occasionally, until sugar is dissolved.

2. In a small bowl, whisk cocoa and remaining milk until smooth. Add to sugar mixture; bring to a boil, whisking constantly.

3. Remove from the heat; stir in chocolate and butter until melted. Stir in vanilla. Keep warm. Serve with cake and fruit.

Spinach Bacon Tartlets

These delicious bites make a lovely presentation, and yes, real men do eat quiche...especially these tartlets!
—**LINDA EVANCOE-COBLE** LEOLA, PENNSYLVANIA

PREP: 25 MIN. • **BAKE:** 15 MIN. • **YIELD:** 2½ DOZEN

- 1 package (8 ounces) reduced-fat cream cheese
- 1 egg white
- ½ cup frozen chopped spinach, thawed and squeezed dry
- 3 tablespoons chopped green onions (white part only)
- 1 teaspoon salt-free seasoning blend
- ¼ teaspoon ground nutmeg
- 2 packages (1.9 ounces each) frozen miniature phyllo tart shells
- 3 turkey bacon strips, diced and cooked

1. In a small bowl, beat the first six ingredients until blended. Spoon filling into tart shells. Place on an ungreased baking sheet.

2. Bake at 350° for 10 minutes. Sprinkle with bacon; bake 2-5 minutes longer or until filling is set and shells are lightly browned. Serve warm.

Crispy Baked Wontons

PREP: 30 MIN. • **BAKE:** 10 MIN. • **YIELD:** ABOUT 4 DOZEN

½　pound ground pork
½　pound extra-lean ground turkey
1　small onion, chopped
1　can (8 ounces) sliced water chestnuts, drained and chopped
⅓　cup reduced-sodium soy sauce
¼　cup egg substitute
1½　teaspoons ground ginger
1　package (12 ounces) wonton wrappers
　Cooking spray
　Sweet-and-sour sauce, optional

1. In a large skillet, cook the pork, turkey and onion over medium heat until meat is no longer pink; drain. Transfer to a large bowl. Stir in the water chestnuts, soy sauce, egg substitute and ginger.

2. Position a wonton wrapper with one point toward you. (Keep remaining wrappers covered with a damp paper towel until ready to use.) Place 2 heaping teaspoons of filling in the center of wrapper. Fold bottom corner over filling; fold sides toward center over filling. Roll toward the remaining point. Moisten top corner with water; press to seal. Repeat with remaining wrappers and filling.

3. Place on baking sheets coated with cooking spray; lightly coat wontons with additional cooking spray.

4. Bake at 400° for 10-12 minutes or until golden brown, turning once. Serve warm with sweet-and-sour sauce if desired.

Layered Shrimp Dip

PREP: 15 MIN. + CHILLING • **YIELD:** 12-16 SERVINGS

- 1 package (3 ounces) cream cheese, softened
- 6 tablespoons salsa, divided
- ½ cup cocktail sauce
- 3 cans (6 ounces each) small shrimp, rinsed and drained
- 1 can (2¼ ounces) sliced ripe olives, drained
- 1 cup (4 ounces) shredded cheddar cheese
- 1 cup (4 ounces) shredded Monterey Jack cheese
- Sliced green onions
- Tortilla chips

1. In a small bowl, combine cream cheese and 3 tablespoons salsa; spread into an ungreased 9-in. pie plate. Combine cocktail sauce and remaining salsa; spread over cream cheese.

2. Arrange shrimp evenly over top. Sprinkle with olives. Combine cheeses; sprinkle over top. Add onions. Chill. Serve with tortilla chips.

delightful dippers

Other delicious dippers to try with the Layered Shrimp Dip include thick slices of seedless cucumber, toasted baguette slices, fresh radish slices or lightly steamed vegetables such as broccoli, cauliflower, carrots, asparagus or zucchini.

Pepperoni Pizza Twists

PREP: 20 MIN. • **BAKE:** 30 MIN. + STANDING • **YIELD:** 8 SERVINGS

- 2 packages (11 ounces each) refrigerated crusty French loaf
- 1 tablespoon all-purpose flour
- 1 cup (4 ounces) shredded part-skim mozzarella cheese
- 1 package (3½ ounces) sliced pepperoni, finely chopped
- 1 jar (14 ounces) pizza sauce, divided
- 1 egg white, beaten
- 2 tablespoons grated Parmesan cheese
- ½ teaspoon Italian seasoning

1. Place one loaf on a lightly floured surface. With a sharp knife, make a lengthwise slit down the center of loaf to within ½ in. of bottom. Open dough so it lies flat; sprinkle with half of flour. Roll into a 14-in. x 5-in. rectangle. Repeat with remaining loaf.

2. In a large bowl, combine mozzarella cheese and pepperoni. Spread half of mozzarella mixture down the center of each rectangle. Drizzle each with 3 tablespoons pizza sauce.

3. Roll up jelly-roll style, starting from a long side; seal seams and ends. Place one loaf seam side down on a greased baking sheet. Place remaining loaf seam side down next to the first loaf. Twist loaves together three times.

4. With a sharp knife, make three shallow 3-in. slashes across top of each loaf; brush with egg white. Sprinkle with Parmesan cheese and Italian seasoning.

5. Bake at 350° for 25 minutes. Cover loosely with foil. Bake 4 minutes longer or until golden brown. Let stand for 10 minutes before slicing. Serve with remaining pizza sauce.

Italian Party Appetizers

Quick, easy, delicious, colorful and impressive! This is one great recipe to serve with a refreshing white wine. It's quick for unexpected guests and easily doubled for a crowd.
—HEATHER NYGREN CUMMING, GEORGIA

PREP/TOTAL TIME: 30 MIN. • **YIELD:** 4 DOZEN

- 4 ounces cream cheese, softened
- 48 Triscuits or other crackers
- ¼ cup prepared pesto
- ¼ cup oil-packed sun-dried tomatoes, patted dry and thinly sliced

1. Spread cream cheese on each cracker. Top with pesto and a tomato slice. Serve immediately.

66 When I entertain guests for brunch, this breakfast pizza is always on the menu. We like it so much that we even enjoy it as a late-night snack!

—**JANELLE LEE** APPLETON, WISCONSIN 99

breakfast & brunch

Morning fare is a snap with the recipes in this chapter. Turn the page for casseroles, crepes, pancakes and more—each calling for items you likely already have on hand!

Peaches & Cream French Toast

PREP: 20 MIN. + CHILLING • **BAKE:** 50 MIN. • **YIELD:** 12 SERVINGS

- 1 **cup packed brown sugar**
- ½ **cup butter, cubed**
- 2 **tablespoons corn syrup**
- 1 **can (29 ounces) sliced peaches, drained**
- 1 **loaf (1 pound) day-old French bread, cubed**
- 1 **package (8 ounces) cream cheese, cubed**
- 12 **eggs**
- 1½ **cups half-and-half cream**
- 1 **teaspoon vanilla extract**

1. In a small saucepan, combine the brown sugar, butter and corn syrup. Cook and stir over medium heat until sugar is dissolved; pour into a greased 13-in. x 9-in. baking dish.

2. Arrange peaches in dish. Place half of the bread cubes over peaches. Layer with cream cheese and remaining bread. Place the eggs, cream and vanilla in a blender; cover and process until smooth. Pour over top. Cover and refrigerate overnight.

3. Remove from the refrigerator 30 minutes before baking. Bake, uncovered, at 350° for 50-60 minutes or until a knife inserted near the center comes out clean.

Apple Spice Waffles

These waffles are cozy and comforting anytime, morning or evening. The smell of toasty waffles with apples is sure to warm you up on even the most blustery of winter days.
—JANE (PAIR) SIMS DE LEON, TEXAS

PREP/TOTAL TIME: 30 MIN. • YIELD: 12 WAFFLES

2 cups biscuit/baking mix
2 teaspoons ground cinnamon
1 teaspoon ground nutmeg
2 eggs
1½ cups milk
6 tablespoons butter, melted
1 cup chopped peeled apple

1. In a large bowl, combine the biscuit mix, cinnamon and nutmeg. In another bowl, combine the eggs, milk and butter; stir into dry ingredients just until moistened. Stir in apple.

2. Bake in a preheated waffle iron according to manufacturer's directions until golden brown.

TO FREEZE WAFFLES: Serve desired amount of waffles. Arrange remaining waffles in a single layer on sheet pans. Freeze overnight or until frozen. Transfer to a resealable plastic freezer bag. Waffles may be frozen for up to 2 months. Reheat waffles in a toaster.

Sweetened sour cream and fruit pie filling add flavor and richness to these pretty rolled pancakes. They're tasty for brunch...or dessert.
—WENDY MOYLAN CRYSTAL LAKE, ILLINOIS

Fruit Pancake Roll-Ups

PREP/TOTAL TIME: 15 MIN. • YIELD: 4 SERVINGS

¼ cup sour cream
½ teaspoon confectioners' sugar
4 large pancakes, warmed
½ cup strawberry or raspberry pie filling
Fresh fruit and additional pie filling, optional

1. In a large bowl, combine the sour cream and sugar. Spread over warm pancakes; top with pie filling. Roll up jelly-roll style. Serve with fruit and additional pie filling if desired.

Scrambled Egg Poppers

These handy grab-and-go breakfast treats are ideal for busy mornings and sure to be a favorite with kids.
—**KATIE WILLIAMS** BLACK CREEK, WISCONSIN

PREP: 15 MIN. • **BAKE:** 25 MIN. • **YIELD:** 8 SERVINGS

- 2 loaves (1 pound each) frozen whole wheat bread dough, thawed
- 8 eggs
- ½ cup fat-free milk
- ¼ teaspoon salt
- ¼ teaspoon pepper
- ½ cup bacon bits, divided
- ½ cup shredded cheddar cheese

1. Divide each loaf into eight pieces. Roll into balls. Place in muffin cups coated with cooking spray. Bake at 350° for 20-25 minutes or until golden brown.

2. Meanwhile, in a large bowl, whisk the eggs, milk, salt and pepper; stir in ¼ cup bacon bits. Coat a large nonstick skillet with cooking spray and place over medium heat. Add egg mixture to skillet (mixture should set immediately at edges).

3. As eggs set, push cooked edges toward the center, letting uncooked portion flow underneath. When the eggs are set, remove from the heat.

4. Using a melon baller, scoop out the center of each roll, leaving a ¼-in. shell (discard removed bread or save for another use). Spoon 3 tablespoons cooked egg mixture into each roll. Top with remaining bacon bits and sprinkle with cheese. Bake 2-3 minutes longer or until cheese is melted.

Breakfast Bake

I wanted to have scrambled eggs and hash browns one morning, and this is the dish I created. My wife loved it, so guess who's making breakfast more often?
—**HOWARD ROGERS** EL PASO, TEXAS

PREP: 15 MIN. • **BAKE:** 50 MIN. • **YIELD:** 6 SERVINGS

- 1½ cups egg substitute
- ½ cup fat-free milk
- 3½ cups frozen O'Brien potatoes, thawed
- 1⅓ cups shredded reduced-fat cheddar cheese, divided
- ½ cup chopped sweet onion
- 4 tablespoons crumbled cooked bacon, divided
- ½ teaspoon salt
- ½ teaspoon salt-free seasoning blend
- ¼ teaspoon chili powder
- 4 green onions, chopped

1. In a large bowl, whisk the egg substitute and milk. Stir in the hash browns, 1 cup cheese, onion, 2 tablespoons bacon, salt, seasoning blend and chili powder. Pour into an 8-in. square baking dish coated with cooking spray.

2. Bake at 350° for 45-50 minutes or until a knife inserted near the center comes out clean. Sprinkle with remaining cheese and bacon. Bake 3-5 minutes longer or until cheese is melted. Sprinkle with green onions. Let stand for 5 minutes before cutting.

Getting children to eat breakfast is a breeze when you offer them these little bundles of goodness packed with hearty ingredients. The recipe is so simple that kids of all ages can help make them.

—BERNICE WILLIAMS
NORTH AURORA, ILLINOIS

Breakfast Bundles

PREP/TOTAL TIME: 30 MIN. • **YIELD:** 2 DOZEN

- ½ **cup butter, softened**
- 2 **tablespoons orange juice concentrate**
- 1 **egg, lightly beaten**
- 1½ **cups all-purpose flour**
- ⅔ **cup sugar**
- ½ **cup Grape-Nuts cereal**
- 1 **teaspoon baking powder**
- ½ **pound sliced bacon, cooked and crumbled**

1. In a bowl, beat butter and orange juice. Add egg; mix well. Combine flour, sugar, cereal and baking powder; stir into butter mixture. Fold in bacon.

2. Drop by rounded tablespoonfuls onto ungreased baking sheets. Bake at 350° for 11-13 minutes or until edges are lightly brown. Store in the refrigerator.

testing 1-2-3

If you're not sure that a container of baking powder is still effective, test it! Place 1 teaspoon of baking powder in a cup and add ⅓ cup of hot tap water. If active bubbling occurs, the product is fine to use. If not, it should be replaced. Be sure to check the expiration date when buying new baking soda.

Breakfast Burritos

PREP/TOTAL TIME: 30 MIN. • YIELD: 5 SERVINGS

- ¼ **pound bulk pork sausage**
- 5 **eggs**
- ⅓ **cup chopped tomato**
- ¼ **cup chopped onion**
- 2 **tablespoons canned chopped green chilies**
- ¼ **teaspoon pepper**
- 5 **slices process American cheese**
- 5 **flour tortillas (10 inches), warmed**
- ½ **cup chunky salsa**
- ½ **cup sour cream**

1. In a large skillet, cook sausage over medium heat until no longer pink; drain.

2. In a large bowl, whisk the eggs, tomato, onion, chilies and pepper. Add to the skillet; cook and stir until set.

3. Place a cheese slice on each tortilla. Spoon filling off center on each tortilla. Top with salsa and sour cream. Fold sides and ends over filling and roll up.

Breakfast Crepes With Berries

PREP/TOTAL TIME: 20 MIN. • **YIELD:** 8 SERVINGS

- 1½ cups fresh raspberries
- 1½ cups fresh blackberries
- 1 cup (8 ounces) sour cream
- ½ cup confectioners' sugar
- 1 carton (6 ounces) orange creme yogurt
- 1 tablespoon lime juice
- 1½ teaspoons grated lime peel
- ½ teaspoon vanilla extract
- ⅛ teaspoon salt
- 8 prepared crepes (9 inches)

1. In a large bowl, combine raspberries and blackberries; set aside. In a small bowl, combine sour cream and confectioners' sugar until smooth. Stir in the yogurt, lime juice, lime peel, vanilla and salt.

2. Spread 2 tablespoons sour cream mixture over each crepe; top with about ⅓ cup berries. Roll up; drizzle with remaining sour cream mixture. Serve immediately.

Chocolate Chip Pancakes

Mornings will get off to a great start with these yummy double-chocolate pancakes. Whip up a batch on the weekend, and you'll have speedy breakfasts the whole family will rave about for days to come.
—**TASTE OF HOME TEST KITCHEN**

PREP: 15 MIN. • **COOK:** 5 MIN./BATCH • **YIELD:** 11 PANCAKES

- 2 cups biscuit/baking mix
- 2 tablespoons instant chocolate drink mix
- 2 teaspoons baking powder
- 1 egg
- 1 cup milk
- ½ cup sour cream
- ¼ cup miniature semisweet chocolate chips
   Maple syrup and butter, optional

1. In a large bowl, combine the biscuit mix, drink mix and baking powder. Combine the egg, milk and sour cream; stir into dry ingredients just until moistened. Fold in chocolate chips.

After a long day of blackberry picking, I whipped up a sauce to dress up some crepes I had on hand. This quick sauce really hit the spot and tied everything together beautifully! The crepes make an elegant addition to any brunch, and the sauce is delectable over warm waffles, too.
—**JENNIFER WEISBRODT**
OCONOMOWOC, WISCONSIN

2. Pour batter by ¼ cupfuls onto a greased hot griddle. Turn when bubbles form on top; cook until second side is golden brown. Serve with maple syrup and butter if desired.

3. Cool remaining pancakes; arrange in a single layer on baking sheets. Freeze overnight or until frozen. Transfer to a resealable plastic freezer bag. May be frozen for up to 2 months.

TO USE FROZEN PANCAKES: Place on a lightly greased baking sheet. Bake at 400° for 4-6 minutes or until heated through. Serve with maple syrup and butter if desired.

Tex-Mex Quiche

PREP: 10 MIN. • **BAKE:** 45 MIN. + COOLING • **YIELD:** 6 SERVINGS

1	teaspoon chili powder
1	unbaked pie shell (9 inches)
1	cup (4 ounces) shredded cheddar cheese
1	cup (4 ounces) shredded Monterey Jack cheese
1	tablespoon all-purpose flour
3	eggs, beaten
1½	cups half-and-half cream
1	can (4 ounces) chopped green chilies, well drained
1	can (2¼ ounces) sliced ripe olives, drained
1	teaspoon salt
¼	teaspoon pepper

1. Sprinkle chili powder over the inside of the pie shell. Combine shredded cheeses with flour and place in pie shell.

2. Combine eggs, cream, chilies, olives, salt and pepper. Pour over cheese.

3. Bake at 325° for 45-55 minutes or until a knife inserted in the center comes out clean. Cool for 10 minutes before cutting into wedges.

half-and-half substitute

For dishes that are cooked or baked, you may substitute 4 ½ teaspoons melted butter plus enough whole milk to equal 1 cup for each cup of half-and-half cream. One cup of evaporated milk may also be substituted.

Sunrise Frittata

My family and friends find this hard to resist. It is an impressive dish to serve breakfast and brunch guests, and it is oh-so easy to prepare.
—**JOSEPHINE PIRO** EASTON, PENNSYLVANIA

PREP: 20 MIN. • **COOK:** 15 MIN. • **YIELD:** 6 SERVINGS

1½	cups frozen O'Brien potatoes
2	teaspoons canola oil
1½	cups cubed fully cooked lean ham
8	egg whites
4	eggs
½	cup shredded fontina cheese, divided
⅓	cup fat-free milk
1	teaspoon minced fresh oregano or ¼ teaspoon dried oregano
¾	cup julienned roasted sweet red pepper
¾	cup salsa
¼	cup minced fresh cilantro

1. In a large ovenproof skillet coated with cooking spray, cook and stir the potatoes in oil over medium heat until tender. Stir in ham; heat through.

2. In a small bowl, whisk the egg whites, eggs, ¼ cup cheese, milk and oregano; add to the pan. Arrange red pepper strips over egg mixture to resemble the spokes of a wheel. Cover and cook over low heat for 8-12 minutes or until almost set.

3. Uncover; broil 6 in. from the heat for 3-5 minutes or until the eggs are set and frittata is golden brown. Sprinkle with remaining cheese; let stand until melted. Cut into wedges.

4. Meanwhile, in a small saucepan, combine salsa and cilantro; heat through. Serve with frittata.

Baked Blueberry Pancake

Baking these flapjacks in the oven takes the fuss out of morning meals. For a quick breakfast, I make the pancake while I fix supper the night before, then I cut it into squares. The next morning, I top servings with butter and syrup before placing them in the microwave.
—**NORNA DETIG** LINDENWOOD, ILLINOIS

PREP/TOTAL TIME: 20 MIN. • **YIELD:** 6 SERVINGS

2	cups pancake mix
1½	cups fat-free milk
1	egg
1	tablespoon canola oil
1	teaspoon ground cinnamon
1	cup fresh or frozen blueberries
	Butter and maple syrup

1. In a large bowl, combine the pancake mix, milk, egg, oil and cinnamon just until blended (batter will be lumpy). Fold in blueberries.

2. Spread into a greased 15-in. x 10-in. x 1-in. baking pan. Bake at 400° for 10-12 minutes or until golden brown. Serve with butter and syrup.

EDITOR'S NOTE: If using frozen blueberries, use without thawing to avoid discoloring the batter.

Speedy Sausage Squares

Whenever I want to serve something special for a family brunch, this is usually what I prepare. I'll gather the ingredients together the night before, so it's a snap to bake the next morning.
—**MIRIAM YODER** HOUSTONIA, MISSOURI

PREP: 15 MIN. • **BAKE:** 30 MIN. • **YIELD:** 12 SERVINGS

- 1 tube (8 ounces) refrigerated crescent rolls
- 1 pound bulk pork sausage
- ¼ cup chopped onion
- 6 eggs, lightly beaten
- ¾ cup 2% milk
- 2 tablespoons chopped green pepper
- ½ teaspoon dried oregano
- ½ teaspoon pepper
- ¼ teaspoon garlic salt
- 1 cup (4 ounces) part-skim shredded mozzarella cheese

1. Unroll crescent dough into a greased 13-in. x 9-in. baking dish; seal seams and perforations. Bake at 375° for 6 minutes or until golden brown.

2. Meanwhile, in a large skillet, cook sausage and onion over medium heat until meat is no longer pink; drain. In a small bowl, combine the eggs, milk, green pepper, oregano, pepper and garlic salt; pour over crust. Sprinkle with sausage mixture.

3. Bake for 15-20 minutes or until a knife inserted near the center comes out clean. Sprinkle with cheese; bake 5 minutes longer or until cheese is melted.

Sweet Onion Pie

Chock-full of sweet onions, this creamy, quichelike pie makes a scrumptious addition to a morning buffet. By using less butter to cook the onions and substituting lighter ingredients, I cut calories and fat from this tasty dish—but not flavor!
—**BARBARA REESE** CATAWISSA, PENNSYLVANIA

PREP: 35 MIN. • **BAKE:** 20 MIN. • **YIELD:** 8 SERVINGS

- 2 sweet onions, halved and sliced
- 1 tablespoon butter
- 1 unbaked pastry shell (9 inches)
- 1 cup egg substitute
- 1 cup fat-free evaporated milk
- 1 teaspoon salt
- ¼ teaspoon pepper

1. In a large nonstick skillet, cook onions in butter over medium-low heat for 30 minutes or until very tender. Meanwhile, line unpricked pastry shell with a double thickness of heavy-duty foil.

2. Bake at 450° for 6 minutes. Remove foil; cool on a wire rack. Reduce heat to 425°.

3. Spoon onions into pastry shell. In a small bowl, whisk the egg substitute, milk, salt and pepper; pour over onions. Bake for 20-25 minutes or until a knife inserted near the center comes out clean. Let stand for 5-10 minutes before cutting.

Sausage
Hash Brown Bake

PREP: 15 MIN. • **BAKE:** 55 MIN. • **YIELD:** 10-12 SERVINGS

- 2 **pounds bulk pork sausage**
- 2 **cups (8 ounces) shredded cheddar cheese, divided**
- 1 **can (10¾ ounces) condensed cream of chicken soup, undiluted**
- 1 **cup (8 ounces) sour cream**
- 1 **carton (8 ounces) French onion dip**
- 1 **cup chopped onion**
- ¼ **cup chopped green pepper**
- ¼ **cup chopped sweet red pepper**
- ⅛ **teaspoon pepper**
- 1 **package (30 ounces) frozen shredded hash brown potatoes, thawed**

1. In a large skillet, cook sausage over medium heat until no longer pink; drain on paper towels. In a large bowl, combine 1 ¾ cups cheese and the next seven ingredients; fold in potatoes.

2. Spread half into a greased shallow 3-qt. baking dish. Top with sausage and remaining potato mixture. Sprinkle with remaining cheese. Cover and bake at 350° for 45 minutes. Uncover; bake 10 minutes longer or until heated through.

Scrambled Egg Brunch Bread

PREP: 25 MIN. • **BAKE:** 25 MIN. • **YIELD:** 6 SERVINGS

- 2 **tubes (8 ounces each) refrigerated crescent rolls**
- 4 **ounces thinly sliced deli ham, julienned**
- 4 **ounces cream cheese, softened**
- ½ **cup milk**
- 8 **eggs**
- ¼ **teaspoon salt**
  Dash pepper
- ¼ **cup chopped sweet red pepper**
- 2 **tablespoons chopped green onion**
- 1 **teaspoon butter**
- ½ **cup shredded cheddar cheese**

1. Unroll each tube of crescent dough (do not separate rectangles). Place side by side on a greased baking sheet with long sides touching; seal seams and perforations. Arrange ham lengthwise down center third of rectangle.

2. In a large bowl, beat cream cheese and milk until smooth. Separate one egg; set egg white aside. Beat in the egg yolk, salt, pepper and remaining eggs to cream cheese mixture. Stir in red pepper and onion.

3. In a large skillet, melt butter; add egg mixture. Cook and stir over medium heat just until set. Remove from the heat. Spoon scrambled eggs over ham. Sprinkle with cheese.

4. On each long side of dough, cut 1-in.-wide strips to the center to within ½ in. of filling. Starting at one end, fold alternating strips at an angle across the filling. Pinch ends to seal and tuck under.

5. Beat reserved egg white; brush over dough. Bake at 375° for 25-28 minutes or until golden brown.

Wake-Up Wonton Cups

PREP/TOTAL TIME: 20 MIN. • **YIELD:** 10 WONTON CUPS

- 10 **wonton wrappers**
  Cooking spray
- 4 **eggs**
- ½ **teaspoon garlic powder**
- ¼ **teaspoon salt**
- 1 **medium tomato, seeded and chopped**
- 10 **drops hot pepper sauce**

1. Press wonton wrappers into miniature muffin cups coated with cooking spray. Spritz wrappers with cooking spray. Bake at 350° for 10-12 minutes or until lightly browned.

2. Meanwhile, in a small bowl, whisk the eggs, garlic powder and salt. Heat a small nonstick skillet coated with cooking spray until hot. Add the egg mixture; cook and stir over medium heat until eggs are completely set.

3. Spoon eggs into cups. Top each with chopped tomato and a drop of pepper sauce.

handling wonton wrappers

One thing to remember when using wonton wrappers is that they are delicate and dry out quickly. To avoid having them dry out and crack, place a clean damp towel over the opened package of wontons while using them, and an additional damp towel over the finished wontons until serving.

Corned Beef
Hash and Eggs

PREP: 15 MIN. • **BAKE:** 20 MIN. • **YIELD:** 4 SERVINGS

1	**package (32 ounces) frozen cubed hash browns**
1½	**cups chopped onion**
½	**cup canola oil**
4	**to 5 cups chopped cooked corned beef**
½	**teaspoon salt**
8	**eggs**
2	**tablespoons minced fresh parsley**
	Salt and pepper to taste

1. In a large ovenproof skillet, cook the hash browns
and onion in oil until the potatoes are browned and
onion is tender. Remove from the heat; stir in corned
beef and salt.

2. Make eight wells in the hash browns. Break one egg
into each well. Sprinkle with salt and pepper. Cover
and bake at 325° for 20-25 minutes or until eggs reach
desired doneness. Garnish with parsley.

Chocolate-Cherry Cream Crepes

My teenage son calls me a gourmet cook whenever I make his favorite crepes. Sometimes, for a change, I substitute apple pie filling for the cherries and top the golden crepes with warm caramel sauce.

—KIMBERLY WITT MINOT, NORTH DAKOTA

PREP: 30 MIN. + CHILLING • **COOK:** 15 MIN. • **YIELD:** 8 SERVINGS

- 1¼ cups milk
- 3 eggs
- 2 tablespoons butter, melted
- ¾ cup all-purpose flour
- 1 tablespoon sugar
- ¼ teaspoon salt
- 1 package (8 ounces) cream cheese, softened
- ½ cup confectioners' sugar
- 1 teaspoon vanilla extract
- 1 can (21 ounces) cherry pie filling
  Chocolate fudge ice cream topping and whipped topping

1. In a large bowl, combine the milk, eggs and butter. Combine the flour, sugar and salt; add to egg mixture and mix well. Cover and refrigerate for 1 hour. For filling, in a small bowl, beat cream cheese until fluffy. Beat in confectioners' sugar and vanilla until smooth; set aside.

2. Heat a lightly greased 8-in. nonstick skillet; pour 2 tablespoons batter into the center of skillet. Lift and tilt pan to evenly coat bottom. Cook until top appears dry; turn and cook 15-20 seconds longer.

3. Remove to a wire rack. Repeat with remaining batter, greasing skillet as needed. Stack crepes with waxed paper between. Cover and freeze 10 crepes for another use. Crepes may be frozen for up to 3 months.

4. Pipe filling onto the center of each remaining crepe. Top with 2 tablespoons pie filling. Fold side edges of crepe to the center. Drizzle with fudge topping and garnish with whipped topping. Serve immediately.

Apple Cinnamon Turnovers

Refrigerated biscuit dough speeds up the prep work of these wonderful turnovers. Sprinkled with cinnamon and sugar, they get rave reviews at potlucks. People say the taste reminds them of apple pie.

—ROBIN STEVENS CADIZ, KENTUCKY

PREP: 20 MIN. • **BAKE:** 10 MIN. • **YIELD:** 10 SERVINGS

- 1 medium tart apple, peeled and chopped
- ½ cup applesauce
- ¾ teaspoon ground cinnamon, divided
  Dash ground nutmeg
- 1 tube (7½ ounces) refrigerated biscuits
- 1 tablespoon butter, melted
- 2 tablespoons sugar

1. In a large bowl, combine the apple, applesauce, ¼ teaspoon cinnamon and nutmeg. Separate biscuits; roll out each into a 6-in. circle.

2. Place on a greased baking sheet. Place a heaping tablespoonful of apple mixture in the center of each. Fold in half and pinch edges to seal. Brush with butter. Combine sugar and remaining cinnamon; sprinkle over tops.

3. Bake at 400° for 8-10 minutes or until edges are golden brown. Serve warm.

My family favorite makes a wonderful morning meal served with muffins and fresh fruit. It's also a great way to use up extra taco meat. Adjust the heat by choosing a hotter or milder salsa.
—**MICHELLE JIBBEN**
SPRINGFIELD, MINNESOTA

Spicy Egg Bake

PREP/TOTAL TIME: 30 MIN. • **YIELD:** 8 SERVINGS

- 1 tube (8 ounces) refrigerated crescent rolls
- 10 eggs
- ⅓ cup water
- 3 tablespoons butter
- 1½ cups prepared taco meat
- 1 cup (4 ounces) shredded cheddar cheese
- 1 cup (4 ounces) shredded Monterey Jack cheese
- 1 cup salsa

1. Unroll the crescent roll dough into a greased 13-in. x 9-in. baking dish. Seal the seams and perforations; set aside.

2. In a small bowl, whisk eggs and water. In a large skillet, heat butter until hot. Add egg mixture; cook and stir over medium heat until eggs are almost set. Remove from the heat.

3. Sprinkle taco meat over dough. Layer with eggs, cheeses and salsa. Bake, uncovered, at 375° for 14-16 minutes or until bubbly and cheese is melted.

Brunch Pizza

PREP: 15 MIN. • **BAKE:** 25 MIN. • **YIELD:** 6-8 SERVINGS

1	**pound bulk pork sausage**
1	**tube (8 ounces) refrigerated crescent rolls**
1	**cup frozen shredded hash browns**
1	**cup (4 ounces) shredded cheddar cheese**
5	**eggs**
¼	**cup milk**
½	**teaspoon salt**
¼	**teaspoon pepper**
2	**tablespoons grated Parmesan cheese**

1. Cook and crumble sausage; drain and set aside. Separate crescent roll dough into eight triangles and place on an ungreased 12-in. round pizza pan with points toward center. Press over the bottom and up the sides to form a crust; seal perforations. Spoon the sausage over the crust; sprinkle with hash browns and cheddar cheese.

2. In a bowl, beat eggs, milk, salt and pepper; pour over cheese. Sprinkle with Parmesan. Bake at 375° for 25-30 minutes or until crust is golden.

save time and money...

...by buying bulk sausage on sale, browning it, then packing it in small resealable plastic bags. Label and date the bags, then freeze. You'll have cooked bulk sausage available whenever you need it!

Your family will adore this pretty, puffy casserole, and you'll love that it can be made ahead so you don't have to fuss in the morning.
—SUZETTE JURY
KEENE, CALIFORNIA

Italian Sausage Strata

PREP: 25 MIN. + CHILLING • **BAKE:** 1 HOUR + STANDING
YIELD: 12 SERVINGS

1	**pound bulk Italian sausage**
1	**loaf sourdough bread (1 pound), cubed**
1	**jar (4½ ounces) sliced mushrooms, drained**
¼	**cup thinly sliced green onions**
10	**eggs, lightly beaten**
3	**cups half-and-half cream**
1	**teaspoon ground mustard**
½	**teaspoon salt**
1	**cup (4 ounces) shredded Italian cheese blend**

1. In a large skillet, cook sausage over medium heat until no longer pink; drain. Place bread cubes in a greased 13-in. x 9-in. baking dish. Layer with mushrooms, onions and sausage.

2. In a large bowl, whisk the eggs, cream, mustard and salt. Pour over top; sprinkle with cheese. Cover and refrigerate overnight.

3. Remove from the refrigerator 30 minutes before baking. Bake, uncovered, at 350° for 60-65 minutes or until a knife inserted near the center comes out clean. (Cover loosely with foil if top browns too quickly.) Let stand for 10 minutes before serving.

4. Serve immediately or before refrigerating and baking, cover and freeze casserole for up to 3 months.

TO USE FROZEN CASSEROLE: Thaw in the refrigerator overnight. Remove from the refrigerator 30 minutes before baking. Bake according to directions.

Breakfast Biscuits 'n' Eggs

Breakfast sandwiches are such a satisfying way to start the day, and they don't take much time at all. I can fix this quick breakfast using leftover biscuits or with ones baked fresh the same morning. You'll want to try these!
—**TERESA HUFF** NEVADA, MISSOURI

PREP/TOTAL TIME: 15 MIN. • **YIELD:** 4 BISCUITS

- 4 **individually frozen biscuits**
- 2 **teaspoons butter**
- 4 **eggs**
- 4 **slices process American cheese**
- 4 **thin slices deli ham**

1. Prepare biscuits according to package directions. Meanwhile, in a large skillet, heat the butter until hot. Add the eggs; reduce heat to low. Fry until whites are completely set and the yolks begin to thicken but are not hard.

2. Split the biscuits. Layer the bottom of each biscuit with cheese, ham and an egg; replace top. Microwave, uncovered, for 30-45 seconds or until cheese is melted.

EDITOR'S NOTE: This recipe was tested in a 1,100-watt microwave.

If you find it difficult to peel hard-cooked eggs, you may be using eggs that are too fresh. Store eggs in cartons in the refrigerator for about a week before hard-cooking them.
—**LINDA BRAUN** PARK RIDGE, ILLINOIS

Brunch Enchiladas

PREP/TOTAL TIME: 30 MIN. • **YIELD:** 8 SERVINGS

- 8 **hard-cooked eggs, chopped**
- 1 **can (8¼ ounces) cream-style corn**
- ⅔ **cup shredded cheddar cheese**
- 1 **can (4 ounces) chopped green chilies**
- 2 **teaspoons taco seasoning**
- ¼ **teaspoon salt**
- 8 **corn tortillas, warmed**
- 1 **bottle (8 ounces) mild taco sauce**
  Sour cream, optional

1. Combine the first six ingredients; spoon ½ cup down the center of each tortilla. Roll up tightly. Place, seam side down, in a greased 13-in. x 9-in. baking dish. Top with taco sauce.

2. Bake, uncovered, at 350° for 15 minutes or until heated through. Serve with sour cream if desired.

2. Meanwhile, in a small bowl, whisk the eggs and water. In a small skillet, heat remaining oil until hot. Add eggs; cook and stir over medium heat until completely set.

3. Spoon eggs over crust. Sprinkle with bacon and cheeses. Bake 5-7 minutes longer or until cheese is melted.

Zucchini Pie

For a light lunch or brunch that costs just pennies per serving, fix this quiche-like dish made with crescent roll dough. The zucchini pie is delicious, easy and inexpensive.
—**MELISSA COLLINS** SOUTH DAYTONA, FLORIDA

PREP: 25 MIN. • **BAKE:** 25 MIN. • **YIELD:** 6 SERVINGS

- 1 tube (8 ounces) refrigerated crescent rolls
- 3 medium zucchini, thinly sliced
- 1 garlic clove, minced
- 2 tablespoons butter
- 2 teaspoons minced fresh parsley
- 1 teaspoon snipped fresh dill
- ¼ teaspoon salt
- ¼ teaspoon pepper
- 1 cup (4 ounces) shredded Monterey Jack cheese, divided
- 2 eggs, lightly beaten

1. Separate crescent dough into eight triangles; place in a greased 9-in. pie plate with points toward the center. Press onto the bottom and up the sides of plate to form a crust; seal perforations.

2. In a large skillet, saute zucchini and garlic in butter until crisp-tender. Add the parsley, dill, salt, pepper and ½ cup cheese. Spoon into the crust. Pour eggs over the top; sprinkle with remaining cheese.

3. Cover the edges loosely with foil. Bake at 375° for 25-30 minutes or until a knife inserted near the center comes out clean. Let stand for 5 minutes before cutting

I used to make this for my morning drivers when I worked at a pizza-delivery place. And they just loved it! It's a quick and easy eye-opener that appeals to all ages.
—**CATHY SHORTALL** EASTON, MARYLAND

Breakfast Pizza

PREP/TOTAL TIME: 25 MIN. • **YIELD:** 8 SLICES

- 1 tube (13.8 ounces) refrigerated pizza crust
- 2 tablespoons olive oil, divided
- 6 eggs
- 2 tablespoons water
- 1 package (3 ounces) real bacon bits
- 1 cup (4 ounces) shredded Monterey Jack cheese
- 1 cup (4 ounces) shredded cheddar cheese

1. Unroll crust into a greased 15-in. x 10-in. x 1-in. baking pan; flatten dough and build up edges slightly. Brush with 1 tablespoon oil. Prick dough thoroughly with a fork. Bake at 400° for 7-8 minutes or until lightly browned.

Overnight Raisin French Toast

PREP: 15 MIN. + CHILLING • **BAKE:** 45 MIN.
YIELD: 12 SERVINGS

- 1 **loaf (1 pound) cinnamon-raisin bread, cubed**
- 1 **package (8 ounces) cream cheese, cubed**
- 8 **eggs, lightly beaten**
- 1½ **cups half-and-half cream**
- ½ **cup sugar**
- ½ **cup maple syrup**
- 2 **tablespoons vanilla extract**
- 1 **tablespoon ground cinnamon**
- ⅛ **teaspoon ground nutmeg**

1. Place half of the bread cubes in a greased 13-in. x 9-in. baking dish. Top with cream cheese and remaining bread.

2. In a large bowl, whisk the remaining ingredients. Pour over top. Cover and refrigerate overnight.

3. Remove from the refrigerator 30 minutes before baking. Cover and bake at 350° for 30 minutes. Uncover; bake 15-20 minutes longer or until a knife inserted near the center comes out clean.

66 My family and I operate a busy fruit farm, and because I cook every day, I love that I can prepare a side dish a day ahead and bake it just before we're ready to eat. Ranch Potato Casserole is especially good in place of baked potatoes. 99

—**LYDIA SCHNITZLER** KINGSBURG, CALIFORNIA

standout side dishes

Choose from a variety of perfect partners to round out any entree. From hearty casserole and stuffing recipes to colorful veggie dishes and fresh salads, you'll find it here.

Savory Mediterranean Orzo

PREP: 25 MIN. • **BAKE:** 20 MIN.
YIELD: 12 SERVINGS (⅔ CUP EACH)

- 4 **cups reduced-sodium chicken broth**
- 1 **package (16 ounces) orzo pasta**
- 1 **medium onion, finely chopped**
- 2 **tablespoons olive oil**
- 4 **garlic cloves, minced**
- 2 **cups (8 ounces) crumbled feta cheese, divided**
- 1 **package (10 ounces) frozen chopped spinach, thawed and squeezed dry**
- 1 **jar (7½ ounces) roasted sweet red peppers, drained and chopped**
- 1 **small yellow summer squash, finely chopped**
- ½ **teaspoon salt**
- ½ **teaspoon pepper**

1. In a large saucepan, bring broth to a boil. Stir in orzo; cook over medium heat for 6-8 minutes. Remove from the heat.

2. In a small skillet, saute onion in oil until tender. Add garlic; cook 1 minute longer. Stir into orzo mixture. Stir in 1 cup cheese, spinach, red peppers, squash, salt and pepper.

3. Transfer to a greased 13-in. x 9-in. baking dish; sprinkle with the remaining cheese. Bake at 350° for 20-25 minutes or until heated through.

Antipasto Potato Bake

PREP: 15 MIN. • **BAKE:** 20 MIN. • **YIELD:** 10 SERVINGS

- 2 cans (14½ ounces each) sliced potatoes, drained
- 2 cans (14 ounces each) water-packed artichoke hearts, rinsed and drained
- 2 jars (7 ounces each) roasted sweet red peppers, drained
- 1 can (3.8 ounces) sliced ripe olives, drained
- ¼ cup grated Parmesan cheese
- 1½ teaspoons minced garlic
- ⅓ cup olive oil
- ½ cup seasoned bread crumbs
- 1 tablespoon butter, melted

1. In a large bowl, combine the potatoes, artichokes, peppers, olives, cheese and garlic. Drizzle with oil; toss gently to coat. Transfer to a greased 3-qt. baking dish. Toss bread crumbs and butter; sprinkle over the top.

2. Bake, uncovered, at 375° for 20-25 minutes or until lightly browned.

This hearty side dish has a surprising Mediterranean flavor. Red peppers and black olives add color, making this casserole a pretty addition to any buffet.
—KELLEY BUTLER-LUDINGTON
EAST HAVEN, CONNECTICUT

seasoned bread crumbs

One slice of dried bread yields about ¼ cup of fine dry bread crumbs. To make your own seasoned crumbs, break slices of dried bread into pieces and process to a fine texture. Season according to your taste. You may try adding dried basil and oregano, garlic and onion powder, grated Parmesan, salt or paprika.

I jazzed up a package of stuffing mix with pork sausage, mushrooms, celery and onion to make this stuffing. It impressed my in-laws at a family gathering and has since become a popular side dish with my husband and children.

—JENNIFER LYNN CULLEN
TAYLOR, MICHIGAN

Skillet Sausage Stuffing

PREP/TOTAL TIME: 25 MIN. • **YIELD:** 8 SERVINGS

1   **pound bulk pork sausage**
1¼   **cups chopped celery**
½   **cup chopped onion**
½   **cup sliced fresh mushrooms**
1½   **teaspoons minced garlic**
1½   **cups reduced-sodium chicken broth**
1   **teaspoon rubbed sage**
1   **package (6 ounces) stuffing mix**

1. In a large skillet, cook the sausage, celery, onion and mushrooms over medium heat until meat is no longer pink. Add garlic; cook 1 minute longer; drain. Stir in broth and sage.

2. Bring to a boil. Stir in stuffing mix. Cover and remove from the heat; let stand for 5 minutes. Fluff with a fork.

Dressed-Up French Green Beans

We add lemon juice, bacon crumbles and Dijon mustard to transform frozen green beans into a standout partner for all kinds of entrees. Plus, it couldn't be easier to make!
—TASTE OF HOME TEST KITCHEN

PREP/TOTAL TIME: 20 MIN. • **YIELD:** 4 SERVINGS

- 4 cups frozen French-style green beans
- 2 tablespoons crumbled cooked bacon
- 2 teaspoons lemon juice
- 2 teaspoons olive oil
- 2 teaspoons Dijon mustard
- ½ teaspoon sugar
- ½ teaspoon garlic powder
- ½ teaspoon dill weed
- ¼ teaspoon pepper

1. Cook green beans according to package directions. Meanwhile, in a small bowl, combine the remaining ingredients. Drain beans; add bacon mixture and gently stir to coat.

EDITOR'S NOTE: This recipe was tested in a 1,100-watt microwave.

Ranch Potato Casserole

PREP: 30 MIN. • **BAKE:** 40 MIN. • **YIELD:** 8 SERVINGS

- 6 to 8 medium red potatoes (about 2 to 2½ pounds)
- ½ cup sour cream
- ½ cup prepared ranch-style dressing
- ¼ cup bacon bits or crumbled cooked bacon
- 2 tablespoons minced fresh parsley
- 1 cup (4 ounces) shredded cheddar cheese

TOPPING:
- ½ cup (2 ounces) shredded cheddar cheese
- 2 cups coarsely crushed cornflakes
- ¼ cup butter, melted

1. Cook the potatoes until tender; quarter (leaving skins on if desired) and set aside.

2. Combine the sour cream, dressing, bacon, parsley and 1 cup cheese. Place potatoes in a greased 13-in. x 9-in. baking dish. Pour sour cream mixture over potatoes and gently toss. Top with ½ cup of cheese. Combine cornflakes and butter; sprinkle over top. Bake at 350° for 40-45 minutes.

My family and I operate a busy fruit farm, and because I cook every day, I love that I can prepare a side dish a day ahead and bake it just before we're ready to eat! Ranch Potato Casserole is especially good in place of baked potatoes.
—LYDIA SCHNITZLER
KINGSBURG, CALIFORNIA

Creamy Spinach Casserole

Rich and comforting, this savory spinach casserole is a welcome addition to the table. You will love the short prep time and the decadent taste.

—ANNETTE MARIE YOUNG WEST LAFAYETTE, INDIANA

PREP: 10 MIN. • **BAKE:** 35 MIN. • **YIELD:** 10 SERVINGS

- 2 cans (10¾ ounces each) reduced-fat reduced-sodium condensed cream of chicken soup, undiluted
- 1 package (8 ounces) reduced-fat cream cheese, cubed
- ½ cup fat-free milk
- ½ cup grated Parmesan cheese
- 4 cups herb seasoned stuffing cubes
- 2 packages (10 ounces each) frozen chopped spinach, thawed and squeezed dry

1. In a large bowl, beat the soup, cream cheese, milk and Parmesan cheese until blended. Stir in stuffing cubes and spinach.

2. Spoon into a 2-qt. baking dish coated with cooking spray. Bake, uncovered, at 350° for 35-40 minutes or until heated through.

All dressed up with crispy apples, bacon and a creamy bottled dressing, this crisp salad makes a refreshing, versatile side dish.
—SHERRY THOMPSON SENECA, SOUTH CAROLINA

Fresh Broccoli Salad

PREP/TOTAL TIME: 15 MIN. • **YIELD:** 6 SERVINGS

- ¾ pound chopped fresh broccoli
- 1 small tart apple, chopped
- ½ cup chopped red onion
- 3 tablespoons real bacon bits
- ½ cup ranch salad dressing
- 4½ teaspoons sugar

1. In a large bowl, combine the broccoli, apple, onion and bacon. In a small bowl, combine salad dressing and sugar. Pour over broccoli mixture; toss to coat.

Spanish Hominy

PREP: 15 MIN. • **COOK:** 6 HOURS • **YIELD:** 12 SERVINGS

- 4 **cans (15½ ounces each) hominy, rinsed and drained**
- 1 **can (14½ ounces) diced tomatoes, undrained**
- 1 **can (10 ounces) diced tomatoes and green chilies, undrained**
- 1 **can (8 ounces) tomato sauce**
- ¾ **pound sliced bacon, diced**
- 1 **large onion, chopped**
- 1 **medium green pepper, chopped**

1. In a 5-qt. slow cooker, combine the hominy, tomatoes and tomato sauce.

2. In a large skillet, cook bacon until crisp; remove with a slotted spoon to paper towels. Drain, reserving 1 tablespoon drippings.

3. In the same skillet, saute onion and green pepper in drippings until tender. Stir onion mixture and bacon into hominy mixture. Cover and cook on low for 6-8 hours or until heated through.

It's hard to improve on the taste Mother Nature gives to fresh green beans, but Mom has for years been using this recipe. I've always thought the crunchy almonds were a super addition.

—BRENDA DUFRESNE MIDLAND, MICHIGAN

Green Beans Amandine

PREP/TOTAL TIME: 20 MIN. • **YIELD:** 6 SERVINGS

- 1 **pound fresh or frozen green beans, cut into 2-inch pieces**
- ½ **cup water**
- ¼ **cup slivered almonds**
- 2 **tablespoons butter**
- 1 **teaspoon lemon juice**
- ¼ **teaspoon seasoned salt, optional**

1. Place beans in a large saucepan and cover with water. Bring to a boil. Cover and cook for 10-15 minutes or until crisp-tender; drain and set aside.

2. In a large skillet, cook almonds in butter over low heat. Stir in lemon juice and seasoned salt if desired. Add beans and heat through.

Easy Spanish Rice

With less sodium and fewer calories, this Spanish rice rivals any store-bought brand. Thanks to convenience items, it goes from start to finish in a fast 15 minutes.

—SUSAN LE BRUN SULPHUR, LOUISIANA

PREP/TOTAL TIME: 15 MIN. • **YIELD:** 4 SERVINGS

- 2 **cups water**
- 2 **cups instant brown rice**
- 1 **envelope enchilada sauce mix**
- 1 **cup picante sauce**

1. In a large saucepan, bring the water to a boil; stir in rice and sauce mix. Return to a boil. Reduce heat; cover and simmer for 5 minutes. Remove from the heat; stir in picante sauce. Let stand for 5 minutes before serving.

Broccoli Bean Bake

PREP: 15 MIN. • **BAKE:** 20 MIN. • **YIELD:** 8 SERVINGS

- 6 **cups fresh broccoli florets**
- ⅓ **cup chopped onion**
- 1 **teaspoon minced garlic**
- 3 **tablespoons butter, divided**
- 1 **can (15½ ounces) great northern beans, rinsed and drained**
- 1 **jar (4 ounces) diced pimientos, drained**
- 1 **teaspoon dried oregano**
- ½ **teaspoon salt**
- ⅛ **teaspoon pepper**
- 2 **cups (8 ounces) shredded cheddar cheese**
- 3 **tablespoons dry bread crumbs**

1. Place broccoli in a saucepan; add 1 in. of water. Bring to a boil. Reduce heat; cover and simmer for 5-8 minutes or until crisp-tender. Meanwhile, in a skillet, saute the onion and garlic in 1 tablespoon butter. Spread into a greased 11-in. x 7-in. baking dish.

2. Drain broccoli; place over onion mixture. Top with beans and pimientos. Sprinkle with oregano, salt, pepper, cheese and bread crumbs. Melt remaining butter; pour over the top. Bake, uncovered, at 375° for 20-25 minutes or until heated through.

Corn & Bean Bake

PREP: 10 MIN. • **BAKE:** 35 MIN. • **YIELD:** 6 SERVINGS

Surprise your family when you bring this flavorful green bean dish to the table. Adding whole kernel corn and buttery crackers to the creamy casserole brings a whole new twist to a time-honored tradition.
—**NELLIE PERDUE**
SUMMER SHADE, KENTUCKY

- 1 package (16 ounces) frozen cut green beans
- 1 can (15¼ ounces) whole kernel corn, drained
- 1 can (10¾ ounces) condensed cream of mushroom soup, undiluted
- 1 cup (4 ounces) shredded cheddar cheese, divided
- ½ cup crushed butter-flavored crackers (about 12 crackers)

1. In a large bowl, combine the beans, corn, soup and ½ cup cheese. Spoon into a greased 2-qt. baking dish. Top with crackers and remaining cheese.

2. Bake, uncovered, at 350° for 35 minutes or until heated through.

MICROWAVE CORN & BEAN BAKE: Spoon bean mixture into a greased microwave-safe 2-qt. dish. Cover and microwave on high for 10 minutes; stir once. Sprinkle with crackers and remaining cheese. Microwave, uncovered, for 3-5 minutes or until heated through.

For a festive fall look, I like to hollow out a pumpkin and serve this creamy, hearty polenta inside it. To add crunchy texture, try sprinkling some pumpkin seeds on top.
—**DEBI GEORGE**
MANSFIELD, TEXAS

Creamy Pumpkin Polenta

PREP/TOTAL TIME: 25 MIN. • **YIELD:** 6 SERVINGS

5⅓	**cups water**
1	**teaspoon salt**
1⅓	**cups yellow cornmeal**
½	**teaspoon ground nutmeg**
¾	**cup canned pumpkin**
½	**cup cream cheese, cubed**

Salted pumpkin seeds or pepitas, optional

1. In a large heavy saucepan, bring the water and salt to a boil.

2. Reduce heat to a gentle boil; slowly whisk in cornmeal and nutmeg. Cook and stir with a wooden spoon for 15-20 minutes or until polenta is thickened and pulls away cleanly from the sides of the pan. Stir in pumpkin and cream cheese until smooth. Sprinkle each serving with pumpkin seeds if desired.

polenta, please

Polenta is an Italian-style dish prepared from cornmeal and water; it is often flavored with cheese. It is cooked until thickened and smooth and served as a side dish, similar to rice or mashed potatoes. Polenta makes a great accompaniment with main courses that have a sauce or gravy.

Southern Coleslaw

PREP/TOTAL TIME: 15 MIN. • **YIELD:** 6 SERVINGS

- 3 cups coleslaw mix
- ½ cup shredded cheddar cheese
- ¼ cup canned Mexicorn
- 1 jalapeno pepper, seeded and chopped
- 2 tablespoons chopped red onion
- 1 tablespoon minced fresh cilantro
- ½ cup ranch salad dressing
- 1½ teaspoons lime juice
- ½ teaspoon ground cumin

1. In a large bowl, combine the first six ingredients. In a small bowl, whisk the salad dressing, lime juice and cumin. Pour over coleslaw; toss to coat. Refrigerate until serving.

EDITOR'S NOTE: Wear disposable gloves when cutting hot peppers; the oils can burn skin. Avoid touching your face.

Colorful Rice Medley

With only a gram of fat and less than 200 calories per serving, this delightful side dish is sure to brighten up any meal. I like to boost the nutritional value with shredded carrot, red onion and fresh parsley.
—**TERRI GRIFFIN** SALISBURY, MARYLAND

PREP/TOTAL TIME: 15 MIN. • **YIELD:** 4 SERVINGS

- 2 cups water
- 2 cups uncooked instant rice
- ⅓ cup shredded carrot
- ¼ cup finely chopped red onion
- 1½ teaspoons steak sauce
- 1 teaspoon butter
- ½ to 1½ teaspoons salt
- ½ teaspoon pepper
- 1 teaspoon minced fresh parsley

1. In a large saucepan, bring water to a boil. Stir in rice. Remove from the heat; cover and let stand for 3 minutes. Stir in the remaining ingredients. Cover and let stand 5 minutes longer.

Liven up canned corn with green pepper, cream of celery soup and cheddar cheese for a deluxe side dish. With a butter-flavored cracker topping, this comfort food is sure to disappear in a hurry!

—LINDA ROBERSON
COLLIERVILLE, TENNESSEE

Shoepeg Corn Supreme

PREP: 10 MIN. • **BAKE:** 25 MIN. • **YIELD:** 8 SERVINGS

- 1 **small green pepper, chopped**
- 1 **small onion, chopped**
- 1 **celery rib, chopped**
- 2 **tablespoons olive oil**
- 3 **cans (7 ounces each) white or shoepeg corn, drained**
- 1 **can (10¾ ounces) condensed cream of celery soup, undiluted**
- 1 **cup (8 ounces) sour cream**
- ½ **cup shredded sharp cheddar cheese**
- ¼ **teaspoon pepper**
- 1½ **cups crushed butter-flavored crackers**
- 3 **tablespoons butter, melted**

1. In a large skillet, saute the green pepper, onion and celery in oil until tender. Remove from the heat; stir in the corn, soup, sour cream, cheese and pepper. Transfer to a greased 11-in. x 7-in. baking dish.

2. Combine cracker crumbs and butter; sprinkle over the top. Bake, uncovered, at 350° for 25-30 minutes or until bubbly.

Colorful Pasta Salad

Here's a bright side that features sweet pineapple, crunchy vegetables and refreshing cilantro in a tangy dressing with pasta. It requires just 15 minutes of prep time, so it's also perfect for a quick lunch or on-the-go dinner.
—**MARY TALLMAN** ARBOR VITAE, WISCONSIN

PREP/TOTAL TIME: 15 MIN. • **YIELD:** 5 SERVINGS

  1½ **cups uncooked tricolor spiral pasta**
   1 **can (8 ounces) unsweetened pineapple chunks**
   1 **cup fresh snow peas, halved**
  ½ **cup thinly sliced carrot**
  ½ **cup sliced cucumber**
   1 **tablespoon minced fresh cilantro**
  ¼ **cup Italian salad dressing**

1. Cook pasta according to package directions. Meanwhile, drain pineapple, reserving ¼ cup juice. In a large bowl, combine the pineapple, snow peas, carrot, cucumber and reserved pineapple juice.

2. Drain pasta and rinse with cold water. Add to pineapple mixture. Sprinkle with cilantro. Drizzle with salad dressing and toss to coat. Chill until serving.

Early-Bird Asparagus Supreme

PREP/TOTAL TIME: 10 MIN. • **YIELD:** 6 SERVINGS

   3 **pounds fresh asparagus, cut into 1-inch pieces**
   3 **tablespoons butter, melted**
   1 **envelope onion soup mix**
   1 **cup (4 ounces) shredded mozzarella or Monterey Jack cheese**

1. In a large saucepan, bring ½ in. of water to a boil. Add asparagus; cover and boil for 3 minutes. Drain and immediately place asparagus in ice water. Drain and pat dry.

2. Place in a 13-in. x 9-in. baking dish coated with cooking spray. Combine butter and soup mix; drizzle over asparagus. Sprinkle with cheese.

3. Bake, uncovered, at 425° for 10-12 minutes or until asparagus is tender and cheese is melted.

Fresh asparagus is so delicious in the springtime, and my vegetable side dish highlights its spectacular seasonal flavor.
—**JOYCE SPECKMAN** HOLT, CALIFORNIA

Celebrate the last garden harvest with this satisfying side dish. Simply cook the carrots, squash and zucchini in oil that's been spiced up with ranch dressing mix. You'll be able to dish out hot and hearty helpings in minutes!
—TASTE OF HOME TEST KITCHEN

Skillet Ranch Vegetables

PREP/TOTAL TIME: 20 MIN. • **YIELD:** 4 SERVINGS

- 1 tablespoon canola oil
- 1 envelope buttermilk ranch salad dressing mix
- 2 medium carrots, thinly sliced
- 2 medium yellow squash, sliced
- 2 medium zucchini, sliced

1. In a skillet, combine the oil and salad dressing mix. Add carrots; cook over medium heat for 4-5 minutes or until crisp-tender. Add squash and zucchini; cook 4-5 minutes longer or until all of the vegetables are tender. Remove with a slotted spoon to serving dish.

summer squash

Zucchini, pattypan and yellow are the most common varieties of summer squash. Generally, small squash are more tender. To store, refrigerate in a plastic bag for up to 5 days. One pound of summer squash equals about 3 medium or 2 ½ cups chopped.

Squash Dressing

PREP: 30 MIN. + COOLING • **BAKE:** 40 MIN. • **YIELD:** 8 SERVINGS

1   package (8½ ounces) corn bread/muffin mix
½   cup water
4   cups chopped yellow summer squash
½   cup each chopped onion, celery and green pepper
½   cup butter, cubed
1   can (10¾ ounces) condensed cream of chicken soup, undiluted
1   cup milk
1   teaspoon salt
½   teaspoon pepper

1. Prepare corn bread according to package directions. Cool and crumble; set aside. In a large saucepan bring ½ in. of water to a boil. Add squash; cook, covered, for 3-5 minutes or until crisp-tender. Drain.

2. In a large skillet, saute the onion, celery and green pepper in butter until tender. Stir in corn bread and squash. In a small bowl, combine the soup, milk, salt and pepper; add to squash mixture. Transfer to a greased 11-in. x 7-in. baking dish. Bake, uncovered, at 350° for 40-45 minutes or until golden brown.

Instant Fried Rice

Instant rice and a seasoning packet cut the prep time for this fast, fuss-free and delicious fried-rice recipe. Peas and onion add a bit of nutrition!

—AMY CORLEW-SHERLOCK
LAPEER, MICHIGAN

PREP/TOTAL TIME: 20 MIN. • YIELD: 4 SERVINGS

- 1 envelope fried rice seasoning
- 2 tablespoons water
- 2 green onions, chopped
- 2 tablespoons canola oil
- 1 egg, lightly beaten
- 3 cups cold cooked instant rice
- ½ cup peas

1. In a small bowl, combine seasoning mix and water; set aside. In a large skillet or wok, stir-fry onions in oil for 2-3 minutes. Add egg; stir until scrambled.

2. Add rice and peas; stir-fry until heated through. Stir in seasoning mixture; stir-fry 3-4 minutes longer or until heated through.

Speedy Sweet Potatoes

PREP/TOTAL TIME: 15 MIN. • YIELD: 6 SERVINGS

- 2 cans (15¾ ounces each) sweet potatoes, drained
- ½ teaspoon salt
- 1 can (8 ounces) crushed pineapple, drained
- ¼ cup coarsely chopped pecans
- 1 tablespoon brown sugar
- 1 cup miniature marshmallows, divided
  Ground nutmeg

1. In a 1 ½-qt. microwave-safe dish, layer sweet potatoes, salt, pineapple, pecans, brown sugar and ½ cup marshmallows. Cover and microwave on high for 3 to 6 minutes or until bubbly around the edges. Top with the remaining marshmallows.

2. Microwave, uncovered, on high for 1-2 minutes or until marshmallows puff. Sprinkle with nutmeg.

EDITOR'S NOTE: This recipe was tested in a 1,100-watt microwave.

I discovered this scrumptious sweet potato recipe years ago. There's no need for lots of butter and sugar because the pineapple and marshmallows provide plenty of sweetness. It's a holiday favorite at our house.
—BETH BUHLER LAWRENCE, KANSAS

With a mild hint of cumin, these veggies go with just about any dish. And because they're so colorful, they're sure to perk up any plate!
—**LINDA FOREMAN**
LOCUST GROVE, OKLAHOMA

Carrots with Sugar Snap Peas

PREP/TOTAL TIME: 15 MIN. • **YIELD:** 4 SERVINGS

1 package (16 ounces) frozen sliced carrots, thawed and patted dry
3 tablespoons butter
¼ cup chicken broth
3 tablespoons sugar
¼ teaspoon salt
¼ teaspoon pepper
½ pound fresh sugar snap peas
1 teaspoon cumin seeds, toasted or ¼ teaspoon ground cumin

1. In a large skillet, saute the carrots in butter for 2 minutes. Add the broth, sugar, salt and pepper. Cover and cook for 2-5 minutes or until carrots are crisp-tender.

2. Add peas and cumin. Cook and stir 3-4 minutes longer or until peas are crisp-tender.

toasting cumin seeds

Heat a small skillet over medium high heat. When the pan is hot, add the seeds (do not use any oil in the pan). Continually shake the skillet to keep the seeds moving; they should be done in about 1 minute, when they give off a pleasant aroma. Immediately transfer seeds to a plate or bowl so they stop cooking; allow to cool.

Squash Stuffing Casserole

My friends rave about this creamy side dish. It jazzes up summer squash, zucchini and carrots with canned soup and stuffing mix.
—PAMELA THORSON
HOT SPRINGS, ARKANSAS

PREP: 15 MIN. • **COOK:** 4 HOURS • **YIELD:** 8 SERVINGS

- ¼ cup all-purpose flour
- 1 can (10¾ ounces) condensed cream of chicken soup, undiluted
- 1 cup (8 ounces) sour cream
- 2 medium yellow summer squash, cut into ½-inch slices
- 1 small onion, chopped
- 1 cup shredded carrots
- 1 package (8 ounces) stuffing mix
- ½ cup butter, melted

1. In a large bowl, combine the flour, soup and sour cream until blended. Add the vegetables and gently stir to coat.

2. Combine the stuffing mix and butter; sprinkle half into a 5-qt. slow cooker. Top with vegetable mixture and remaining stuffing mixture. Cover and cook on low for 4-5 hours or until vegetables are tender.

During autumn, apple cider is abundant in our state. My family looks forward to the sweet and tart flavor it brings to this bean dish!
—**MARA MCAULEY** HINSDALE, NEW YORK

Autumn Beans

PREP/TOTAL TIME: 30 MIN. • **YIELD:** 4 SERVINGS

- 8 bacon strips, chopped
- ¼ cup finely chopped onion
- 1 cup apple cider
- 2 cans (16 ounces each) baked beans, undrained
- ¼ to ½ cup raisins
- ½ teaspoon ground cinnamon

1. In a skillet, lightly fry bacon. Remove to paper towel to drain. Set aside 2 tablespoons drippings. Saute onion in the drippings until tender.

2. Stir in the remaining ingredients. Bring to a boil; reduce heat and simmer, uncovered, 20-25 minutes, stirring occasionally.

Mixed Veggies

Crunchy water chestnuts give a nice contrast in texture to the tender peas in my snappy side dish. I prepare it often for company. Guests would never guess that it costs only pennies per serving.
—**JUDY BENNETT** VACAVILLE, CALIFORNIA

PREP/TOTAL TIME: 25 MIN. • **YIELD:** 8 SERVINGS

- 2 cups sliced fresh mushrooms
- ½ cup chopped onion
- 2 tablespoons butter
- 2 packages (16 ounces each) frozen peas, thawed
- 1 can (8 ounces) sliced water chestnuts, drained and halved
- ¼ cup soy sauce

1. In a large saucepan, saute the mushrooms and onion in butter. Add the peas, water chestnuts and soy sauce. Cook until heated through, about 10 minutes.

Baked Vegetable Medley

PREP: 35 MIN. + CHILLING • **BAKE:** 40 MIN. • **YIELD:** 12 SERVINGS

- 1 **medium head cauliflower, broken into florets**
- 1 **bunch broccoli, cut into florets**
- 6 **medium carrots, sliced**
- 1 **pound sliced fresh mushrooms**
- 1 **bunch green onions, sliced**
- ¼ **cup butter, cubed**
- 1 **can (10¾ ounces) condensed cream of chicken soup, undiluted**
- ½ **cup milk**
- ½ **cup process cheese sauce**

1. Place the cauliflower, broccoli and carrots in a steamer basket; place in a large saucepan over 1 in. of water. Bring to a boil; cover and steam for 7-9 minutes or until crisp-tender. Meanwhile, in a large skillet, saute mushrooms and onions in butter until tender.

2. Drain vegetables. In a large bowl, combine the soup, milk and cheese sauce. Add vegetables and mushroom mixture; toss to coat. Transfer to a greased 2-qt. baking dish. Cover and refrigerate overnight.

3. Remove from the refrigerator 30 minutes before baking. Bake, uncovered, at 350° for 40-45 minutes or until bubbly.

Stuffing Baskets

Instant stuffing mix makes these individual mini casseroles a snap to prepare, and their fun shape won't soon be forgotten by your guests!
—TASTE OF HOME TEST KITCHEN

PREP: 10 MIN. • **BAKE:** 30 MIN. • **YIELD:** 1 DOZEN

- 1 medium green pepper, chopped
- ¼ cup butter, cubed
- 1 jar (4½ ounces) sliced mushrooms
- 1 package (6 ounces) instant stuffing mix
- ½ cup chopped pecans

1. In a large saucepan, saute green pepper in butter until crisp-tender. Drain mushrooms, reserving liquid; set mushrooms aside. Add water to liquid to measure 1⅔ cups. Add to green pepper. Bring to a boil; stir in the stuffing mix.

2. Remove from the heat. Cover and let stand for 5 minutes. Add mushrooms and pecans; fluff with a fork. Spoon into paper-lined muffin cups; pack lightly. Bake at 350° for 30-35 minutes.

And the Beets Go On

PREP/TOTAL TIME: 15 MIN. • **YIELD:** 8 SERVINGS

- 2 cans (13¼ ounces each) sliced beets, drained
- 1 can (14 ounces) whole-berry cranberry sauce
- ¼ cup thawed orange juice concentrate

1. In a large saucepan, combine the beets, cranberry sauce and orange juice concentrate. Cook and stir over low heat until heated through. Serve with a slotted spoon.

Think you don't like beets? Try these! Their ruby red color and tangy flavor make them an excellent choice for Valentine's Day.
—ALCY THORNE LOS MOLINOS, CALIFORNIA

Broccoli Rice Casserole

PREP: 15 MIN. • **BAKE:** 30 MIN. • **YIELD:** 8 SERVINGS

1½   **cups water**
½   **cup butter, cubed**
1   **tablespoon dried minced onion**
2   **cups uncooked instant rice**
1   **package (16 ounces) frozen chopped broccoli, thawed**
1   **can (10¾ ounces) condensed cream of mushroom soup, undiluted**
1   **jar (8 ounces) process cheese sauce**

1. In a large saucepan, bring the water, butter and onion to a boil. Stir in rice. Remove from the heat; cover and let stand for 5 minutes or until water is absorbed.

2. Stir in the broccoli, soup and cheese sauce. Transfer to a greased 2-qt. baking dish. Bake, uncovered, at 350° for 30-35 minutes or until bubbly.

When I was little, serving this dish was the only way my mother could get me to eat broccoli. It's an excellent recipe that is especially good with chicken and turkey.
—JENNIFER FULLER
BALLSTON SPA, NEW YORK

Squash Bake

PREP: 20 MIN. • **BAKE:** 25 MIN. • **YIELD:** 8-10 SERVINGS

8	cups sliced yellow squash (about 2 pounds)
½	cup chopped onion
¾	cup shredded carrots
¼	cup butter
1	can (10¾ ounces) condensed cream of chicken soup, undiluted
½	cup sour cream
2	cups herb stuffing croutons, divided

1. Cook squash in lightly salted boiling water for 3 to 4 minutes or until crisp-tender; drain well.

2. In a large skillet, saute onion and carrots in butter until tender.

3. Combine onion and carrots with soup, sour cream and 1½ cups croutons. Add squash and mix lightly. Spoon into a lightly greased 11-in. x 7-in. baking dish. Sprinkle with the remaining croutons.

4. Bake, uncovered, at 350° for 25 minutes or until heated through.

Nacho Hash Brown Casserole

My tasty slow cooker recipe will free up your oven and produce the best hash browns ever. Soft and super cheesy, they make a comforting side dish for meat or poultry.
—**PAT HABIGER** SPEARVILLE, KANSAS

PREP: 15 MIN. • **COOK:** 3¼ HOURS • **YIELD:** 8 SERVINGS

- 1 package (32 ounces) frozen cubed hash brown potatoes, thawed
- 1 can (10¾ ounces) condensed cream of celery soup, undiluted
- 1 can (10¾ ounces) condensed nacho cheese soup, undiluted
- 1 large onion, finely chopped
- ⅓ cup butter, melted
- 1 cup (8 ounces) reduced-fat sour cream

1. In a greased 3-qt. slow cooker, combine the first five ingredients. Cover and cook on low for 3-4 hours or until potatoes are tender. Stir in sour cream. Cover and cook 15-30 minutes longer or until heated through.

Tangy Caesar Salad

PREP/TOTAL TIME: 15 MIN. • **YIELD:** 6-8 SERVINGS

- 8 cups torn romaine
- ¼ cup creamy Caesar salad dressing
- 1 tablespoon lemon juice
- ½ teaspoon pepper
- 1 cup Caesar salad croutons
- ⅓ cup grated Parmesan cheese

1. Place romaine in a large salad bowl. In a small bowl, whisk the salad dressing, lemon juice and pepper; drizzle over romaine and toss to coat. Top with croutons and cheese.

When time is tight, I like to toss together this zippy salad. It's a breeze to make with bottled Caesar dressing and Caesar salad croutons.
—**PAULA STEWART**
CRAWFORDVILLE, GEORGIA

bountiful breads

The scrumptious recipes in this chapter prove that fresh baked goods don't have to be a chore. Choose from sweet rolls, breads, biscuits, coffee cakes and more.

Banana Nut Bread

PREP: 10 MIN. • **BAKE:** 40 MIN. + COOLING
YIELD: 2 LOAVES (12 SLICES EACH)

- 1 **package (18¼ ounces) yellow cake mix**
- 1 **egg**
- ½ **cup 2% milk**
- 1 **cup mashed ripe bananas (about 2 medium)**
- ½ **cup chopped pecans**

1. In a large bowl, combine the cake mix, egg and milk. Add bananas; beat on medium speed for 2 minutes. Stir in pecans.

2. Pour into two greased 8-in. x 4-in. loaf pans. Bake at 350° for 40-45 minutes or until a toothpick inserted near the center comes out clean. Cool for 10 minutes before removing from pans to wire racks to cool completely.

Sour Cream Pan Biscuits

These golden brown biscuits make a convenient meal accompaniment since they bake at a similar temperature to many roast chicken entrees. The biscuits are fluffy and tender on the inside with just a hint of sweetness.
—**JENNIFER HOEFT** THORNDALE, TEXAS

PREP/TOTAL TIME: 25 MIN. • **YIELD:** 6 SERVINGS

- 2 **cups biscuit/baking mix**
- 1 **teaspoon sugar**
- ½ **cup club soda**
- 3 **tablespoons sour cream**

1. In a small bowl, combine all ingredients; stir just until moistened. Drop into six mounds on a 9-in. round baking pan coated with cooking spray.

2. Bake at 400° for 20 minutes or until golden brown. Serve warm.

I made this hearty bread for a golf outing my husband attended and it received many compliments. Several men asked for the recipe, and they've told me they make it often. It makes a hefty appetizer or sandwich for lunch.

—LORELEI HULL
LULING, LOUISIANA

Three-Meat Stromboli

PREP: 20 MIN. • **BAKE:** 35 MIN.
YIELD: 2 LOAVES (12-16 SLICES EACH)

- 2 **loaves (1 pound each) frozen bread dough, thawed**
- 2 **tablespoons Dijon mustard**
- ½ **cup grated Parmesan cheese, divided**
- ¼ **pound pastrami, finely chopped**
- ¼ **pound pepperoni, finely chopped**
- ¼ **pound hard salami, finely chopped**
- 1 **cup (4 ounces) shredded Swiss cheese**
- 1 **egg, beaten**

1. Roll each loaf of bread dough into a 12-in. x 7-in. rectangle. Spread mustard to within 1 in. of edges. Sprinkle each with 2 tablespoons Parmesan cheese.

2. Combine the pastrami, pepperoni, salami and Swiss cheese; sprinkle over dough. Top with remaining Parmesan cheese. Brush edges of dough with egg. Roll up, jelly-roll style, beginning with a long side. Seal seam and ends.

3. Place seam side down on a greased baking sheet; cut three slits in the top of each loaf. Bake at 350°for 35-40 minutes or until golden brown. Slice; serve warm.

THREE-CHEESE MEAT STROMBOLI: Substitute a ¼ pound chopped fully cooked ham for the pastrami and omit the pepperoni. Use ¾ cup each shredded mozzarella and cheddar cheeses for the Swiss cheese. Add ¼ cup chopped roasted red pepper to the meat-cheese mixture. Proceed as recipe directs.

Garlic Poppy Seed Spirals

This is a fast, easy way to dress up plain crescent rolls. Adjust the seasoning to your family's taste...or use a little powdered ranch dressing mix as an alternative.
—**STACEY SCHERER** MACOMB, MICHIGAN

PREP/TOTAL TIME: 25 MIN. • **YIELD:** 10 SERVINGS

- 3 tablespoons butter, melted
- 1 teaspoon garlic powder
- 1 teaspoon dried minced onion
- ½ teaspoon poppy seeds
- 1 tube (8 ounces) refrigerated crescent rolls

1. In a small bowl, combine the butter, garlic powder, onion and poppy seeds; set aside. Remove crescent dough from tube; do not unroll. Cut dough into 10 slices; dip one side in butter mixture.

2. Place buttered side up in an ungreased 9-in. round baking pan. Brush with remaining butter mixture. Bake at 350° for 14-16 minutes or until golden brown. Serve warm.

Mexican Corn Bread

PREP: 10 MIN. • **BAKE:** 50 MIN. • **YIELD:** 18-24 SERVINGS

- 2 packages (8½ ounces each) corn bread/muffin mix
- 1 medium onion, chopped
- 2 cups (8 ounces) shredded cheddar cheese
- 1 can (14¾ ounces) cream-style corn
- 1½ cups (12 ounces) sour cream
- 4 eggs, lightly beaten
- 1 can (4 ounces) chopped green chilies
- ⅓ cup canola oil
- 1 tablespoon finely chopped jalapeno pepper

1. In a large bowl, combine corn bread mix and onion. Combine the remaining ingredients; add to the corn bread mixture just until moistened. Pour into a greased 13-in. x 9-in. baking dish.

2. Bake at 350° for 50-55 minutes or until lightly browned and the edges pull away from sides of pan and a toothpick inserted near the center comes out clean. Serve warm. Refrigerate leftovers.

EDITOR'S NOTE: Wear disposable gloves when cutting hot peppers; the oils can burn skin. Avoid touching your face.

I work at an elementary school, and a couple of times a year we have a gathering where everyone brings a favorite dish to pass. A friend shared this delicious corn bread and it was a big hit.
—**SANDY GAULITZ** SPRING, TEXAS

Here's a luscious make-and-take recipe for any holiday brunches you're invited to. It couldn't be simpler or quicker, and you can vary the flavor using what preserves you have on hand.
—**HOLLY BAUER** WEST BEND, WISCONSIN

Apricot & White Chocolate Coffee Cake

PREP: 15 MIN. • **BAKE:** 20 MIN. • **YIELD:** 12 SERVINGS

- 2 **cups biscuit/baking mix**
- 2 **tablespoons sugar**
- 1 **egg**
- ⅔ **cup 2% milk**
- 2 **tablespoons canola oil**
- ½ **cup white baking chips**
- ½ **cup apricot preserves**

TOPPING:

- ⅓ **cup biscuit/baking mix**
- ⅓ **cup sugar**
- 2 **tablespoons cold butter**

1. In a large bowl, combine the biscuit mix and sugar. Whisk the egg, milk and oil; stir into dry ingredients just until moistened. Fold in chips. Pour into a greased 9-in. round baking pan.

2. Drop preserves by teaspoonfuls over batter. Cut through batter with a knife to swirl the preserves.

3. For topping, combine biscuit mix and sugar in small bowl; cut in butter until crumbly. Sprinkle over batter.

4. Bake at 400° for 20-25 minutes or until golden brown. Serve warm.

Herb Focaccia Bread

PREP: 30 MIN. + RISING • **BAKE:** 15 MIN.
YIELD: 2 BREAD LOAVES (10 WEDGES EACH)

1 **package (16 ounces) hot roll mix**
1 **cup warm water (120° to 130°)**
1 **egg, lightly beaten**
2 **tablespoons plus 2 teaspoons olive oil, divided**
1 **cup finely chopped onion**
1 **teaspoon dried rosemary, crushed**
1 **teaspoon dried thyme**

1. In a large bowl, combine the contents of the roll mix and yeast packets. Stir in the warm water, egg and 2 tablespoons oil; beat for 2 minutes or until dough pulls away from sides of bowl.

2. Turn onto a floured surface; knead until smooth and elastic, about 5 minutes. Place in a bowl coated with cooking spray, turning once to grease top. Let rest for 5 minutes.

3. Divide dough in half. Roll each half into a 12-in. circle. Transfer to two 12-in. pizza pans coated with cooking spray. Using fingertips, make indentations 1 in. apart on dough; cover.

4. In a small skillet, saute the onion, rosemary and thyme in the remaining oil for 3-4 minutes or until tender. Spread evenly on dough. Cover and let rise in a warm place until doubled, about 30 minutes.

5. Bake at 375° for 14-18 minutes or until golden brown. Remove from pans to wire racks.

Pancake mix is the key to this light and fluffy quick bread that kids will love. These scones are so wonderful with a cup of coffee, milk or herbal tea.
—MARGARET WILSON
SUN CITY, CALIFORNIA

Chocolate-Orange Scones

PREP/TOTAL TIME: 25 MIN. • **YIELD:** 8 SCONES

- 1½ **cups complete buttermilk pancake mix**
- ¾ **cup heavy whipping cream**
- 2 **to 3 teaspoons grated orange peel**
- 2 **milk chocolate candy bars (1.55 ounces each), chopped**

1. In a small bowl, combine the pancake mix, cream and orange peel. Turn onto a lightly floured surface, knead 6 times. Knead in chocolate.

2. Pat into a 9-in. circle. Cut into eight wedges. Separate wedges and place on a greased baking sheet. Bake at 400° for 9-11 minutes or until lightly browned. Serve warm.

successful scones

To ensure that your scones come out perfectly, here are some tips: 1. Use cold butter and/or cream; 2. When slicing, dip the knife in flour to prevent sticking; 3. After cutting, if the wedges are separated, the scones will have a crisper crust. If the wedges are cut and not separated, the scones will have a softer crust; 4. Scones are best on the day they're baked.

Lemon Pull-Apart Coffee Cake

PREP/TOTAL TIME: 30 MIN. • **YIELD:** 10 SERVINGS

¼ **cup sugar**
¼ **cup chopped walnuts**
¼ **cup golden raisins**
2 **tablespoons butter, melted**
2 **teaspoons grated lemon peel**
1 **tube (12 ounces) refrigerated buttermilk biscuits**
GLAZE:
½ **cup confectioners' sugar**
1 **tablespoon lemon juice**

1. In a large bowl, combine the first five ingredients. Separate biscuits and cut each into quarters; toss with sugar mixture. Place in a greased 9-in. round baking pan.

2. Bake at 400° for 20-25 minutes or until golden brown. Immediately invert onto a wire rack. Combine glaze ingredients until smooth; drizzle over warm coffee cake.

French Onion Drop Biscuits

These simple drop biscuits have a golden color and mild onion flavor. They're fast to fix and fabulous!
—**GALELAH DOWELL** FAIRLAND, OKLAHOMA

PREP/TOTAL TIME: 20 MIN. • **YIELD:** 1 DOZEN

- 2 cups biscuit/baking mix
- 1 carton (8 ounces) French onion dip
- ¼ cup 2% milk

1. In a large bowl, combine baking mix and onion dip. Stir in milk just until moistened. Drop by rounded tablespoonfuls 2 in. apart onto a baking sheet coated with cooking spray.

2. Bake at 450° for 10-14 minutes or until golden brown. Serve warm.

Caramel Sweet Rolls

PREP: 10 MIN. • **BAKE:** 25 MIN. • **YIELD:** 6 SERVINGS

- ½ cup packed brown sugar
- ⅓ cup heavy whipping cream
- ¼ cup chopped walnuts
- 1 tube (11 ounces) refrigerated breadsticks
- 2 tablespoons sugar
- 1 teaspoon ground cinnamon

1. In a small bowl, combine brown sugar and cream until sugar is dissolved. Spread into a greased 8-in. square baking dish. Sprinkle with walnuts.

2. On a lightly floured surface, unroll breadstick dough (do not separate). Combine sugar and cinnamon; sprinkle over dough. Reroll, starting with a short end. Cut into six slices. Place cut side down in prepared pan.

3. Bake at 350° for 25-30 minutes or until golden brown. Cool for 1 minute before inverting onto a serving plate. Serve warm.

Our family loves sweet rolls. This is my favorite recipe because it's super-easy and calls for a tube of ready-made breadstick dough. The sweet rolls take just minutes to assemble but taste like you spent hours making them!
—**KRISTA SMITH** MENTONE, CALIFORNIA

Italian Cloverleaf Rolls

A sprinkling of seasonings on top of these simple rolls gives them a wonderful flavor. Consider doubling the recipe because these are guaranteed to disappear!
—**HEIDI HALL** NORTH ST. PAUL, MINNESOTA

PREP: 20 MIN. + RISING • **BAKE:** 15 MIN. • **YIELD:** 1 DOZEN

- 1 package (16 ounces) hot roll mix
- 2 tablespoons butter, melted
- 3 tablespoons grated Parmesan cheese
- 1 tablespoon sesame seeds
- ¾ teaspoon dill weed
- ¾ teaspoon dried basil
- ½ teaspoon garlic salt

1. Prepare roll mix according to package directions. Divide dough into 12 portions; divide each into three pieces. Shape each into a ball; place three balls in each greased muffin cup. Brush with butter.

2. Combine the cheese, sesame seeds, dill, basil and garlic salt; sprinkle over tops. Cover and let rise in a warm place until doubled, about 20 minutes.

3. Bake at 375° for 15-20 minutes or until golden brown. Remove from pan to a wire rack. Serve warm.

Hazelnut Crescent Rolls

Tender dough gives way to warm and wonderful chocolate with a hint of hazelnut flavor. This simple treat is sure to please everyone. Yum!
—**PHYLLIS ADKINS** SOUTH CHARLESTON, WEST VIRGINIA

PREP/TOTAL TIME: 25 MIN. • **YIELD:** 8 SERVINGS

- 1 tube (8 ounces) refrigerated crescent rolls
- ½ cup Nutella, warmed
- ⅓ cup chocolate-covered English toffee bits
  Confectioners' sugar

1. Unroll crescent roll dough; separate into triangles. Spread each with 1 tablespoon Nutella; sprinkle with toffee bits. Roll up from the wide end and place pointed side down 2 in. apart on greased baking sheets. Curve ends to form crescents.

2. Bake at 375° for 11-13 minutes or until lightly browned. Dust with confectioners' sugar.

Easy Orange Rolls

PREP: 15 MIN. • **BAKE:** 25 MIN. • **YIELD:** 12-16 SERVINGS

- **1 cup sugar**
- **½ cup butter, cubed**
- **¼ cup orange juice**
- **2 tablespoons grated orange peel**
- **3 tubes (10 ounces each) refrigerated biscuits**

1. In a small saucepan, combine the sugar, butter, orange juice and peel. Heat until sugar is dissolved and the butter is melted. Pour into a greased 10-in. fluted tube pan.

2. Place 12 biscuits on their sides in a ring around the outer edge, overlapping slightly. Arrange remaining biscuits in the same manner, creating two more rings (one of 10 biscuits and one of eight).

3. Bake at 350° for 25-30 minutes or until golden brown. Immediately turn upside down onto serving platter. Serve warm.

Apple Pinwheels

PREP: 20 MIN. • **BAKE:** 20 MIN. • **YIELD:** ABOUT 2 DOZEN

- ⅓ **cup water**
- ⅓ **cup butter**
- 1⅓ **cups sugar, divided**
- 2 **tubes (8 ounces each) refrigerated crescent rolls**
- 3 **cups finely chopped peeled tart apples**
- 1 **teaspoon apple pie spice**

1. In a saucepan, combine water, butter and 1 cup of sugar; cook over medium heat until butter is melted and sugar is dissolved. Set aside.

2. Unroll each tube of crescent roll dough into a rectangle; seal seams and perforations.

3. Combine the apples, pie spice and remaining sugar; sprinkle over dough to within 1 in. of edges. Roll up, jelly-roll style, starting with a long side. Cut into 1-in. rolls; place in a greased 13-in. x 9-in. x 1-in. baking dish. Pour syrup over rolls.

4. Bake at 350° for 20-25 minutes or until golden brown. Serve warm.

Pepperoni Pizza Muffins

PREP: 20 MIN. • **BAKE:** 20 MIN. • **YIELD:** 14 MUFFINS

- 3 **cups biscuit/baking mix**
- 1 **can (10¾ ounces) condensed tomato soup, undiluted**
- ¾ **cup water**
- ½ **cup shredded part-skim mozzarella cheese**
- ½ **cup shredded cheddar cheese**
- ½ **cup diced pepperoni**
- 2 **tablespoons chopped ripe olives**
- 1 **tablespoon dried minced onion**
- 1 **teaspoon Italian seasoning**

1. Place biscuit mix in a large bowl. Combine the remaining ingredients; stir into biscuit mix just until moistened. Fill greased muffin cups three-fourths full.

2. Bake at 350° for 17-20 minutes or until a toothpick inserted near the center comes out clean. Cool for 5 minutes before removing from pans to wire racks. Serve warm. Refrigerate leftovers.

Loaded with pizza flavor, I serve these moist muffins regularly. They're great for lunch but also make good appetizers when baked in mini muffin cups. Try adding chopped mushrooms or green pepper to the batter.
—**ANDREA MCGEE**
PORT ALSWORTH, ALASKA

Speedy Cinnamon Rolls

On special occasions when we were growing up, my mother would make as many as four batches of these delicious cinnamon rolls to satisfy the appetites of her eight ravenous children. Today this recipe is still a hit.
—**NICOLE WEIR** HAGER CITY, WISCONSIN

PREP: 10 MIN. + RISING • **BAKE:** 25 MIN. • **YIELD:** 1½ DOZEN

- 1 **loaf (1 pound) frozen bread dough, thawed**
- 2 **tablespoons butter, melted**
- ⅔ **cup packed brown sugar**
- ½ **cup chopped walnuts**
- 1 **teaspoon ground cinnamon**
- ½ **cup heavy whipping cream**

1. On a floured surface, roll dough into an 18-in. x 6-in. rectangle; brush with butter.

2. In a large bowl, combine the brown sugar, walnuts and cinnamon; sprinkle over dough. Roll up, jelly-roll style, starting with a long side; pinch seams to seal. Cut into 16 slices.

3. Place, cut side down, in two greased 8-in. round baking pans. Cover and let rise until doubled, about 50 minutes.

4. Pour ¼ cup cream over each pan. Bake at 350° for 25-30 minutes or until golden brown. Immediately invert onto serving plates.

Cherry Danish

These delightful Danish use only five ingredients plus water. They are so quick to fix—you don't even have to uncoil the refrigerated breadsticks. We prefer them with cherry pie filling, but you can also use peach or blueberry.
—**MARGARET MCNEIL** GERMANTOWN, TENNESSEE

PREP/TOTAL TIME: 30 MIN. • **YIELD:** 1 DOZEN

2	**tubes (11 ounces each) refrigerated breadsticks**
⅓	**cup butter, melted**
1	**tablespoon sugar**
1	**cup cherry pie filling**
1	**cup confectioners' sugar**
1½	**teaspoons water**

1. Separate each tube of breadsticks into six sections but leave coiled. Place in a greased 15-in. x 10-in. x 1-in. baking pan. Brush generously with butter and sprinkle with sugar.

2. Make an indentation in the top of each coil; fill with about 1 tablespoon of pie filling. Bake at 400° for 15-20 minutes or until golden brown. Combine the confectioners' sugar and water until smooth; drizzle over the warm rolls.

The ABC abbreviation in the title of these muffins stands for Applesauce, Bran and Cinnamon. They are an absolute favorite at our house. In fact, my husband asks for them instead of birthday cake!
—**SUSAN SMITH** NEWARK, OHIO

ABC Muffins

PREP: 15 MIN. • **BAKE:** 20 MIN. • **YIELD:** 1½ DOZEN

3	**eggs**
¾	**cup canola oil**
½	**cup applesauce**
¼	**cup honey**
1	**package (18¼ ounces) yellow cake mix**
1½	**cups wheat bran**
2	**teaspoons ground cinnamon**

1. In a bowl, beat eggs, oil, applesauce and honey. Combine the dry cake mix, bran and cinnamon; add to egg mixture. Mix just until blended.

2. Fill greased or paper-lined muffin cups two-thirds full. Bake at 350° for 20-25 minutes or until muffins are done.

Lemon Poppy Seed Bread

PREP: 10 MIN. • **BAKE:** 35 MIN. + COOLING
YIELD: 2 LOAVES (16 SLICES EACH)

- 1 **package (18¼ ounces) white cake mix**
- 1 **package (3.4 ounces) instant lemon pudding mix**
- 1 **cup warm water**
- 4 **eggs**
- ½ **cup canola oil**
- 4 **teaspoons poppy seeds**

1. In a large bowl, combine the cake mix, pudding mix, water, eggs and oil; beat on low speed for 30 seconds. Beat on medium for 2 minutes. Fold in poppy seeds.

2. Pour into two greased 9-in. x 5-in. loaf pans. Bake at 350° for 35-40 minutes or until a toothpick inserted near the center comes out clean. Cool in pans for 10 minutes before removing to a wire rack.

If the days that you have time for baking are few and far between, try this extra-quick bread. You'll love the ease of preparation, the handful of ingredients and the delicious flavor.
—KAREN DOUGHERTY FREEPORT, ILLINOIS

freezing bread

To freeze bread, after it is cooled (make sure it isn't iced or frosted), wrap tightly in freezer-safe plastic bags, plastic wrap in foil, or freezer paper and store in the freezer. Wrapped like this, bread will keep in the freezer up to a month. To thaw, unwrap slightly and thaw at room temperature for 2 to 3 hours.

Teddy Bear Biscuits

PREP/TOTAL TIME: 20 MIN. • **YIELD:** 3 BEARS

- 1 tube (7½ ounces) refrigerated buttermilk biscuits (10 biscuits)
- 1 egg, lightly beaten
- 2 tablespoons sugar
- ¼ teaspoon ground cinnamon
- 9 miniature semisweet chocolate chips

1. For each bear, shape one biscuit into an oval for the body and place on a greased baking sheet. Cut one biscuit into four pieces; shape into balls for arms and legs. Place next to body.

2. Cut one biscuit into two small pieces and one large piece; shape into head and ears and place above body. Brush with egg. Combine sugar and cinnamon; sprinkle over bears.

3. Bake at 425° for 8-10 minutes (the one remaining biscuit can be baked with the bears) or until golden brown. Place chocolate chips on head for eyes and nose while the biscuits are still warm.

French Onion Bread

PREP: 25 MIN. + RISING • **BAKE:** 30 MIN. • **YIELD:** 3 LOAVES

2	packages (¼ ounce each) active dry yeast
1	cup warm water (110° to 115°)
5¼	to 5¾ cups all-purpose flour, divided
4	tablespoons sugar, divided
¾	teaspoon salt
1¼	cups hot water (120° to 130°)
1	envelope onion soup mix
3	tablespoons shortening

1. In a bowl, dissolve yeast in warm water. Add ½ cup flour, 2 tablespoons sugar and salt; beat until smooth, about 1 minute. Cover and let rise in a warm place for 20 minutes.

2. In a small bowl, combine hot water, soup mix, shortening and remaining sugar. Cool to 115°. Add to yeast mixture with 2 cups flour; mix for 1-2 minutes. Stir in enough remaining flour to form a soft dough.

3. Turn onto a floured surface; knead until smooth and elastic, about 6-8 minutes. Place in a greased bowl, turning once to grease top. Cover and let rise in a warm place until doubled, about 1 hour.

4. Punch the dough down; divide into thirds. Shape into loaves; place in three greased 8-in. x 4-in. loaf pans. Cover and let rise until doubled, about 30 minutes.

5. Bake at 375° for 30 minutes or until golden brown. Remove from pans to cool on wire racks.

Rum Sweet Rolls

PREP: 25 MIN. + RISING • **BAKE:** 25 MIN. + COOLING
YIELD: 1 DOZEN

These sweet tender rolls are a great choice for breakfast, a coffee break or even special occasions. Because they are so easy to make, I bake several batches for the holidays.
—**KAREN HUGHES** CHESTER, VIRGINIA

　1　**package (16 ounces) hot roll mix**
　3　**tablespoons butter, softened**
　2　**cups confectioners' sugar**
4½　**teaspoons water**
3½　**teaspoons rum extract**
　½　**teaspoon ground cinnamon**

1. Prepare hot roll mix according to package directions. Turn dough onto a lightly floured surface; gently knead for 5 minutes. Cover with a bowl and let rest for 5 minutes. Roll into a 12-in. x 10-in. rectangle. Spread with butter to within ½ in. of edges.

2. In a large bowl, combine the confectioners' sugar, water and extract until smooth. Spread half of the mixture over butter. Sprinkle with cinnamon.

3. Roll up jelly-roll style, starting with a long side; pinch seam to seal. Cut into 12 rolls. Place cut side up in a greased 11-in. x 7-in. baking dish. Cover and let rest until nearly doubled, about 25 minutes.

4. Bake at 375° for 20-25 minutes or until golden brown. Cool for 5 minutes before removing from pan to a wire rack. Cool for 15 minutes. Drizzle with remaining confectioners' sugar mixture. Serve warm.

Pesto Breadsticks

PREP/TOTAL TIME: 20 MIN. • **YIELD:** 1 DOZEN

- 1 tube (11 ounces) refrigerated breadsticks
- 2 tablespoons prepared pesto
- ¼ teaspoon garlic pepper blend
- 1 tablespoon butter, melted
- 2 tablespoons shredded Parmesan cheese

1. Unroll and separate breadsticks; place on an ungreased baking sheet. Combine pesto and garlic pepper; brush over breadsticks. Twist each breadstick three times.

2. Brush with butter; sprinkle with cheese. Bake at 375° for 10-13 minutes or until golden brown. Serve warm.

Our Test Kitchen created these savory breadsticks flavored with garlic pepper and pesto. Whether you serve them with soup, salad or even a pasta supper, these cute twists add fun to any menu.
—**TASTE OF HOME TEST KITCHEN**

Oat Cinnamon Rolls

Dried cranberries add a holiday touch to these special rolls made from convenient frozen bread dough. My husband loves marmalade, so when I spotted this recipe that used it as icing, I knew I had to try it. Now it's one of his favorites.
—**MARGARET WILSON** SUN CITY, CALIFORNIA

PREP: 15 MIN. + RISING • **BAKE:** 30 MIN. • **YIELD:** 9 ROLLS

- 1 cup quick-cooking oats
- ⅓ cup packed brown sugar
- 2 teaspoons ground cinnamon
- 1 cup dried cranberries
- ⅓ cup butter, melted
- 1 pound frozen bread dough, thawed
- ¼ cup orange marmalade

1. In a large bowl, combine the oats, brown sugar and cinnamon. Stir in cranberries and butter; set aside.

2. On a lightly floured surface, roll the dough into a 12-in. x 10-in. rectangle. Sprinkle with oat mixture. Roll up, jelly-roll style, starting with a long side; seal seam. Cut into 9 rolls. Place rolls, cut side up, in a greased 9-in. square baking pan. Cover and let rise in a warm place until doubled, about 30 minutes.

3. Bake at 350° for 30-35 minutes or until golden brown. Cool for 10 minutes before removing from pan to a wire rack. Brush with marmalade. Serve warm.

a bit about oats

Old-fashioned oats are groats that are steamed and flattened with huge rollers. They take about 15 minutes to cook. Quick-cooking oats are groats that have been cut into pieces before being steamed and rolled. They take about 5 minutes to prepare. Both can be used interchangeably, although old-fashioned oats may give your recipe more texture.

Cranberry Cream Cheese Muffins

PREP: 15 MIN. • **BAKE:** 20 MIN. • **YIELD:** 1 DOZEN

- 1 package (3 ounces) cream cheese, softened
- 4 tablespoons sugar, divided
- 1 package (15.6 ounces) cranberry-orange quick bread mix
- 1 cup milk
- ⅓ cup canola oil
- 1 egg

1. In a small bowl, beat cream cheese and 2 tablespoons sugar until smooth; set aside. Place the bread mix in another bowl. Combine the milk, oil and egg; stir into bread mix just until moistened.

2. Fill paper-lined muffin cups one-fourth full with batter. Place 2 teaspoons cream cheese mixture in the center of each; top with remaining batter. Sprinkle with remaining sugar.

3. Bake at 400° for 18-20 minutes or until a toothpick inserted near the center comes out clean. Cool for 5 minutes before removing from pan to a wire rack. Serve warm.

Rippled Coffee Cake

PREP: 10 MIN. • **BAKE:** 30 MIN. • **YIELD:** 16-20 SERVINGS

- 1 **package (18¼ ounces) yellow cake mix**
- 1 **cup (8 ounces) sour cream**
- 4 **eggs**
- ⅔ **cup canola oil**
- 1 **cup packed brown sugar**
- 1 **tablespoon ground cinnamon**

ICING:
- 2 **cups confectioners' sugar**
- ¼ **cup milk**
- 2 **teaspoons vanilla extract**

1. In a large bowl, combine the dry cake mix, sour cream, eggs and oil; beat well. Spread half of the batter into a greased 13-in. x 9-in. baking pan.

2. Combine brown sugar and cinnamon; sprinkle over batter. Carefully spread remaining batter on top.

3. Bake at 350° for 30-35 minutes or until a toothpick inserted near the center comes out clean. Combine icing ingredients; drizzle over warm cake.

sour cream substitute

Plain yogurt can be substituted in equal amounts for sour cream in baking recipes as well as in casseroles, dips and sauces. Nonfat yogurt doesn't work well in recipes that are baked.

66 I came across this recipe years ago at a church recipe exchange. I don't know who created the soup, but my husband and son thank me for it by helping themselves to seconds and thirds!

—ELLEN MCCLEARY SCOTLAND, ONTARIO 99

sensational soups

There's no need to wait hours for a hearty bowl of homemade soup. With the simple recipes in this chapter, you can have this popular comfort food in as little as 10 minutes.

Ground Beef Noodle Soup

PREP: 15 MIN. • **COOK:** 20 MIN.
YIELD: 8 SERVINGS (2 QUARTS)

1½	pounds lean ground beef (90% lean)
½	cup each chopped onion, celery and carrot
7	cups water
1	envelope au jus mix
2	tablespoons beef bouillon granules
2	bay leaves
⅛	teaspoon pepper
1½	cups uncooked egg noodles

1. In a large saucepan, cook the beef, onion, celery and carrot over medium heat until the meat is no longer pink; drain.

2. Add the water, au jus mix, bouillon, bay leaves and pepper; bring to a boil. Stir in the noodles. Return to a boil. Cook, uncovered, for 15 minutes or until noodles are tender, stirring occasionally. Discard bay leaves.

Simple Chicken Soup

I revised a recipe that my family loved so it would be lighter and easier to make. Served with a green salad and fresh bread, the soup makes a hearty yet healthy meal.
—**SUE WEST** ALVORD, TEXAS

PREP/TOTAL TIME: 20 MIN. • **YIELD:** 6 SERVINGS

2	cans (14½ ounces each) reduced-sodium chicken broth
1	tablespoon dried minced onion
1	package (16 ounces) frozen mixed vegetables
2	cups cubed cooked chicken breast
2	cans (10¾ ounces each) reduced-fat reduced-sodium condensed cream of chicken soup, undiluted

1. In a large saucepan, bring broth and onion to a boil. Reduce heat. Add the vegetables; cover and cook for 6-8 minutes or until crisp-tender. Stir in chicken and soup; heat through.

Chicken Wild Rice Chowder

PREP/TOTAL TIME: 25 MIN. • **YIELD:** 4 SERVINGS

- 2 **cups sliced fresh carrots**
- ½ **cup chopped onion**
- ½ **cup chopped celery**
- 2 **tablespoons butter**
- 3 **tablespoons all-purpose flour**
- 2 **cans (14½ ounces each) chicken broth**
- 2⅔ **cups cubed cooked chicken breasts**
- 1 **package (8.8 ounces) ready-to-serve long grain and wild rice**
- ¼ **cup half-and-half cream**
- ⅛ **teaspoon pepper**

1. In a large saucepan, saute the carrots, onion and celery in butter until tender. Stir in flour until blended; gradually add broth. Bring to a boil; cook and stir for 2 minutes or until thickened. Stir in the chicken, rice, cream and pepper; heat through.

This tasty soup, which is perfect for helping you power through a cold day, is comfort food at its finest. You'll love the fact that it's table-ready in just 25 minutes.
—TASTE OF HOME TEST KITCHEN

add a special touch to soup

Adding a garnish to soup before serving adds color, flavor and texture. A garnish might include: finely chopped green onions or chives, minced fresh parsley, shredded cheddar cheese, grated or shredded Parmesan, a dollop of sour cream or croutons.

Hearty Wild Rice Soup

I tasted this thick and hearty soup at a food fair that I helped judge. The original recipe called for uncooked wild rice, but I use a quick-cooking rice blend to speed things up.
—**KATHY HERINK** GLADBROOK, IOWA

PREP/TOTAL TIME: 20 MIN.
YIELD: 8 SERVINGS (ABOUT 2 QUARTS)

- 1 **pound ground beef**
- 2 **cups chopped celery**
- 2 **cups chopped onion**
- 3 **cups hot water**
- 1 **can (14½ ounces) chicken broth**
- 1 **can (10¾ ounces) condensed cream of mushroom soup, undiluted**
- 1 **package (6.75 ounces) quick-cooking long grain and wild rice mix**
- 5 **bacon strips, cooked and crumbled**

1. In a large saucepan, cook the beef, celery and onion over medium heat until meat is no longer pink and vegetables are tender; drain.

2. Add the water, broth, soup, rice and contents of the seasoning packet. Bring to a boil. Reduce heat; cover and simmer for 5 minutes or until heated through. Garnish with bacon.

Hot Dog Bean Soup

PREP/TOTAL TIME: 10 MIN. • **YIELD:** 4 SERVINGS

- 3   hot dogs, halved lengthwise and cut into ¼-inch pieces
- 1   teaspoon canola oil
- 1   can (16 ounces) kidney beans, rinsed and drained
- 1   can (11½ ounces) condensed bean and bacon soup, undiluted
- 1¼ cups water
- 1   teaspoon dried minced onion
- ¼   teaspoon pepper

1. In a large skillet, cook hot dogs in oil over medium heat for 3-4 minutes or until browned.

2. Meanwhile, in a 2-qt. microwave-safe bowl, combine the remaining ingredients. Cover and microwave on high for 2-3 minutes or until heated through, stirring once. Stir in hot dogs.

EDITOR'S NOTE: This recipe was tested in a 1,100-watt microwave.

My husband fixed this soup for our three kids years ago. They always loved it and now prepare it for their own kids. It's a real favorite on family camping trips.
—**MARY ANN KIME** STURGIS, MICHIGAN

Pepperoni Pizza Chili

I came up with this recipe one day when I was craving pizza but didn't want to fuss with making a crust. I just put the ingredients for a pizza in a bowl instead.
—**MARILOUISE WYATT** COWEN, WEST VIRGINIA

PREP: 5 MIN. • **COOK:** 40 MIN. • **YIELD:** 8 SERVINGS

- 1   pound ground beef
- 1   can (16 ounces) kidney beans, rinsed and drained
- 1   can (15 ounces) pizza sauce
- 1   can (14½ ounces) Italian stewed tomatoes
- 1   can (8 ounces) tomato sauce
- 1½ cups water
- 1   package (3½ ounces) sliced pepperoni
- ½   cup chopped green pepper
- 1   teaspoon pizza seasoning or Italian seasoning
- 1   teaspoon salt
      Shredded part-skim mozzarella cheese, optional

1. In a large saucepan, cook beef over medium heat until no longer pink; drain. Stir in the beans, pizza sauce, tomatoes, tomato sauce, water, pepperoni, green pepper, pizza seasoning and salt. Bring to a boil. Reduce heat; simmer, uncovered, for 30 minutes or until chili reaches desired thickness. Sprinkle with cheese if desired.

Ramen Corn Chowder

PREP/TOTAL TIME: 15 MIN. • **YIELD:** 4 SERVINGS

- 2 cups water
- 1 package (3 ounces) chicken ramen noodles
- 1 can (15¼ ounces) whole kernel corn, drained
- 1 can (14¾ ounces) cream-style corn
- 1 cup 2% milk
- 1 teaspoon dried minced onion
- ¼ teaspoon curry powder
- ¾ cup shredded cheddar cheese
- 1 tablespoon crumbled cooked bacon
- 1 tablespoon minced fresh parsley

1. In a small saucepan, bring water to a boil. Break noodles into large pieces. Add noodles and contents of seasoning packet to water. Reduce heat to medium. Cook, uncovered, for 2-3 minutes or until noodles are tender.

2. Stir in the corn, cream-style corn, milk, onion and curry; heat through. Stir in the cheese, bacon and parsley until blended.

Creamy Tomato Basil Soup

PREP/TOTAL TIME: 25 MIN. • **YIELD:** 6 SERVINGS

- 2 tablespoons chopped green onion
- 2 garlic cloves, minced
- 1½ teaspoons olive oil
- 1 can (28 ounces) crushed tomatoes
- 1 can (10½ ounces) condensed chicken broth, undiluted
- 1⅓ cups water
- ¼ teaspoon pepper
- ¾ cup heavy whipping cream
- 2 tablespoons sherry or additional chicken broth
- 2 tablespoons minced fresh basil
- 2 teaspoons sugar

1. In a large saucepan, saute onion and garlic in oil until tender. Add the tomatoes, broth, water and pepper. Bring to a boil. Reduce heat; simmer for 10 minutes.

2. Stir in the cream, sherry or additional broth, basil and sugar. Cook for 1 minute or until heated through (do not boil).

We often eat easy-to-make soups when there's not a lot of time to cook. I replaced the wild rice requested in the original recipe with a boxed rice mix. This creamy concoction is now a family favorite.
—**LISA HOFER**
HITCHCOCK
SOUTH DAKOTA

Cheesy Wild Rice Soup

PREP/TOTAL TIME: 30 MIN. • **YIELD:** 8 SERVINGS

- 1 package (6.2 ounces) fast-cooking long grain and wild rice mix
- 4 cups 2% milk
- 1 can (10¾ ounces) condensed cream of potato soup, undiluted
- 8 ounces process cheese (Velveeta), cubed
- ½ pound bacon strips, cooked and crumbled

1. In a large saucepan, prepare the rice mix according to package directions. Add the milk, soup and process cheese. Cook and stir until the cheese is melted. Garnish with bacon.

what is process cheese?

Process cheese is a blend of different cheeses that is similar in flavor to the natural cheese from which it's made. Generally, it is stable at room temperature and stays smooth and creamy when it is heated. The most common brand name of process American cheese is Velveeta.

Zesty Potato Cheese Soup

PREP/TOTAL TIME: 10 MIN. • **YIELD:** 6 SERVINGS

3 cans (10¾ ounces each) condensed cream of potato soup, undiluted
2 cans (12 ounces each) evaporated milk
¾ cup shredded cheddar cheese
¾ cup shredded pepper jack cheese
6 slices ready-to-serve fully cooked bacon, crumbled

1. In a large saucepan, combine the potato soup and milk. Cook over medium heat for 5-7 minutes or until heated through. Ladle into serving bowls. Sprinkle with cheeses and bacon.

Ground Beef And Barley Soup

PREP: 10 MIN. • **COOK:** 1 HOUR
YIELD: 12 SERVINGS (3 QUARTS)

1½ pounds ground beef
3 celery ribs, sliced
1 medium onion, chopped
3 cans (10½ ounces each) condensed beef consomme, undiluted
1 can (28 ounces) diced tomatoes, undrained
4 medium carrots, sliced
2 cups water
1 can (10¾ ounces) condensed tomato soup, undiluted
½ cup medium pearl barley
1 bay leaf

1. In a Dutch oven, cook the beef, celery and onion over medium heat until the meat is no longer pink; drain. Add the remaining ingredients; bring to a boil. Reduce heat; simmer, uncovered, for 45-50 minutes or until barley is tender. Discard bay leaf.

Tortellini Soup

This soup is delicious, pretty and unbelievably fast to make. For a creamy variation, I sometimes substitute cream of mushroom soup for the French onion soup. If there are any leftovers, they taste even better the next day.
—MARSHA FARLEY BANGOR, MAINE

PREP/TOTAL TIME: 30 MIN. • **YIELD:** 6-8 SERVINGS

1 pound ground beef
3½ cups water
1 can (28 ounces) diced tomatoes, undrained
1 can (10½ ounces) condensed French onion soup, undiluted
1 package (9 ounces) frozen cut green beans
1 package (9 ounces) refrigerated cheese tortellini
1 medium zucchini, chopped
1 teaspoon dried basil

1. In a large saucepan, cook beef over medium heat until no longer pink; drain. Add the remaining ingredients; bring to a boil. Cook, uncovered, for 7-9 minutes or until tortellini is tender.

I came across this recipe years ago at a church recipe exchange. I don't know who created the soup, but my husband and son thank me for preparing it by helping themselves to seconds and thirds!
—ELLEN MCCLEARY SCOTLAND, ONTARIO

Corn and Squash Soup

This hearty soup pairs squash and cream-style corn for such a pleasant taste. My family says this is their favorite squash recipe, and friends also comment on its wonderful flavor.

—JANICE ZOOK
WHITE RIVER JUNCTION, VERMONT

PREP/TOTAL TIME: 25 MIN. • **YIELD:** 8 SERVINGS (2½ QUARTS)

12	bacon strips, diced
1	medium onion, chopped
1	celery rib, chopped
2	tablespoons all-purpose flour
1	can (14½ ounces) chicken broth
6	cups mashed cooked butternut squash
2	cans (8¾ ounces each) cream-style corn
2	cups half-and-half cream
1	tablespoon minced fresh parsley
1½	teaspoons salt
½	teaspoon pepper
	Sour cream, optional

1. In a large saucepan, cook bacon over medium heat until crisp. Remove to paper towels; drain, reserving 2 tablespoons drippings.

2. In the drippings, saute onion and celery until tender. Stir in flour until blended. Gradually stir in broth. Bring to a boil; cook and stir for 2 minutes or until slightly thickened.

3. Reduce heat to medium. Stir in the squash, corn, cream, parsley, salt, pepper and bacon. Cook and stir until heated through. Garnish with sour cream if desired.

Broccoli Cheese Soup

My husband is diabetic, and I'm watching my weight. This soup fits our lifestyle perfectly. Friends and family will never guess it only takes just 15 minutes to make!
—**CAROL COLVIN** DERBY, NEW YORK

PREP/TOTAL TIME: 15 MIN. • **YIELD:** 8 SERVINGS

- 1 can (10¾ ounces) reduced-fat reduced-sodium condensed cream of celery soup, undiluted
- 1 can (10¾ ounces) reduced-fat reduced-sodium condensed cream of chicken soup, undiluted
- 3 cups fat-free milk
- 1 tablespoon dried minced onion
- 1 teaspoon dried parsley flakes
- ½ teaspoon garlic powder
- ¼ teaspoon pepper
- 3 cups frozen chopped broccoli, thawed
- 1 can (14½ ounces) sliced potatoes, drained
- ½ cup shredded reduced-fat cheddar cheese

1. In a large saucepan, combine the soups, milk, onion, parsley, garlic powder and pepper. Stir in broccoli and potatoes; heat through. Just before serving, sprinkle with cheese.

Pantry-Shelf Salmon Chowder

PREP/TOTAL TIME: 20 MIN. • **YIELD:** 4 SERVINGS

- 1 small onion, thinly sliced
- 1 tablespoon butter
- 1 can (10¾ ounces) condensed cream of celery soup, undiluted
- 1⅓ cups milk
- 1 can (15 ounces) cream-style corn
- 1 can (7½ ounces) salmon, drained, bones and skin removed
- 1 tablespoon minced fresh parsley

1. In a large saucepan, saute onion in butter until tender. Stir in the soup, milk and corn; bring to a boil. Reduce heat; add salmon and parsley. Simmer, uncovered, until heated through.

I always joke that if you can open a can, you can prepare this hearty chowder! It takes mere minutes to make, but people will think you fussed a lot longer.
—**KATHRYN AWE** INTERNATIONAL FALLS, MINNESOTA

Mac 'n' Cheese Soup

PREP/TOTAL TIME: 30 MIN. • **YIELD:** 8 SERVINGS (2 QUARTS)

1 package (14 ounces) deluxe macaroni and cheese dinner mix
9 cups water, divided
1 cup fresh broccoli florets
2 tablespoons finely chopped onion
1 can (10¾ ounces) condensed cheddar cheese soup, undiluted
2½ cups 2% milk
1 cup chopped fully cooked ham

1. Set aside the cheese sauce packet from macaroni and cheese mix. In a large saucepan, bring 8 cups water to a boil. Add macaroni; cook for 8-10 minutes or until tender.

2. Meanwhile, in another large saucepan, bring remaining water to a boil. Add broccoli and onion; cook, uncovered, for 3 minutes. Stir in the soup, milk, ham and contents of cheese sauce packet; heat through. Drain macaroni; stir into soup.

BROCCOLI MAC 'N' CHEESE SOUP: Double the broccoli and omit the ham for a meatless take on this soup.

Roasted Red Pepper Soup

PREP: 10 MIN. • **COOK:** 25 MIN. • **YIELD:** 6 SERVINGS

- 1 **large sweet onion, chopped**
- 2 **teaspoons butter**
- 2 **garlic cloves, minced**
- 2 **jars (15½ ounces each) roasted sweet red peppers, drained**
- 2 **cups vegetable broth**
- ½ **teaspoon dried basil**
- ¼ **teaspoon salt**
- 1 **cup half-and-half cream**

1. In a large saucepan, saute onion in butter for 2-3 minutes or until tender. Add garlic; cook 1 minute longer. Stir in the red peppers, broth, basil and salt. Bring to a boil. Reduce heat; cover and simmer for 20 minutes. Cool slightly.

2. In a blender, cover and process soup in batches until smooth. Remove 1 cup to a small bowl; stir in cream. Return remaining puree to pan. Stir in the cream mixture; heat through (do not boil).

Creamy Pumpkin Soup

A few years ago when our pumpkin harvest was very plentiful, I experimented in the kitchen and came up with this recipe.
—**EMMI SCHNEIDER** OAK LAKE, MANITOBA

PREP/TOTAL TIME: 30 MIN. • **YIELD:** 6 SERVINGS (1½ QUARTS)

- 1 medium onion, chopped
- 2 tablespoons butter
- 2 cans (14½ ounces each) chicken broth
- 2 cups sliced peeled potatoes
- 1 can (15 ounces) solid-pack pumpkin
- 2 to 2½ cups milk
- ½ teaspoon ground nutmeg
- ½ teaspoon salt
- ¼ teaspoon pepper
- 1 cup (8 ounces) sour cream
- 1 tablespoon chopped fresh parsley
- 3 bacon strips, cooked and crumbled

1. In a large saucepan, saute onion in butter until tender. Add the broth, potatoes and pumpkin; cook until the potatoes are tender, about 15 minutes. Remove from the heat; cool.

2. Puree half of the mixture at a time in a blender or food processor until smooth; return all to the pan. Add the milk, nutmeg, salt and pepper; heat through.

3. Meanwhile, combine the sour cream and parsley. Spoon soup into bowls; top each with a dollop of sour cream and sprinkle with bacon.

This fresh-tasting soup is packed with colorful, nutritious vegetables. I've recommended it to my friends for years.
—**VERA BATHURST**
ROGUE RIVER, OREGON

Speedy Vegetable Soup

PREP/TOTAL TIME: 25 MIN.
YIELD: 11 SERVINGS (ABOUT 3 QUARTS)

- 2 cans (one 49 ounces, one 14½ ounces) reduced-sodium chicken broth
- 2 celery ribs, thinly sliced
- 1 medium green pepper, chopped
- 1 medium onion, chopped
- 2 medium carrots, chopped
- 1 envelope onion soup mix
- 1 bay leaf
- ¼ teaspoon garlic powder
- ¼ teaspoon pepper
- 1 can (14½ ounces) diced tomatoes, undrained

1. In a Dutch oven, combine the first nine ingredients; bring to a boil over medium heat. Reduce heat; cover and simmer for 15-20 minutes or until vegetables are tender. Add tomatoes; heat through. Discard bay leaf.

You'll think you're on Cape Cod when you taste this thick wholesome chowder made from a recipe I've treasured for many years. It's one of my husband's favorites. He likes it more and more, because over the years I've "customized" the basic recipe by including ingredients he enjoys.

—LINDA LAZAROFF
HEBRON, CONNECTICUT

Country Fish Chowder

PREP: 15 MIN. • **COOK:** 25 MIN.
YIELD: 8-10 SERVINGS (2½ QUARTS)

- 1 **cup chopped onion**
- 4 **bacon strips**
- 3 **tablespoons butter**
- 3 **cans (12 ounces each) evaporated milk**
- 1 **can (15¼ ounces) whole kernel corn, undrained**
- 1 **can (6½ ounces) chopped clams, undrained**
- 3 **medium potatoes, peeled and cubed**
- 1 **teaspoon salt**
- ¾ **teaspoon pepper**
- 1 **pound fish fillets (haddock, cod or flounder), cooked and broken into pieces**
   Crumbled cooked bacon, optional
   Minced chives, optional
   Additional butter, optional

fresher fish

When purchasing fresh fish, choose fish that smells and looks good, whether it is refrigerated or frozen. Good-quality fresh saltwater fish doesn't have a heavy fish odor—it should smell like the ocean. Fillets and steaks should have a fresh-cut appearance with no discoloration or browning around the edges, and the texture should be springy to the touch.

1. In a large saucepan, cook onion and bacon in butter until onion is tender. Add milk, corn, clams, potatoes, salt and pepper. Cover and cook over medium heat, stirring occasionally, until potatoes are tender, about 20 minutes. Stir in fish and heat through. Ladle into bowls. If desired, top with bacon, chives and/or a pat of butter.

Chicken Tortellini Soup

PREP/TOTAL TIME: 30 MIN.
YIELD: 8 SERVINGS (ABOUT 2 QUARTS)

- 2 **cans (14½ ounces each) chicken broth**
- 2 **cups water**
- ¾ **pound boneless skinless chicken breasts, cut into 1-inch cubes**
- 1½ **cups frozen mixed vegetables**
- 1 **package (9 ounces) refrigerated cheese tortellini**
- 2 **celery ribs, thinly sliced**
- 1 **teaspoon dried basil**
- ½ **teaspoon garlic salt**
- ½ **teaspoon dried oregano**
- ¼ **teaspoon pepper**

1. In a large saucepan, bring broth and water to a boil; add chicken. Reduce heat; cook for 10 minutes.

2. Add the remaining ingredients; cook 10-15 minutes longer or until chicken is no longer pink and vegetables are tender.

a great way to freeze soup

After making a big batch of soup, it's easy to freeze individual portions. Line bowls with plastic wrap, pour in the cooled soup and freeze. Once frozen, the soup can be popped out of the bowls and stored in large freezer bags.

Asian Shrimp Soup

PREP/TOTAL TIME: 20 MIN. • **YIELD:** 4 SERVINGS

- 1 **ounce uncooked thin spaghetti, broken into 1-inch pieces**
- 3 **cups plus 1 tablespoon water, divided**
- 3 **teaspoons reduced-sodium chicken bouillon granules**
- ½ **teaspoon salt**
- ½ **cup sliced fresh mushrooms**
- ½ **cup fresh or frozen corn**
- 1 **teaspoon cornstarch**
- 1½ **teaspoons reduced-sodium teriyaki sauce**
- 1 **cup thinly sliced romaine lettuce**
- 1 **can (6 ounces) small shrimp, rinsed and drained**
- 2 **tablespoons sliced green onion**

1. Cook pasta according to package directions.

2. In a large saucepan, combine 3 cups water, bouillon and salt; bring to a boil. Stir in the mushrooms and corn. Reduce heat; cook, uncovered, until the vegetables are tender.

3. Combine the cornstarch, teriyaki sauce and remaining water until smooth; stir into soup. Bring to a boil; cook and stir for 1-2 minutes or until slightly thickened. Reduce heat. Drain pasta; add the pasta, lettuce, shrimp and green onion to the soup; heat through.

66 With nutritious vegetables and zippy beef and beans, these stuffed peppers stand out from others. This tasty dish is easy to make, so I serve it often in the summer and fall...much to my family's delight. 99

—NANCY MCDONALD BURNS, WYOMING

memorable main courses

The classics in this chapter are proof that homemade goodness doesn't require hours of prep time. Serve these reliable family-friendly dishes on your busiest nights.

My grandmother gave me this recipe, which I lightened up. My children loved it when they were little, and now my grandchildren ask for it when they come over. The peaches are delicious hot off the grill.
—**LINDA MCCLUSKEY**
CULLMAN, ALABAMA

Grilled Chicken With Peaches

PREP: 15 MIN. • **GRILL:** 20 MIN. • **YIELD:** 8 SERVINGS

- 1 **cup 100% peach spreadable fruit**
- 2 **tablespoons olive oil**
- 4 **teaspoons reduced-sodium soy sauce**
- 1 **tablespoon ground mustard**
- 1 **garlic clove, minced**
- ½ **teaspoon salt**
- ¼ **teaspoon pepper**
- ¼ **teaspoon cayenne pepper**
- 8 **boneless skinless chicken breast halves (4 ounces each)**
- 8 **medium ripe peaches, halved and pitted**

1. In a small bowl, combine the first eight ingredients; set aside. Using long-handled tongs, moisten a paper towel with cooking oil and lightly coat the grill rack.

2. Grill the chicken, covered, over medium heat for 5-7 minutes on each side or until a meat thermometer reads 170°, basting occasionally with some of the reserved glaze. Transfer to a serving platter and keep warm.

3. Grill peaches cut side down for 8-10 minutes or until tender, turning and basting every 2 minutes with remaining glaze. Serve with chicken.

Braided Pizza Loaf

PREP: 50 MIN. + RISING • **BAKE:** 30 MIN. • **YIELD:** 1 LOAF

- 1 loaf (1 pound) frozen bread dough, thawed
- 1 pound ground beef
- 1 medium onion, finely chopped
- 1 can (8 ounces) tomato sauce
- 1 teaspoon salt
- 1 teaspoon dried oregano
- 1 teaspoon paprika
- 1 teaspoon pepper
- ½ teaspoon garlic salt
- 1 cup (4 ounces) shredded cheddar cheese
- 1 cup (4 ounces) shredded part-skim mozzarella cheese
  Melted butter

1. Place dough in a greased bowl, turning once to grease top. Cover and let rise in a warm place until doubled, about 1 hour.

2. Meanwhile, in a large skillet, cook beef and onion over medium heat until meat is no longer pink; drain. Stir in tomato sauce and seasonings. Bring to a boil. Reduce heat; simmer, uncovered, for 30 minutes, stirring occasionally.

3. Cool completely. Punch dough down. Turn onto a lightly floured surface; roll into a 15-in. x 12-in. rectangle. Place on a greased baking sheet. Spread filling lengthwise down center third of rectangle. Sprinkle cheeses over filling.

4. On each long side, cut 1½-in.-wide strips 2½ in. into center. Starting at one end, fold alternating strips at an angle across filling. Brush with butter.

5. Bake at 350° for 30-35 minutes or until golden brown. Serve warm. Refrigerate leftovers.

Working women can take the frozen bread dough out in the morning and then prepare this hearty loaf when they get home. It's important to let the filling cool completely before spreading it on the dough.
—**DEBBIE MEDUNA** PLAZA, NORTH DAKOTA

Peachy Ginger Pork

Sliced peaches and red pepper strips add pretty color to these quick-to-fix pork slices, while a hint of Dijon mustard and gingerroot perks up the slightly sweet sauce.
—**TERRI GLAUSER** APPLETON, WISCONSIN

PREP/TOTAL TIME: 25 MIN. • **YIELD:** 4 SERVINGS

- 1 pork tenderloin (1 pound), cut into ½-inch slices
- ½ teaspoon salt
- ⅛ teaspoon pepper
- 1 teaspoon olive oil
- 1 medium sweet red pepper, julienned
- 1 cup canned sliced peaches in extra-light syrup
- ½ cup reduced-sodium chicken broth
- ⅓ cup peach spreadable fruit
- 1 tablespoon Dijon mustard
- 2 teaspoons minced fresh gingerroot

1. Flatten pork to ¼-in. thickness; sprinkle with salt and pepper. In a large nonstick skillet coated with cooking spray, saute pork in oil in batches until meat is no longer pink. Remove and keep warm.

2. In the same skillet, saute red pepper and peaches until red pepper is tender. Add the broth, spreadable fruit, mustard and ginger. Cook and stir over medium heat for 4 minutes. Return pork to the pan. Reduce heat; cover and simmer until heated through.

Italian Pot Roast

PREP: 20 MIN. • **BAKE:** 2 HOURS
YIELD: 8-10 SERVINGS (3 CUPS GRAVY)

- 1 tablespoon all-purpose flour
- 1 large oven roasting bag
- 1 boneless beef chuck roast (3 pounds)
- 1⅔ cups water
- 1 can (10¾ ounces) condensed tomato soup, undiluted
- 1 envelope onion soup mix
- 1½ teaspoons Italian seasoning
- 1 garlic clove, minced
- ¼ cup cornstarch
- ¼ cup cold water

1. Sprinkle flour into oven bag; shake to coat. Place in a 13-in. x 9-in. baking pan; add roast. In a small bowl, combine the water, tomato soup, soup mix, Italian seasoning and garlic; pour into oven bag.

I had so many requests for this recipe that I made up cards to hand out whenever I serve it at a get-together. My husband and son think it's world-class eating!
—CAROLYN WELLS
NORTH SYRACUSE, NEW YORK

2. Cut six ½-in. slits in top of bag; close with tie provided. Bake at 325° for 2 to 2 ½ hours or until meat is tender.

3. Remove roast to a serving platter and keep warm. Transfer cooking juices to a small saucepan; skim fat. Bring to a boil. Combine cornstarch and cold water until smooth; stir into cooking juices. Return to a boil; cook and stir for 2 minutes or until thickened. Slice roast; serve with gravy.

Every year my sisters and I have a Sisters Day, which includes a special lunch. This fast and easy pizza is one of our favorites. Served with a garden salad it makes a light, nutritious meal.
—**DEBORAH PREVOST**
BARNET, VERMONT

Greek Pizza

PREP/TOTAL TIME: 20 MIN. • **YIELD:** 12 PIECES

- 1 **prebaked 12-inch thin whole wheat pizza crust**
- 3 **tablespoons prepared pesto**
- 2 **medium tomatoes, thinly sliced**
- ¾ **cup water-packed artichoke hearts, rinsed, drained and chopped**
- ½ **cup crumbled reduced-fat feta cheese**
- ¼ **cup sliced ripe olives**

1. Place the crust on an ungreased 12-in. pizza pan; spread with pesto. Top with tomatoes, artichokes, cheese and olives.

2. Bake at 450° for 10-12 minutes or until heated through.

easy tomato slices

The best way to cut through the skin of a tomato is with a serrated, not straight-edged, knife. Cut a tomato vertically, from stem end to blossom end, for slices that will be less juicy and hold their shape better.

Colorful Crab Stir-Fry

PREP/TOTAL TIME: 30 MIN. • **YIELD:** 4 SERVINGS

- 2   teaspoons cornstarch
- 1   teaspoon chicken bouillon granules
- ¾   cup water
- ½   teaspoon reduced-sodium soy sauce
- 1   cup sliced fresh carrots
- 1   tablespoon canola oil
- 1   cup fresh or frozen snow peas
- ½   cup julienned sweet red pepper
- 1   teaspoon minced fresh gingerroot
- 1   teaspoon minced garlic
- 1   package (8 ounces) imitation crabmeat
    Hot cooked rice, optional

1. In a small bowl, combine the cornstarch, bouillon, water and soy sauce until smooth; set aside. In a large skillet or wok, stir-fry carrots in oil. Add the peas, red pepper, ginger and garlic; stir-fry 1-2 minutes longer or until vegetables are crisp-tender.

2. Stir cornstarch mixture and gradually add to the pan. Bring to a boil; cook and stir for 2 minutes or until thickened. Add crab; heat through. Serve with rice if desired.

Spicy Shrimp Wraps

These hearty grab-and-go wraps are packed with spicy flavor and sweetened with mango. They'll win over family and friends in less time than they take to assemble!

—FRANKIE ALLEN MANN
WARRIOR, ALABAMA

PREP/TOTAL TIME: 20 MIN. • **YIELD:** 6 SERVINGS

- 1 **cup salsa**
- 1 **medium ripe mango, peeled, pitted and diced**
- 1 **tablespoon ketchup**
- 1 **envelope reduced-sodium taco seasoning**
- 1 **tablespoon olive oil**
- 1 **pound uncooked medium shrimp, peeled and deveined**
- 6 **flour tortillas (10 inches), warmed**
- 1½ **cups coleslaw mix**
- 6 **tablespoons reduced-fat sour cream**

1. In a small bowl, combine the salsa, mango and ketchup; set aside. In a large resealable plastic bag, combine taco seasoning and oil; add shrimp. Seal bag and shake to coat.

2. In a nonstick skillet or wok, cook shrimp over medium-high heat for 2-3 minutes or until shrimp turn pink. Top tortillas with coleslaw mix, salsa mixture and shrimp. Fold bottom third of tortilla up over filling; fold sides over. Serve with sour cream.

TEST KITCHEN TIP: Save a little money by shredding cabbage and carrots yourself instead of buying coleslaw mix.

Taco Twists

PREP: 15 MIN. • **BAKE:** 25 MIN. • **YIELD:** 12 SERVINGS

- 1 **pound ground beef**
- 1 **large onion, chopped**
- 2 **cups (8 ounces) shredded cheddar cheese**
- 1 **cup salsa**
- 1 **can (4 ounces) chopped green chilies**
- 1 **teaspoon garlic powder**
- ½ **teaspoon hot pepper sauce**
- ¼ **teaspoon salt**
- ¼ **teaspoon ground cumin**
- 3 **tubes (8 ounces each) refrigerated crescent rolls**

1. In a large skillet, cook beef and onion over medium heat until meat is no longer pink; drain. Stir in the cheese, salsa, chilies, garlic powder, hot pepper sauce, salt and cumin.

2. Unroll crescent roll dough and separate into 12 rectangles. Place on ungreased baking sheets; press perforations to seal. Place ½ cup meat mixture in the center of each rectangle. Bring four corners to the center and twist; pinch to seal.

3. Bake at 350° for 25-30 minutes or until golden brown. You can freeze baked Taco Twists for up to 3 months in a heavy-duty resealable plastic bag.

TO USE FROZEN TACO TWISTS: Bake frozen twists on an ungreased baking sheet at 350° for 20 to 25 minutes or until heated through.

I especially like to use frozen California-blend veggies when making this dish. If you prefer, you can substitute fresh garden vegetables, but it will add a little time. Simply start them in boiling water before adding the pasta. Then add the pasta during the last 3 minutes of cooking the veggies. This makes an easy, colorful and delicious entree!
—**TALENA KEELER**
SILOAM SPRINGS, ARKANSAS

Chicken Fettuccine Alfredo with Veggies

PREP/TOTAL TIME: 15 MIN. • **YIELD:** 4 SERVINGS

- 2 **quarts water**
- 1 **package (9 ounces) refrigerated fettuccine**
- 3 **cups frozen mixed vegetables**
- 1 **package (9 ounces) ready-to-serve roasted chicken breast strips**
- 1½ **cups Alfredo sauce**
- ½ **cup shredded Parmesan cheese**

1. In a Dutch oven, bring water to a boil. Add fettuccine and vegetables; return to a boil. Cook on high for 2-3 minutes or until fettuccine and vegetables are tender; drain. Stir in chicken and Alfredo sauce; heat through. Sprinkle with cheese.

Here is an easy entree elegant enough for company. The sauce has the citrusy flavor of orange along with a little spiciness. It's great with rice and a side salad.
—MITZI SENTIFF
ANNAPOLIS, MARYLAND

Steak with Orange-Thyme Sauce

PREP/TOTAL TIME: 25 MIN. • **YIELD:** 4 SERVINGS

½	cup orange marmalade
2	teaspoons minced fresh thyme or ½ teaspoon dried thyme
1½	teaspoons grated orange peel
1	teaspoon soy sauce
¾	teaspoon seasoned salt
½	teaspoon garlic powder
⅛	teaspoon cayenne pepper
1¼	pounds beef top sirloin steak

1. In a small bowl, combine the first seven ingredients; set aside ⅓ cup for basting.

2. Broil steak 4-6 in. from the heat for 8-10 minutes on each side or until meat reaches desired doneness (for medium-rare, a meat thermometer should read 145°; medium, 160°; well-done, 170°), basting with some of the reserved sauce. Let stand for 5 minutes before slicing. Serve with the remaining sauce.

Asian Beef Noodles

PREP/TOTAL TIME: 30 MIN. • **YIELD:** 4 SERVINGS

- 1 **package (3 ounces) beef-flavored ramen noodles**
- 1 **pound beef top sirloin steak (¾ inch thick)**
- 1 **jalapeno pepper, seeded and finely chopped**
- 1 **tablespoon canola oil**
- 2 **tablespoons water**
- 1 **tablespoon steak sauce**
- 1 **medium carrot, shredded**
- 2 **tablespoons sliced green onion**
- ¼ **cup peanut halves**

We've raised beef the majority of our lives, so I like to try new recipes that feature it. This unique recipe is simply out-of-this-world delicious!
—**MARGERY BRYAN**
MOSES LAKE, WASHINGTON

1. Set aside the seasoning packet from noodles. Prepare noodles according to package directions; drain and set aside.

2. Cut the steak into 3-in. x ½-in. strips. In a large skillet, stir-fry the beef and jalapeno in oil for 1-2 minutes or until the meat is no longer pink. Remove and keep warm.

3. In the same skillet, combine the noodles, water, steak sauce, carrot, onion and contents of seasoning packet. Cook and stir until heated through. Return beef to the pan. Sprinkle with peanuts. Serve immediately.

EDITOR'S NOTE: Wear disposable gloves when cutting hot peppers; the oils can burn skin. Avoid touching your face.

Cheeseburger Biscuit Bake

PREP: 15 MIN. • **BAKE:** 20 MIN. • **YIELD:** 5 SERVINGS

- 1 **pound ground beef**
- ¼ **cup chopped onion**
- 1 **can (8 ounces) tomato sauce**
- ¼ **cup ketchup**
  Dash pepper
- 2 **cups (8 ounces) shredded cheddar cheese, divided**
- 1 **tube (12 ounces) refrigerated buttermilk biscuits, separated into 10 biscuits**

1. In a large skillet, cook beef and onion over medium heat until meat is no longer pink; drain. Stir in the tomato sauce, ketchup and pepper. Spoon half into a greased 8-in. square baking dish; sprinkle with half of the cheese. Repeat layers.

2. Place biscuits around edges of dish. Bake, uncovered, at 400° for 18-22 minutes or until the meat mixture is bubbly and biscuits are golden brown.

Roasted Pepper Tortellini

PREP/TOTAL TIME: 25 MIN. • **YIELD:** 6 SERVINGS

- 1 package (20 ounces) refrigerated cheese tortellini
- 5 Italian sausage links
- 2 tablespoons olive oil
- 2 jars (7 ounces each) roasted sweet red peppers, drained
- 1 can (15 ounces) pizza sauce
- 1 cup (4 ounces) shredded part-skim mozzarella cheese
- 2 tablespoons shredded Parmesan cheese

1. Cook tortellini according to package directions. Meanwhile, in a large skillet, cook the sausage in oil over medium heat until no longer pink; drain. Cut into ¼-in. slices.

2. Place the red peppers in a blender; cover and process until smooth. Drain tortellini. Add the tortellini, pureed peppers and pizza sauce to the skillet; stir to combine. Cook for 5 minutes or until heated through. Sprinkle with cheeses; cover and heat until cheese is melted.

Savory Stuffed Pork Chops

Who'd ever guess stuffed chops could be so simple? Stuffing mix and baby spinach and are the secrets to this savory recipe.
—**REBECCA NOSSAMAN** HURRICANE, WEST VIRGINIA

PREP: 10 MIN. • **BAKE:** 40 MIN. • **YIELD:** 8 SERVINGS

- 8 boneless pork loin chops (1 inch thick and 8 ounces each)
- 1 small onion, chopped
- ½ cup butter, cubed
- 5 cups fresh baby spinach
- 1 package (6 ounces) sage stuffing mix
- 1½ cups (12 ounces) sour cream
- ½ teaspoon rubbed sage
- ½ teaspoon lemon-pepper seasoning

1. Using a sharp knife, cut a pocket in each pork chop. In a large skillet, saute onion in butter until tender. Add spinach, cook until wilted. Stir in the stuffing mix, sour cream and sage.

Refrigerated tortellini cooks fast in this family staple, but you can also use dried tortellini.
—**TASTE OF HOME TEST KITCHEN**

2. Fill each chop with about ⅓ cup stuffing mixture; secure with toothpicks if necessary. Place on a greased 15-in. x 10-in. x 1-in. baking pan. Sprinkle with lemon-pepper seasoning.

3. Bake, uncovered, at 350° for 35-40 minutes or until a meat thermometer reads 160°. Discard toothpicks.

Taco-Filled Peppers

PREP/TOTAL TIME: 30 MIN. • **YIELD:** 4 SERVINGS

- **1 pound ground beef**
- **1 envelope taco seasoning**
- **¾ cup canned kidney beans, rinsed and drained**
- **1 cup salsa**
- **4 medium green peppers**
- **1 medium tomato, chopped**
- **½ cup shredded cheddar cheese**
- **½ cup sour cream**

1. In a large skillet, cook beef over medium heat until no longer pink; drain. Stir in the taco seasoning, kidney beans and salsa. Bring to a boil; reduce heat and simmer for 5 minutes.

2. Cut peppers in half lengthwise; remove stems and discard seeds. In a stockpot, cook peppers in boiling water for 3-5 minutes. Drain and rinse in cold water.

3. Spoon about ½ cup meat mixture into each pepper half. Place in an ungreased 13-in. x 9-in. baking dish. Cover and bake at 350° for 15-20 minutes or until the peppers are crisp-tender and the filling is heated through. Top each with tomato and cheese. Serve with sour cream.

A wonderful blend of fruity flavors with just the right touch of ginger makes this fabulous stir-fry a winner with our gang. I came up with the recipe one night while experimenting with new ways to use beef sirloin strips.

—JILL COX
LINCOLN, NEBRASKA

Ginger Sirloin Strips

PREP/TOTAL TIME: 20 MIN. • **YIELD:** 7 SERVINGS

- 1 **can (14 ounces) pineapple tidbits**
- 1 **can (11 ounces) mandarin oranges**
- 2 **tablespoons cornstarch**
- 1½ **pounds beef top sirloin steak, cut into strips**
- 4½ **teaspoons minced fresh gingerroot**
- 1 **tablespoon olive oil**
- 1 **can (14 ounces) whole-berry cranberry sauce**
- 1 **cup thinly sliced green onions**
  Hot cooked rice

1. Drain pineapple and oranges, reserving juice; set fruit aside. In a small bowl, combine cornstarch and juices until smooth; set aside.

2. In a large skillet or wok, stir-fry beef and ginger in oil until meat is no longer pink. Add the cranberry sauce, onions and pineapple. Stir cornstarch mixture and gradually add to skillet; cook and stir until slightly thickened. Gently stir in oranges. Serve with rice.

fresh gingerroot

Fresh gingerroot should have a smooth skin. If wrinkled and cracked, the root is past its prime. When stored in a resealable plastic bag, unpeeled gingerroot can be frozen for up to 1 year. When needed, simply peel and grate.

Pepperoni and mozzarella cheese punch up pork chops with a taste diners of all ages are sure to love. I like to dress up this speedy supper by using portobello mushrooms and serving it with steamed fresh broccoli or green beans.
—**VANCE WERNER JR.** FRANKLIN, WISCONSIN

Pizza Pork Chops

PREP/TOTAL TIME: 30 MIN. • **YIELD:** 4 SERVINGS

- 2 cups sliced fresh mushrooms
- 2 tablespoons butter
- 4 boneless pork loin chops
  (½ inch thick and 4 ounces each)
- ¼ teaspoon salt
- ¼ teaspoon pepper
- 2 tablespoons olive oil
- 2 cups marinara or spaghetti sauce
- 16 slices pepperoni
- 1 cup (4 ounces) shredded part-skim mozzarella cheese

1. In a large skillet, saute mushrooms in butter until tender. Remove and keep warm. Sprinkle pork chops with salt and pepper. In the same skillet, brown chops in oil on both sides; drain.

2. Add marinara sauce; bring to a boil. Reduce heat; simmer, uncovered, for 4-5 minutes on each side or until a thermometer reads 145°. Layer pork with pepperoni, mushrooms and cheese. Remove from the heat. Cover and let stand for 5 minutes before serving.

Chicken a la King

My comforting recipe has a thick and creamy sauce that's just perfect over biscuits. I've been making this for 30 years, and it's a wonderful way to create a quick lunch or dinner with leftover chicken.
—**RUTH LEE** TROY, ONTARIO

PREP/TOTAL TIME: 25 MIN. • **YIELD:** 4 SERVINGS

- 4 individually frozen biscuits
- 1¾ cups sliced fresh mushrooms
- ¼ cup chopped onion
- ¼ cup chopped celery
- ⅓ cup butter, cubed
- ¼ cup all-purpose flour
- ⅛ to ¼ teaspoon salt
- 1 cup chicken broth
- 1 cup milk
- 2 cups cubed cooked chicken
- 2 tablespoons diced pimientos

1. Bake biscuits according to package directions. Meanwhile, in a large skillet, saute the mushrooms, onion and celery in butter until crisp-tender. Stir in flour and salt until blended. Gradually stir in broth and milk. Bring to a boil; cook and stir for 2 minutes or until thickened.

2. Add chicken and pimientos. Bring to a boil. Reduce heat; simmer, uncovered, for 4-6 minutes or until heated through. Serve with biscuits.

Crescent Chicken Bundles

PREP: 15 MIN. • **BAKE:** 20 MIN. • **YIELD:** 8 SERVINGS

- **2 packages (3 ounces each) cream cheese, softened**
- **4 tablespoons butter, melted, divided**
- **2 tablespoons minced chives**
- **2 tablespoon milk**
- **½ teaspoon salt**
- **¼ teaspoon pepper**
- **4 cups cubed cooked chicken**
- **2 tubes (8 ounces each) refrigerated crescent rolls**
- **1 cup crushed seasoned stuffing**

1. In a small bowl, beat the cream cheese, 2 tablespoons butter, chives, milk, salt and pepper until blended. Stir in chicken.

2. Unroll crescent roll dough and separate into eight rectangles; press perforations together. Spoon about ½ cup chicken mixture in the center of each rectangle. Bring edges up to the center and pinch to seal. Brush with remaining butter. Sprinkle with crushed croutons, lightly pressing down.

3. Transfer to two ungreased baking sheets. Cover one baking sheet and freeze until firm; transfer squares to a covered freezer container. May be frozen for up to 2 months. Bake remaining squares at 350° for 20-25 minutes or until golden brown.

TO USE FROZEN SQUARES: Thaw in the refrigerator and bake as directed.

Saucy Chicken Strips

PREP/TOTAL TIME: 25 MIN. • **YIELD:** 4 SERVINGS

- 1 **pound boneless skinless chicken breast halves**
- 2 **tablespoons butter**
- ½ **cup chopped onion**
- ½ **cup chopped green pepper**
- 1 **can (4 ounces) mushroom stems and pieces, drained**
- 1 **envelope onion soup mix**
- 1¼ **cups water**
- 1 **tablespoon Worcestershire sauce**
- 1 **tablespoon cornstarch**
- 3 **tablespoons cold water**

1. Cut chicken breast in 2-in. x ½-in. strips. Melt butter in a large skillet; add chicken and brown on all sides. Remove chicken from skillet, reserving the drippings.

2. Add the onion, green pepper and mushrooms to the pan; saute until crisp-tender. Return chicken to skillet. In a small bowl, combine the soup mix, water and Worcestershire sauce; pour over chicken. Reduce heat; cover and simmer for 10 minutes.

3. Remove chicken to a warm platter. Combine cornstarch and water until smooth; add to sauce. Bring to a boil. Cook and stir for 2 minutes or until thickened and bubbly. Pour over chicken.

Sirloin in Wine Sauce

This recipe is a family favorite as well as a quick but impressive company dish. The tender sirloin is coated in a hearty mushroom-wine sauce that is fantastic over pasta.

—BARBARA KAMM WILMINGTON, DELAWARE

PREP/TOTAL TIME: 30 MIN. • **YIELD:** 4 SERVINGS

- 2 tablespoons all-purpose flour
- ⅛ teaspoon ground mustard
- 1 pound beef top sirloin steak, thinly sliced
- 2 tablespoons butter
- 1 can (10½ ounces) condensed beef consomme, undiluted
- ½ cup dry red wine or beef broth
- 1 jar (4½ ounces) sliced mushrooms, drained
- ¼ cup chopped green onions
- 1 teaspoon Worcestershire sauce
  Hot cooked linguine

1. In a large resealable plastic bag, combine flour and mustard. Add beef, a few pieces at a time, and shake to coat. In a large skillet, brown beef in butter until meat reaches desired doneness.

2. Add consomme and wine. Stir in the mushrooms, onions and Worcestershire sauce. Bring to a boil. Reduce heat; simmer, uncovered, for 10-15 minutes or until sauce is thickened. Serve with linguine.

Turkey Stir-Fry

PREP/TOTAL TIME: 20 MIN. • **YIELD:** 4 SERVINGS

- 1 pound turkey breast tenderloins, cubed
- 1 tablespoon canola oil
- 1 package (16 ounces) frozen stir-fry vegetable blend
- 1 medium onion, cut into wedges
- ½ cup stir-fry sauce
- ⅓ cup shredded carrot
  Hot cooked rice

1. In a large skillet or wok, stir-fry the turkey in oil for 3-4 minutes or until no longer pink. Remove with a slotted spoon.

2. Stir-fry the mixed vegetables, onion, stir-fry sauce and carrot for 4-6 minutes or until vegetables are tender. Add turkey; heat through. Serve with rice.

Need a nourishing meal in minutes? Toss together these seven ingredients for a colorful and delicious main dish the whole family will love. Frozen veggies make it extra quick, and a garnish of fresh cilantro adds extra flavor.

—MILDRED SHERRER FORT WORTH, TEXAS

This colorful combination is just one example of the many flavorful uses for spaghetti squash.
—**CLARA COULSON MINNEY**
WASHINGTON COURT HOUSE, OHIO

Salsa Spaghetti Squash

PREP/TOTAL TIME: 30 MIN. • **YIELD:** 4 SERVINGS

- 1 **medium spaghetti squash**
- ½ **cup chopped onion**
- 2 **cups salsa**
- 1 **can (15 ounces) black beans, rinsed and drained**
- 3 **tablespoons minced fresh cilantro**
- 1 **medium ripe avocado, peeled and cubed**

1. Cut squash in half lengthwise; discard seeds. Place squash cut side down on a microwave-safe plate. Microwave, uncovered, on high for 15-18 minutes or until tender.

2. Meanwhile, in a nonstick skillet coated with cooking spray, cook onion until tender. Stir in the salsa, beans and cilantro; heat through. Gently stir in avocado; cook 1 minute longer.

3. When squash is cool enough to handle, use a fork to separate strands. Divide squash among four plates; top with salsa mixture.

EDITOR'S NOTE: This recipe was tested in a 1,100-watt microwave.

Pesto Halibut

PREP/TOTAL TIME: 20 MIN. • **YIELD:** 6 SERVINGS

- 2 tablespoons olive oil
- 1 envelope pesto sauce mix
- 1 tablespoon lemon juice
- 6 halibut fillets (4 ounces each)

1. In a small bowl, combine the oil, sauce mix and lemon juice; brush over both sides of fillets. Place in a greased 13-in. x 9-in. baking dish.

2. Bake, uncovered, at 450° for 12-15 minutes or until fish flakes easily with a fork.

Artichoke Ham Puffs

This recipe is wonderful for a special brunch with family or friends. With lots of cheese and chunks of ham, the filling is delicious and satisfying. I like to serve the puffs along with fresh fruit and sweet rolls or bread.
—**SUZANNE MERRILL** MODESTO, CALIFORNIA

PREP: 10 MIN. • **COOK:** 20 MIN. • **YIELD:** 6 SERVINGS

- 6 frozen puff pastry shells
- ½ pound sliced fresh mushrooms
- 6 tablespoons butter, divided
- 3 tablespoons all-purpose flour
- ¼ teaspoon ground mustard
- ¼ teaspoon minced fresh tarragon
- 2 cups milk
- 2½ cups (10 ounces) shredded cheddar cheese
- ⅛ teaspoon coarsely ground pepper
- 3 cups cubed fully cooked ham
- 1 can (14 ounces) water-packed artichoke hearts, rinsed, drained, patted dry and quartered

1. Bake pastry shells according to package directions. Meanwhile, in a large skillet, saute mushrooms in 2 tablespoons butter for 3-4 minutes or until tender. Add the remaining butter; cook for 2-3 minutes over medium heat until melted.

2. Stir in the flour, mustard and tarragon until blended. Gradually add milk. Bring to a boil; cook and stir for 2 minutes or until thickened.

In this entree, the mildness of halibut contrasts perfectly with the deep flavor of pesto. It literally takes minutes to get the fillets ready for the oven, so you can quickly start on your side dishes. Nearly anything goes well with this fish.
—**APRIL SHOWALTER**
INDIANAPOLIS, INDIANA

3. Reduce heat to medium. Add cheese and pepper; cook and stir for 3-4 minutes or until cheese is melted. Remove from the heat; stir in ham and artichokes. Remove tops from pastry shells; fill with ham mixture. Replace tops.

1. In a large skillet, cook the chicken, green peppers and onion in 2 tablespoons oil over medium heat for 6-8 minutes or until chicken juices run clear. Stir in barbecue sauce. Bring to a boil. Reduce heat; simmer for 1-2 minutes or until heated through.

2. Sprinkle cheese down the center of each tortilla; top with chicken mixture. Fold sides and ends over filling and roll up.

3. In a large skillet, brown burritos in remaining oil on all sides over medium heat. Serve with lime wedges, sour cream, lettuce and tomatoes if desired.

Turkey Cordon Bleu Pasta

What a great way to use up extra turkey and ham! This creamy pasta recipe has undergone a few changes over the years, but it remains one of my best.
—**SANDRA NETHERTON** MARIETTA, GEORGIA

PREP/TOTAL TIME: 30 MIN. • **YIELD:** 4 SERVINGS

2	**cups sliced fresh mushrooms**
½	**cup sliced green onions**
¼	**cup chopped green pepper**
2	**tablespoons butter**
2	**cups cubed cooked turkey**
1	**cup cubed fully cooked ham**
1	**can (10¾ ounces) condensed cream of mushroom soup, undiluted**
½	**cup water**
¼	**cup sherry or chicken broth**
Hot cooked linguine	
¼	**cup shredded Swiss cheese**

1. In a large skillet, saute the mushrooms, onions and green pepper in butter for 4-5 minutes or until crisp-tender.

2. In a large bowl, combine the turkey, ham, soup, water and sherry. Stir into vegetables. Bring to a boil. Reduce heat to medium; cook, uncovered, for 3-4 minutes or until heated through. Serve with linguine. Sprinkle with cheese.

We always have the ingredients for these treats on hand. My husband came up with the recipe, and it turned out to be a hit!
—**AMY DANDO**
APALACHIN, NEW YORK

Barbecue Chicken Burritos

PREP/TOTAL TIME: 30 MIN. • **YIELD:** 4 SERVINGS

½	**pound boneless skinless chicken breasts, cut into ½-inch cubes**
1½	**cups julienned green peppers**
1	**cup chopped onion**
4	**tablespoons canola oil, divided**
½	**cup barbecue sauce**
1½	**cups (6 ounces) shredded Mexican cheese blend**
4	**flour tortillas (10 inches), warmed**
	Lime wedges, sour cream, shredded lettuce and chopped tomatoes, optional

I found this wonderful, quick recipe in a book years ago. It's been a favorite for special occasions ever since! I like to serve it with twice-baked potatoes and a spinach salad.
—**JANET SINGLETON**
BELLEVUE, OHIO

Glazed Beef Tournedos

PREP/TOTAL TIME: 20 MIN. • **YIELD:** 4 SERVINGS

- **3 tablespoons steak sauce**
- **2 tablespoons ketchup**
- **2 tablespoons orange marmalade**
- **1 tablespoon lemon juice**
- **1 tablespoon finely chopped onion**
- **1 garlic clove, minced**
- **4 beef tenderloin steaks (6 ounces each)**

1. In a small bowl, combine the steak sauce, ketchup, marmalade, lemon juice, onion and garlic. Set aside ¼ cup for serving.

2. Moisten a paper towel with cooking oil; using long-handled tongs, lightly coat the grill rack. Grill steaks, uncovered, over medium heat or broil 4 in. from the heat for 5-7 minutes on each side or until meat reaches desired doneness (for medium-rare, a thermometer should read 145°; medium, 160°; well-done, 170°), basting frequently with remaining sauce.

3. Just before serving, brush the steaks with the reserved sauce.

66 Frozen green peas add lovely color to this comforting meal in one. It's an easy, cheesy dish and a terrific way to use up extra baked ham. No one feels like they're eating leftovers! 99

—RENEE SCHWEBACH DUMONT, MINNESOTA

all-in-one dinners

For robust meals that combine ease and satisfaction, turn to these delicious one-dish dinners. From steamy casseroles to hearty pasta dishes, they're perfect for busy cooks like you!

Fold-Over Tortilla Bake

PREP: 20 MIN. • **BAKE:** 20 MIN. • **YIELD:** 6 SERVINGS

- 1 **pound ground beef**
- 1 **cup chopped onion**
- 2 **cans (14½ ounces each) stewed tomatoes**
- 1 **cup enchilada sauce**
- 1 **to 2 teaspoons ground cumin**
- ½ **teaspoon salt**
- ¼ **teaspoon pepper**
- 12 **flour or corn tortillas (6 inches)**
- 2 **packages (3 ounces each) cream cheese, softened**
- 1 **can (4 ounces) chopped green chilies, drained**
- 1 **cup (4 ounces) shredded Monterey Jack cheese**

1. In a large skillet, cook ground beef and onion until beef is no longer pink; drain. Stir in the tomatoes, enchilada sauce and seasonings. Bring to a boil. Reduce heat and simmer, covered, for 5 minutes. Pour half of the meat sauce into a 13-in. x 9-in. baking dish. Set aside.

2. Wrap the stack of tortillas in foil; warm at 350° for 8-10 minutes. Spread warm tortillas with cream cheese and top with chilies. Fold tortillas in half. Arrange folded tortillas over meat sauce; pour remaining sauce over top.

3. Cover and bake at 350° for 15 minutes. Sprinkle with cheese; bake 5 minutes longer or until cheese is melted.

Try something a little different with your tacos tonight. This recipe is special enough for potlucks or dinner guests.
—DEBORAH SMITH DEWITT, NEBRASKA

keeping it lean

To reduce the fat when using ground beef, buy 97% extra-lean. Browning the ground beef in fat-free broth instead of oil will help it keep its moist texture and beefy flavor.

Tuna in the Straw Casserole

PREP/TOTAL TIME: 30 MIN. • **YIELD:** 4 SERVINGS

- 1 can (10¾ ounces) condensed cream of mushroom soup, undiluted
- 1 can (5 ounces) evaporated milk
- 1 can (5 ounces) albacore white tuna in water
- 1 can (4 ounces) mushroom stems and pieces, drained
- 1 cup frozen mixed vegetables
- 2 cups potato sticks, divided

1. In a large bowl, combine soup and milk until blended. Stir in the tuna, mushrooms, vegetables and 1½ cups potato sticks.

2. Transfer to a greased 1½-qt. baking dish. Bake, uncovered, at 375° for 20 minutes. Sprinkle with the remaining potatoes. Bake 5-10 minutes longer or until bubbly and potatoes are crisp.

Cranberry Sweet-and-Sour Pork

PREP/TOTAL TIME: 20 MIN. • **YIELD:** 6 SERVINGS

- 1 **tablespoon cornstarch**
- ½ **cup unsweetened pineapple juice**
- 1 **cup whole-berry cranberry sauce**
- ½ **cup barbecue sauce**
- 1½ **pounds pork tenderloin, cut into ½-inch cubes**
- 1 **tablespoon canola oil**
- ½ **teaspoon salt**
- ¼ **teaspoon pepper**
- 1 **medium green pepper, cut into strips**
- ¾ **cup pineapple tidbits**
  Hot cooked rice or chow mein noodles

1. In a small bowl, combine cornstarch and pineapple juice until smooth. Stir in cranberry and barbecue sauces; set aside.

2. In a large skillet, stir-fry pork in oil for 3 minutes or until meat is no longer pink. Sprinkle with salt and pepper. Remove from the pan and keep warm.

3. Add green pepper and pineapple to pan; stir-fry for 2 minutes. Stir cornstarch mixture and add to skillet. Bring to a boil. Cook and stir for 2 minutes or until thickened. Add pork; heat through. Serve with rice or noodles.

Your family is going to gobble up this cheesy, Southwestern chicken bake, and ask for it again and again. This is real comfort food!

—MELANIE BURNS
PUEBLO WEST, COLORADO

Chicken Enchilada Bake

PREP: 20 MIN. • **BAKE:** 50 MIN. + STANDING
YIELD: 10 SERVINGS

4½   cups cubed rotisserie chicken
1   can (28 ounces) green enchilada sauce
1¼   cups (10 ounces) sour cream
9   corn tortillas (6 inches), cut into 1½-inch pieces
4   cups (16 ounces) shredded Monterey Jack cheese

1. In a greased 13-in. x 9-in. baking dish, layer half of the chicken, enchilada sauce, sour cream, tortillas and cheese. Repeat layers.

2. Cover and bake at 375° for 40 minutes. Uncover; bake 10 minutes longer or until bubbly. Let stand for 15 minutes before serving.

all that pizzazz

Add some pizzazz to the Chicken Enchilada Bake by serving it with optional toppings, such as shredded lettuce, lightly crushed tortilla chips, guacamole, chopped green onions, chopped tomatoes and/or sliced black olives.

Easy Chicken Potpie

PREP: 20 MIN. • BAKE: 40 MIN. • YIELD: 6 SERVINGS

- 1 can (10¾ ounces) reduced-fat reduced-sodium condensed cream of chicken soup, undiluted
- 1 can (10¾ ounces) reduced-fat reduced-sodium condensed cream of mushroom soup, undiluted
- ½ cup plus ⅔ cup fat-free milk, divided
- ½ teaspoon dried thyme
- ¼ teaspoon pepper
- ⅛ teaspoon poultry seasoning
- 2 packages (16 ounces each) frozen mixed vegetables, thawed
- 1½ cups cubed cooked chicken breast
- 1½ cups reduced-fat biscuit/baking mix

1. In a large bowl, combine the soups, ½ cup milk, thyme, pepper and poultry seasoning. Stir in vegetables and chicken.

2. Transfer to a 13-in. x 9-in. baking dish coated with cooking spray. In a small bowl, stir biscuit mix and remaining milk just until blended. Drop by 12 rounded tablespoonfuls onto chicken mixture.

3. Bake, uncovered, at 350° for 40-50 minutes or until filling is bubbly and biscuits are golden brown.

Bratwurst Hash

PREP/TOTAL TIME: 30 MIN. • **YIELD:** 4 SERVINGS

- 4 uncooked bratwurst links
- 1 package (20 ounces) refrigerated diced potatoes with onion
- 1 cup fresh or frozen corn
- 1 medium green pepper, chopped
- ¼ cup chopped roasted sweet red peppers
- ¾ cup shredded Colby-Monterey Jack cheese, divided
- ½ teaspoon seasoned salt

1. In a large skillet, cook bratwurst over medium heat until a thermometer reads 160°; drain. Remove from pan; cut meat in half and slice into ¼-in. pieces. Return to pan; stir in the potatoes, corn and green pepper. Cook, covered, over medium heat for 12-15 minutes or until vegetables are tender, stirring occasionally.

2. Stir in the red peppers, ½ cup cheese and seasoned salt; heat through. Sprinkle with remaining cheese.

Looking for something homey that's stick-to-your-ribs good? This satisfying, delicious recipe is for you!
—**TASTE OF HOME TEST KITCHEN**

Chili Tots

Cook once and eat twice with this hearty Southwestern casserole. With help from a few convenience products, it goes together quickly before freezing it or popping in the oven.
—**LINDA BALDWIN** LONG BEACH, CALIFORNIA

PREP: 15 MIN. • **BAKE:** 35 MIN.
YIELD: 2 CASSEROLES (6 SERVINGS EACH)

- 1 pound ground beef
- 2 cans (15 ounces each) chili without beans
- 1 can (8 ounces) tomato sauce
- 1 can (2¼ ounces) sliced ripe olives, drained
- 1 can (4 ounces) chopped green chilies
- 2 cups (8 ounces) shredded cheddar cheese
- 1 package (32 ounces) frozen Tater Tots

1. In a large skillet, cook the beef over medium heat until no longer pink; drain. Stir in the chili, tomato sauce, olives and chilies.

2. Transfer to two greased 8-in. square baking dishes. Sprinkle with cheese; top with Tater Tots. Cover and freeze one casserole for up to 3 months.

3. Cover and bake the remaining casserole at 350° for 35-40 minutes or until heated through.

TO USE FROZEN CASSEROLE: Remove from the freezer 30 minutes before baking (do not thaw). Cover and bake at 350° for 1¼ to 1½ hours or until heated through.

Beef Broccoli Supper

When I put together a cookbook for our family reunion, my sister submitted this recipe. My husband and our boys usually don't care for broccoli, but they sure love this dish!

—**NITA GRAFFIS** DOVE CREEK, COLORADO

PREP: 25 MIN. • **BAKE:** 35 MIN. • **YIELD:** 4-6 SERVINGS

- ¾ cup uncooked long grain rice
- 1 pound ground beef
- 1½ cups fresh broccoli florets
- 1 can (10¾ ounces) condensed broccoli cheese soup, undiluted
- ½ cup milk
- 1 teaspoon salt-free seasoning blend
- 1 teaspoon salt
- ½ teaspoon pepper
- ½ cup dry bread crumbs
- 2 tablespoons butter, melted

1. Cook rice according to package directions. Meanwhile, in a large skillet, cook beef over medium heat until no longer pink; drain. Add the rice, broccoli, soup, milk, seasoning blend, salt and pepper; stir until combined. Transfer to a greased 2-qt. baking dish.

2. Toss the bread crumbs and melted butter; sprinkle over the beef mixture. Cover and bake at 350° for 30 minutes. Uncover and bake 5-10 minutes longer or until heated through.

Turkey and Gravy Baskets

Take advantage of convenience items to put a special entree on the table even when time is tight. Here, we spooned a colorful mix of fresh veggies and packaged cooked turkey and gravy into puff pastry shells from the freezer section. This is also a great way to use up holiday leftovers. Simply use 2 cups leftover turkey plus 1 cup gravy as a substitute for one 18-ounce package of refrigerated turkey breast slices in gravy.

—**TASTE OF HOME TEST KITCHEN**

PREP/TOTAL TIME: 20 MIN. • **YIELD:** 4 SERVINGS

- 1 package (10 ounces) frozen puff pastry shells
- 2 cups fresh broccoli florets
- ½ cup chopped onion
- ½ cup chopped sweet red pepper
- 4 teaspoons canola oil
- 1 package (18 ounces) refrigerated turkey breast slices in gravy
- ½ cup turkey gravy

1. Bake four pastry shells according to package directions; save remaining shells for another use.

2. Meanwhile, in a large skillet, saute the broccoli, onion and red pepper in oil for 5 minutes or until crisp-tender.

3. Cut turkey slices into bite-size pieces; add to skillet with gravy from package and additional gravy. Heat through. Serve in pastry shells.

Ham 'n' Noodle Hot Dish

PREP: 15 MIN. • **BAKE:** 30 MIN. • **YIELD:** 4 SERVINGS

- 3 **tablespoons butter, divided**
- 2 **tablespoons all-purpose flour**
- 1 **cup milk**
- 1 **cup (4 ounces) shredded process cheese (Velveeta)**
- ½ **teaspoon salt**
- 2 **cups diced fully cooked ham**
- 1½ **cups elbow macaroni or medium noodles, cooked and drained**
- 1 **cup frozen peas, thawed**
- ¼ **cup dry bread crumbs**
- ½ **teaspoon dried parsley flakes**

1. In a saucepan, melt 2 tablespoons butter; stir in flour until smooth. Gradually add milk. Bring to a boil over medium heat; cook and stir for 2 minutes. Remove from the heat; stir in cheese and salt until cheese is melted.

2. Add the ham, noodles and peas. Pour into a greased 1-qt. baking dish. Melt remaining butter; add bread crumbs and parsley. Sprinkle over casserole.

3. Bake, uncovered, at 350° for 30 minutes or until heated through.

Savory Steak Salad

PREP/TOTAL TIME: 30 MIN. • **YIELD:** 4 SERVINGS

  2 **tablespoons brown sugar, divided**
  1 **teaspoon salt**
  ¾ **teaspoon ground cinnamon**
  ¼ **teaspoon cayenne pepper**
  ¼ **teaspoon pepper**
  1 **beef top sirloin steak (1 inch thick and 1 pound)**
  ¾ **cup balsamic vinaigrette, divided**
  1 **medium onion, sliced**
  2 **tablespoons butter**
  1 **package (5 ounces) spring mix salad greens**
  ½ **cup dried cranberries**
  ¼ **cup crumbled blue cheese**

1. In a small bowl, combine 1 tablespoon brown sugar, salt, cinnamon, cayenne and pepper. Rub over both sides of steak. Brush with ¼ cup vinaigrette.

2. Place steak on a broiler pan. Broil 4 in. from the heat for 5-6 minutes on each side or until meat reaches desired doneness (for medium-rare, a thermometer should read 145°; medium, 160°; well-done, 170°).

3. Meanwhile, in a large skillet, saute onion in butter for 10 minutes or until tender. Add remaining brown sugar; cook and stir over medium heat for 5-10 minutes or until onion is browned.

4. Cut steak across the grain into thin slices. In a large bowl, combine the greens, cranberries, blue cheese, onion and beef. Drizzle with remaining vinaigrette; toss to coat.

A convenient prebaked crust makes this tasty taco pizza a great supper solution on busy weeknights. I keep the ingredients on hand so that we can whip it up for a filling meal anytime.
—**MARY CASS** BALTIMORE, MARYLAND

Taco Pizza

PREP: 30 MIN. • **BAKE:** 10 MIN.
YIELD: 2 PIZZAS (6-8 SERVINGS EACH)

1 **pound ground beef**
1 **envelope taco seasoning**
1 **cup water**
2 **prebaked 12-inch pizza crusts**
1 **can (16 ounces) refried beans**
¾ **cup salsa**
2 **cups coarsely crushed tortilla chips**
2 **cups (8 ounces) shredded cheddar cheese**
2 **medium tomatoes, chopped, optional**
1 **cup shredded lettuce, optional**

1. In a large saucepan, cook beef over medium heat until no longer pink; drain. Stir in taco seasoning and water. Bring to a boil; reduce heat. Simmer, uncovered, for 10 minutes; set aside.

2. Place crusts on ungreased pizza pans or baking sheets. Combine beans and salsa; spread over crusts. Top with beef mixture, chips and cheese.

3. Bake at 350° for 13-16 minutes or until cheese is melted. Sprinkle with tomatoes and lettuce if desired.

Crab 'n' Penne Casserole

PREP: 20 MIN. • **BAKE:** 40 MIN. • **YIELD:** 6 SERVINGS

- 1½ **cups uncooked penne pasta**
- 1 **jar (15 ounces) Alfredo sauce**
- 1½ **cups imitation crabmeat, chopped**
- 1 **medium yellow summer squash, sliced**
- 1 **medium zucchini, sliced**
- 1 **tablespoon dried parsley flakes**
- ⅛ **to ¼ teaspoon crushed red pepper flakes**
- 1½ **cups (6 ounces) shredded part-skim mozzarella cheese**
- 2 **tablespoons dry bread crumbs**
- 2 **teaspoons butter, melted**

1. Cook pasta according to package directions. Meanwhile, in a large bowl, combine the Alfredo sauce, crab, yellow squash, zucchini, parsley and pepper flakes. Drain pasta; add to sauce mixture and toss to coat.

2. Transfer to a greased 13-in. x 9-in. baking dish. Sprinkle with cheese. Cover and bake at 325° for 35 minutes or until heated through.

3. Toss bread crumbs and butter; sprinkle over casserole. Bake, uncovered, 5-6 minutes longer or until browned.

CRAB AND TWIST BAKE: Substitute spiral pasta for the penne and provolone cheese for the mozzarella.

Pork Chops and Chilies Casserole

PREP: 15 MIN. • **BAKE:** 40 MIN. • **YIELD:** 4 SERVINGS

- 4 **pork rib chops (¾ to 1 inch thick)**
- 1 **tablespoon canola oil**
- 1 **medium onion, chopped**
- 1 **can (4 ounces) chopped green chilies**
- ½ **cup chopped celery**
- 1½ **cups uncooked instant rice**
- 1 **can (10¾ ounces) condensed cream of mushroom soup, undiluted**
- 1⅓ **cups water**
- 3 **tablespoons reduced-sodium soy sauce**

1. In a large skillet, over medium-high heat, cook chops in oil for 2-3 minutes on each side or until chops are lightly browned; drain. Remove and set aside.

2. In the same skillet, saute the onion, chilies and celery until onion is tender. Stir in rice; saute until lightly browned. Add all remaining ingredients.

3. Place in a greased 2-qt. casserole. Top with pork chops. Bake at 350° for about 30-40 minutes or until meat is tender.

Polenta Chili Casserole

PREP: 20 MIN. • **BAKE:** 35 MIN. + STANDING
YIELD: 8 SERVINGS

We created this delicious vegetarian bean and polenta bake by combining spicy chili, mixed veggies and homemade polenta. It's a warm and filling casserole that's sure to please everyone.
—DAN KELMENSON
WEST BLOOMFIELD, MICHIGAN

- 1¼ **cups yellow cornmeal**
- ½ **teaspoon salt**
- 4 **cups boiling water**
- 2 **cups (8 ounces) shredded cheddar cheese, divided**
- 3 **cans (15 ounces each) vegetarian chili with beans**
- 1 **package (16 ounces) frozen mixed vegetables, thawed and well drained**

1. In a large saucepan, combine cornmeal and salt. Gradually whisk in boiling water. Cook and stir over medium heat for 5 minutes or until thickened. Remove from the heat. Stir in ¼ cup cheddar cheese until melted.

2. Spread into a 13-in. x 9-in. baking dish coated with cooking spray. Bake, uncovered, at 350° for 20 minutes. Meanwhile, heat chili according to package directions.

3. Spread vegetables over polenta; top with chili. Sprinkle with remaining cheese. Bake 12-15 minutes longer or until cheese is melted. Let stand for 10 minutes before serving.

Stovetop Beef 'n' Shells

PREP/TOTAL TIME: 30 MIN. • YIELD: 4 SERVINGS

    4   ounces uncooked medium pasta shells
    1   pound lean ground beef (90% lean)
    1   medium onion, chopped
    1   garlic clove, minced
    1   can (15 ounces) crushed tomatoes
    1   can (8 ounces) tomato sauce
    1   teaspoon sugar
    ½   teaspoon salt
    ½   teaspoon pepper

1. Cook pasta according to package directions. Meanwhile, in a large saucepan, cook beef and onion over medium heat until meat is no longer pink. Add garlic; cook 1 minute longer. Drain.

2. Stir in the tomatoes, tomato sauce, sugar, salt and pepper. Bring to a boil. Reduce heat; simmer, uncovered, for 10-15 minutes. Drain pasta; stir into beef mixture and heat through.

Chicken & Corn Bread Bake

Here's Southern comfort food at its best! This casserole is delicious made with chicken or turkey. It's often on the menu when I cook for my husband, our four grown children and their spouses...and our 10 grandkids!

—**ANN HILLMEYER** SANDIA PARK, NEW MEXICO

I make this supper when I'm pressed for time. It's just as tasty as it is fast to fix. I like to round out the meal with salad, bread and fruit.
—**DONNA ROBERTS** MANHATTAN, KANSAS

PREP: 25 MIN. • BAKE: 25 MIN. • YIELD: 8 SERVINGS

    2½ cups reduced-sodium chicken broth
    1   small onion, chopped
    1   celery rib, chopped
    ⅛   teaspoon pepper
    4½ cups corn bread stuffing mix, divided
    4   cups cubed cooked chicken
    1½ cups (12 ounces) sour cream
    1   can (10¾ ounces) condensed cream of chicken soup, undiluted
    3   green onions, thinly sliced
    ¼   cup butter, cubed

1. In a large saucepan, combine the broth, onion, celery and pepper. Bring to a boil. Reduce heat; cover and simmer for 5-6 minutes or until vegetables are tender. Stir in 4 cups stuffing mix.

2. Transfer to a greased 13-in. x 9-in. baking dish. Top with chicken. In a small bowl, combine the sour cream, soup and green onions. Spread over chicken. Sprinkle with remaining stuffing mix; dot with butter.

3. Bake, uncovered, for 325° for 25-30 minutes or until heated through.

CHICKEN BROCCOLI STUFFING BAKE: Top chicken with 1¼ cups thawed frozen broccoli florets before covering chicken with soup mixture. Proceed as directed.

Wild Rice Chicken Dinner

PREP/TOTAL TIME: 30 MIN.
YIELD: 2 CASSEROLES (6-8 SERVINGS EACH)

- 2 **packages (8.8 ounces each) ready-to-serve long grain and wild rice**
- 2 **packages (16 ounces each) frozen French-style green beans, thawed**
- 2 **cans (10¾ ounces each) condensed cream of celery soup, undiluted**
- 2 **cans (8 ounces each) sliced water chestnuts, drained**
- ⅔ **cup chopped onion**
- 2 **jars (4 ounces each) sliced pimientos, drained**
- 1 **cup mayonnaise**
- ½ **cup 2% milk**
- 1 **teaspoon pepper**
- 6 **cups cubed cooked chicken**
- 1 **cup slivered almonds, divided**

1. Heat rice according to package directions. Meanwhile, in a Dutch oven, combine the green beans, soup, water chestnuts, onion, pimientos, mayonnaise, milk and pepper. Bring to a boil. Reduce heat; cover and simmer for 5 minutes. Stir in chicken and rice; cook 3-4 minutes longer or until chicken is heated through.

2. Transfer half of the mixture to a serving dish; sprinkle with ½ cup almonds. Serve immediately. Pour the remaining mixture into a greased 13-in. x 9-in. baking dish; cool. Sprinkle with remaining almonds. Cover and freeze for up to 3 months.

TO USE FROZEN CASSEROLE: Thaw in the refrigerator overnight. Cover and bake at 350° for 40-45 minutes or until heated through.

Burgundy Steak

PREP/TOTAL TIME: 30 MIN. • **YIELD:** 4 SERVINGS

- ¼ cup all-purpose flour
- ¼ teaspoon paprika
- 1 pound beef top sirloin steak, cut into 1-inch strips
- 1 tablespoon canola oil
- 1 can (10½ ounces) condensed French onion soup, undiluted
- ½ cup Burgundy wine or beef broth
- 3 cups hot cooked egg noodles

1. In a large resealable plastic bag, combine the flour and paprika. Add beef, a few pieces at a time, and shake to coat.

2. In a large skillet, brown beef in oil. Add soup and wine; bring to a boil. Reduce heat; simmer, uncovered, for 10-12 minutes or until meat is no longer pink and sauce is thickened. Serve with noodles.

With just a few ingredients, this hearty classic is table-ready in about 30 minutes. Serve it with your favorite green salad or vegetable for a well-rounded and satisfying meal.

—JENNIFER HESS CUPERTINO, CALIFORNIA

what is Burgundy wine?

Burgundy is a region in eastern France. Although the region produces white wines, it is best known for its popular red wines, commonly referred to as "Burgundies." Made from the Pinot Noir grape, red wines in this region can also be produced from other grape varieties, such as Gamay.

Beef Fillets with Grilled Vegetables

PREP/TOTAL TIME: 30 MIN. • **YIELD:** 4 SERVINGS

- 4 **beef tenderloin steaks (1½ inches thick and 4 ounces each)**
- 3 **teaspoons pepper, divided**
- ½ **cup creamy Caesar salad dressing**
- 8 **to 12 romaine leaves**
- 2 **medium tomatoes, cut into 1-inch slices**
- 1 **medium onion, sliced**
- 3 **tablespoons olive oil**
- 2 **tablespoons butter, melted**
- ½ **teaspoon salt**

1. Rub steaks with 2 teaspoons pepper; place in a large resealable plastic bag. Add salad dressing; seal bag and turn to coat. Refrigerate for 10 minutes.

2. Meanwhile, brush romaine, tomatoes and onion with oil. Grill tomatoes and onion, uncovered, over medium heat for 4-5 minutes on each side or until onion is crisp-tender. Grill romaine for 30 seconds on each side or until heated through. Wrap vegetables in foil and set aside.

3. Drain and discard marinade. Grill steaks, covered, over medium heat for 7-8 minutes on each side or until meat reaches desired doneness (for medium-rare, a thermometer should read 145°; medium, 160°; well-done, 170°), basting occasionally with butter.

4. Serve with grilled vegetables. Sprinkle with salt and remaining pepper.

Cheesy Shell Lasagna

PREP: 25 MIN. • **BAKE:** 45 MIN. + STANDING
YIELD: 12 SERVINGS

- 1½ **pounds lean ground beef (90% lean)**
- 2 **medium onions, chopped**
- 1 **garlic clove, minced**
- 1 **can (14½ ounces) diced tomatoes, undrained**
- 1 **jar (14 ounces) meatless spaghetti sauce**
- 1 **can (4 ounces) mushroom stems and pieces, undrained**
- 8 **ounces uncooked small shell pasta**
- 2 **cups (16 ounces) reduced-fat sour cream**
- 11 **slices (8 ounces) reduced-fat provolone cheese**
- 1 **cup (4 ounces) shredded part-skim mozzarella cheese**

1. In a nonstick skillet, cook beef and onions over medium heat until meat is no longer pink. Add garlic; cook 1 minute longer. Drain. Stir in the tomatoes, spaghetti sauce and mushrooms. Bring to a boil. Reduce heat; simmer, uncovered, for 20 minutes.

2. Meanwhile, cook pasta according to package directions; drain.

3. Place half of the pasta in an ungreased 13-in. x 9-in. baking dish. Top with half of the meat sauce, sour cream and provolone cheese. Repeat layers. Sprinkle with mozzarella cheese.

4. Cover and bake at 350° for 35-40 minutes. Uncover; bake 10 minutes longer or until the cheese begins to brown. Let stand for 10 minutes before cutting.

This zesty layered casserole is a real crowd-pleaser. It was one of our children's favorites when they were growing up, and now our grandchildren love it! Plus, it's easier to make than traditional lasagna.
—MRS. LEO MERCHANT JACKSON, MISSISSIPPI

Meat Loaf Dinner

I like the fact that I can pop this meat loaf into the oven in the late afternoon and forget about it until dinner. When in a hurry, I substitute canned potatoes and green beans for fresh.
—FLORENCE DOLLARD GRAND ISLAND, NEW YORK

PREP: 15 MIN. • **BAKE:** 2 HOURS • **YIELD:** 8 SERVINGS

- 1 **egg**
- ½ **cup seasoned bread crumbs**
- ¼ **cup chopped onion**
- ½ **teaspoon seasoned salt**
- 2 **pounds lean ground beef**
- 4 **medium potatoes, quartered**
- ½ **pound fresh or frozen cut green beans**
- 1 **can (14½ ounces) stewed tomatoes**

1. In a large bowl, combine the first four ingredients. Crumble beef over mixture and mix well. Shape into a loaf in a greased roasting pan. Arrange potatoes and green beans around loaf. Pour tomatoes over all.

2. Cover and bake at 350° for 2 hours or until the meat is no longer pink and a meat thermometer reads 160°.

My husband and boys love this recipe because the kabobs are mouthwatering and delicious. I love it because it's so fast and easy!
—**KAREN ENGSTROM** GLASGOW, MONTANA

Barbecue Beef Kabobs

PREP: 25 MIN. + MARINATING • **GRILL:** 20 MIN.
YIELD: 10 KABOBS

- 1 cup ketchup
- ⅓ cup French salad dressing
- ⅓ cup reduced-sodium soy sauce
- 1 tablespoon Worcestershire sauce
- 1 pound boneless beef sirloin steak, cut into 1-inch cubes
- 1 cup fresh baby carrots
- 2 tablespoons water
- 1 pound medium fresh mushrooms, halved
- 1 medium green pepper, cut into 1-inch pieces
- ½ medium onion, cut into 1-inch pieces
  Hot cooked rice, optional

1. In a small bowl, combine the ketchup, salad dressing, soy sauce and Worcestershire sauce. Transfer ⅓ cup to another bowl for basting; cover and refrigerate. Pour remaining marinade into a large resealable plastic bag; add steak. Seal bag and turn to coat; refrigerate for at least 1 hour.

2. Place carrots and water in a microwave-safe dish. Cover and microwave on high for 4 minutes; drain. Drain and discard marinade. On 10 metal or soaked wooden skewers, alternately thread beef and vegetables.

3. Grill, covered, over medium-hot heat for 18-20 minutes or until meat reaches desired doneness, basting frequently with reserved marinade and turning once. Serve with rice if desired.

Great Pork Chop Bake

PREP: 10 MIN. • **BAKE:** 55 MIN. • **YIELD:** 6 SERVINGS

- 6 **bone-in pork loin chops (¾-inch thick and 8 ounces each)**
- 1 **tablespoon canola oil**
- 1 **can (10¾ ounces) condensed cream of chicken soup, undiluted**
- 3 **tablespoons ketchup**
- 2 **tablespoons Worcestershire sauce**
- ½ **teaspoon salt**
- ¼ **teaspoon pepper**
- 4 **medium potatoes, cut into ½-inch wedges**
- 1 **medium onion, sliced into rings**

1. In a large skillet, brown pork chops in oil. Transfer to a greased 13-in. x 9-in. baking dish. In a large bowl, combine the soup, ketchup, Worcestershire sauce, salt and pepper. Add potatoes and onion; toss to coat. Pour over the chops.

2. Cover and bake at 350° for 55-60 minutes or until a meat thermometer reads 160° and potatoes are tender.

cleaner ketchup bottle tops

Ketchup bottle squeeze tops can get messy fast. To keep them clean, save tops from used bottles and run them through the dishwasher. When a top currently on the ketchup bottle gets messy, replace it with a clean spare one.

Church Supper Hot Dish

PREP: 40 MIN. • **BAKE:** 30 MIN. • **YIELD:** 8 SERVINGS

- 1   **pound ground beef**
- 2   **cups sliced peeled potatoes**
- 2   **cups finely chopped celery**
- ¾   **cup finely chopped carrots**
- ¼   **cup finely chopped green pepper**
- ¼   **cup finely chopped onion**
- 2   **tablespoons butter**
- 1   **cup water**
- 2   **cans (10¾ ounces each) condensed cream of mushroom soup, undiluted**
- 1   **can (5 ounces) chow mein noodles, divided**
- 1   **cup (4 ounces) shredded cheddar cheese**

1. In a large skillet, cook beef over medium heat until no longer pink; drain and set aside.

2. In the same skillet, saute the potatoes, celery, carrots, green pepper and onion in butter for 5 minutes. Add water; cover and simmer for 10 minutes or until vegetables are tender. Stir in soup and cooked ground beef until blended.

3. Sprinkle half of the chow mein noodles into a greased shallow 2-qt. baking dish. Spoon meat mixture over noodles. Cover and bake at 350° for 20 minutes. Top with cheese and remaining noodles. Bake, uncovered, 10 minutes longer or until heated through.

Zesty Tacos

Jazz up everyday tacos in a snap! Black-eyed peas and a drizzle of Italian dressing are the surprise ingredients that perk up this recipe with extra flavor.
—**SUSIE BONHAM** FAIRVIEW, OKLAHOMA

PREP/TOTAL TIME: 30 MIN. • **YIELD:** 8 SERVINGS

- 1 **pound ground beef**
- 1 **cup water**
- 1 **envelope taco seasoning**
- 8 **taco shells**
- 1 **can (15½ ounces) black-eyed peas, rinsed and drained**
- 1 **cup chopped tomatoes**
- 1 **cup shredded lettuce**
- 1 **cup (4 ounces) shredded cheddar cheese**
- ½ **cup zesty Italian salad dressing**

1. In a large skillet, cook beef over medium heat for 5-6 minutes or until meat is no longer pink; drain. Stir in water and taco seasoning. Bring to a boil. Reduce heat; simmer, uncovered, for 4-5 minutes or until thickened.

2. Meanwhile, prepare taco shells according to package directions. Stir peas into skillet; heat through. Spoon ¼ cup beef mixture into each taco shell. Top with tomatoes, lettuce and cheese. Drizzle with salad dressing.

With brown rice, whole grains, tomatoes and corn, this super-fast meal is such a tasty way to get your family to eat more fiber; and they won't even realize it's good for them!
—**PENNY HAWKINS**
MEBANE, NORTH CAROLINA

Southwest Chicken and Rice

PREP/TOTAL TIME: 10 MIN. • **YIELD:** 4 SERVINGS

- 2 **packages (8½ ounces each) ready-to-serve Santa Fe whole grain rice medley**
- 2 **packages (6 ounces each) ready-to-use Southwestern chicken strips, cut into chunks**
- 1 **can (10 ounces) diced tomatoes and green chilies, drained**
- ½ **cup shredded Monterey Jack cheese**

1. Heat rice according to package directions. In a 2-qt. microwave-safe dish, combine chicken and tomatoes; stir in rice. Cover and microwave on high for 2-3 minutes. Sprinkle with cheese; cook 1 minute longer or until cheese is melted.

EDITOR'S NOTE: This recipe was tested in a 1,100-watt microwave.

66 In the winter, big bowls of this soup make a warming supper with a salad and biscuits. It's a simple recipe—just saute the onions early in the day and let the soup simmer until dinnertime. 99

—LINDA ADOLPH EDMONTON, ALBERTA

slow cooker cuisine

Let your slow cooker take care of dinner for you with these convenient stick-to-your ribs recipes. Some have a hands-on prep time of only 10 minutes!

Mushroom 'n' Steak Stroganoff

PREP: 15 MIN. • **COOK:** 6¼ HOURS • **YIELD:** 6 SERVINGS

2	tablespoons all-purpose flour
½	teaspoon garlic powder
½	teaspoon pepper
¼	teaspoon paprika
1¾	pounds beef top round steak, cut into 1½-inch strips
1	can (10¾ ounces) condensed cream of mushroom soup, undiluted
½	cup water
¼	cup onion mushroom soup mix
2	jars (4½ ounces each) sliced mushrooms, drained
½	cup sour cream
1	tablespoon minced fresh parsley
	Hot cooked egg noodles, optional

1. In a large resealable plastic bag, combine the flour, garlic powder, pepper and paprika. Add beef strips and shake to coat.

2. Transfer to a 3-qt. slow cooker. In a small bowl, combine the soup, water and soup mix; pour over beef. Cover and cook on low for 6-7 hours or until the meat is tender.

3. Stir in the mushrooms, sour cream, and parsley. Cover and cook 15 minutes longer or until sauce is thickened. Serve with noodles if desired.

Sweet and Savory Brisket

PREP: 10 MIN. • **COOK:** 8 HOURS • **YIELD:** 8-10 SERVINGS

- 1 **beef brisket (3 to 3½ pounds), cut in half**
- 1 **cup ketchup**
- ¼ **cup grape jelly**
- 1 **envelope onion soup mix**
- ½ **teaspoon pepper**

1. Place half of the brisket in a 5-qt. slow cooker. In a small bowl, combine the ketchup, jelly, soup mix and pepper; spread half over meat. Top with the remaining meat and ketchup mixture.

2. Cover and cook on low for 8-10 hours or until meat is tender. Slice brisket; serve with cooking juice.

EDITOR'S NOTE: This is a fresh beef brisket, not corned beef.

I like this recipe not only because it makes such tender and flavorful beef, but because it takes advantage of a slow cooker. It's wonderful to come home from work and have this mouthwatering dish waiting for you.
—**CHRIS SNYDER** BOULDER, COLORADO

keep the lid on

Unless the recipe instructs you to stir in or add ingredients, refrain from lifting the lid while the slow cooker is cooking. Every time you lift the lid, steam is lost and you add 15 to 30 minutes of cooking time.

Apple Granola Dessert

I'd be lost without my slow cooker! Besides using it to prepare many evening meals, I often make desserts in it. One of our favorites is this recipe for tender apples and granola cereal. It fills the house with such a wonderful aroma.
—JANIS LAWRENCE CHILDRESS, TEXAS

PREP: 10 MIN. • **COOK:** 6 HOURS • **YIELD:** 4-6 SERVINGS

- 4 medium tart apples, peeled and sliced
- 2 cups granola cereal with fruit and nuts
- ¼ cup honey
- 2 tablespoons butter, melted
- 1 teaspoon ground cinnamon
- ½ teaspoon ground nutmeg
  Whipped topping, optional

1. In a 1½-qt. slow cooker, combine apples and cereal. In a small bowl, combine the honey, butter, cinnamon and nutmeg; pour over apple mixture and mix well. Cover and cook on low for 6-8 hours. Serve with whipped topping if desired.

Crunchy Candy Clusters

Before I retired, I brought these yummy peanut butter bites to work for special occasions. They're so simple. I still make them for holidays because my family always looks forward to the coated cereal-and-marshmallow clusters.
—FAYE O'BRYAN OWENSBORO, KENTUCKY

PREP: 15 MIN. • **COOK:** 1 HOUR • **YIELD:** 6½ DOZEN

- 2 pounds white candy coating, coarsely chopped
- 1½ cups peanut butter
- ½ teaspoon almond extract, optional
- 4 cups Cap'n Crunch cereal
- 4 cups crisp rice cereal
- 4 cups miniature marshmallows

1. Place candy coating in a 5-qt. slow cooker. Cover and cook on high for 1 hour. Add peanut butter. Stir in extract if desired.

2. In a large bowl, combine the cereals and marshmallows. Stir in the peanut butter mixture until well coated. Drop by tablespoonfuls onto waxed paper. Let stand until set. Store at room temperature.

For a rich, fudgy dessert that's a cross between pudding and cake, try this. I like to serve it warm with a scoop of vanilla ice cream. Whenever I take it to parties, everybody wants the recipe!
—PAIGE ARNETTE
LAWRENCEVILLE, GEORGIA

Chocolate Pudding Cake

PREP: 10 MIN. • **COOK:** 6 HOURS • **YIELD:** 10-12 SERVINGS

1 package (18¼ ounces) chocolate cake mix
1 package (3.9 ounces) instant chocolate pudding mix
2 cups (16 ounces) sour cream
4 eggs
1 cup water
¾ cup canola oil
1 cup (6 ounces) semisweet chocolate chips
    Whipped cream or ice cream, optional

1. In a large bowl, combine the first six ingredients; beat on low speed for 30 seconds. Beat on medium for 2 minutes. Stir in chocolate chips. Pour into a greased 5-qt. slow cooker.

2. Cover and cook on low for 6-8 hours or until a toothpick inserted near the center comes out with moist crumbs. Serve in bowls with whipped cream or ice cream if desired.

This is by far the simplest way to make roast beef and gravy. On busy days, I can put this main dish in the slow cooker and forget about it. My family likes it with mashed potatoes and fruit salad.
—ABBY METZGER LARCHWOOD, IOWA

Hot Chili
Cheese Dip

To simplify party preparation, I use my slow cooker to create this thick, cheesy dip. Your guests won't believe how good it is!
—JEANIE CARRIGAN MADERA, CALIFORNIA

PREP: 20 MIN. • **COOK:** 4 HOURS • **YIELD:** 6 CUPS

- 1   medium onion, finely chopped
- 2   teaspoons canola oil
- 2   garlic cloves, minced
- 2   cans (15 ounces each) chili without beans
- 2   cups salsa
- 2   packages (3 ounces each) cream cheese, cubed
- 2   cans (2¼ ounces each) sliced ripe olives, drained
     Tortilla chips

1. In a small skillet, saute onion in oil until tender. Add garlic; cook 1 minute longer.

2. Transfer to a 3-qt. slow cooker. Stir in the chili, salsa, cream cheese and olives. Cover and cook on low for 4 hours or until heated through, stirring occasionally. Stir before serving with tortilla chips.

Roast Beef
And Gravy

PREP: 15 MIN. • **COOK:** 8 HOURS • **YIELD:** 8-10 SERVINGS

- 1   boneless beef chuck roast (3 pounds)
- 2   cans (10¾ ounces each) condensed cream of mushroom soup, undiluted
- ⅓   cup sherry or beef broth
- 1   envelope onion soup mix

1. Cut roast in half; place in a 3-qt. slow cooker. In a large bowl, combine the remaining ingredients; pour over roast.

2. Cover and cook on low for 8-10 hours or until meat is tender.

This sensational dish is so wonderful to come home to, especially on a cool winter day. It's a delicious way to use up leftover holiday ham, too.
—**JILL PENNINGTON**
JACKSONVILLE, FLORIDA

Slow-Cooked Ham 'n' Broccoli

PREP: 10 MIN. • **COOK:** 2 HOURS + STANDING
YIELD: 6-8 SERVINGS

- 3 **cups cubed fully cooked ham**
- 3 **cups frozen chopped broccoli, thawed**
- 1 **can (10¾ ounces) condensed cream of mushroom soup, undiluted**
- 1 **jar (8 ounces) process cheese sauce**
- 1 **can (8 ounces) sliced water chestnuts, drained**
- 1¼ **cups uncooked instant rice**
- 1 **cup 2% milk**
- 1 **celery rib, chopped**
- 1 **medium onion, chopped**
- ⅛ **to ¼ teaspoon pepper**
- ½ **teaspoon paprika**

1. In a 3-qt. slow cooker, combine the first 10 ingredients. Cover and cook on high for 2-3 hours or until the rice is tender. Let stand for 10 minutes before serving. Sprinkle with paprika.

rice in recipes

Instant rice (which is precooked before packaging) and long grain rice require different amounts of liquid during cooking, so they cannot be substituted measure for measure. Once prepared, you can use either kind of rice interchangeably in a recipe that calls for cooked rice.

My recipe for tender chicken in a creamy sauce gets fast and easy flavor from salad dressing mix. Served over rice or pasta, it's rich, delicious and special enough to serve company.

—MAURA MCGEE
TALLAHASSEE, FLORIDA

Creamy Italian Chicken

PREP: 5 MIN. • **COOK:** 4 HOURS • **YIELD:** 4 SERVINGS

- 4 boneless skinless chicken breast halves (4 ounces each)
- 1 envelope Italian salad dressing mix
- ¼ cup water
- 1 package (8 ounces) cream cheese, softened
- 1 can (10¾ ounces) condensed cream of chicken soup, undiluted
- 1 can (4 ounces) mushroom stems and pieces, drained
  Hot cooked pasta or rice
  Fresh oregano leaves, optional

1. Place the chicken in a 3-qt. slow cooker. Combine salad dressing mix and water; pour over chicken. Cover and cook on low for 3 hours.

2. In a small bowl, beat the cream cheese and soup until blended. Stir in mushrooms. Pour over chicken. Cook 1 hour longer or until a thermometer reaches 170°. Serve with pasta or rice. Garnish with oregano if desired.

Savory Italian Beef Sandwiches

Before leaving for work, I often put these ingredients in the slow cooker. And supper is ready when I get home! Could anything be easier? This recipe is also great for potlucks.

—**CAROL ALLEN** MCLEANSBORO, ILLINOIS

PREP: 15 MIN. • **COOK:** 7 HOURS • **YIELD:** 10-12 SERVINGS

- 1   boneless beef chuck roast (3 to 4 pounds)
- 3   tablespoons dried basil
- 3   tablespoons dried oregano
- 1   cup water
- 1   envelope onion soup mix
- 10   to 12 Italian rolls or sandwich buns

1. Cut roast in half; place in a 5-qt. slow cooker. Combine the basil, oregano and water; pour over roast. Sprinkle with soup mix.

2. Cover and cook on low for 8-10 hours or until meat is tender. Remove meat; shred with two forks and keep warm. Strain broth and skim fat. Serve meat on rolls; use broth for dipping if desired.

Texas Black Bean Soup

PREP: 5 MIN. • **COOK:** 4 HOURS
YIELD: 8-10 SERVINGS (ABOUT 2½ QUARTS)

- 2   cans (15 ounces each) black beans, rinsed and drained
- 1   can (14½ ounces) stewed tomatoes or Mexican stewed tomatoes, cut up
- 1   can (14½ ounces) diced tomatoes or diced tomatoes with green chilies
- 1   can (14½ ounces) chicken broth
- 1   can (11 ounces) Mexicorn, drained
- 2   cans (4 ounces each) chopped green chilies
- 4   green onions, thinly sliced
- 2   to 3 tablespoons chili powder
- 1   teaspoon ground cumin
- ½   teaspoon dried minced garlic

1. In a 3-qt. slow cooker, combine all ingredients. Cover and cook on high for 4-6 hours or until heated through.

This hearty soup is made with convenient canned items and perfect for spicing up a family gathering on a cool day. It tastes fabulous and requires so little time and attention.
—**PAMELA SCOTT** GARLAND, TEXAS

Old-Fashioned Pork Chops

PREP: 20 MIN. • **COOK:** 5 HOURS • **YIELD:** 6 SERVINGS

- ½   **cup all-purpose flour**
- 1½   **teaspoons ground mustard**
- ½   **teaspoon garlic salt**
- ½   **teaspoon pepper**
- 6   **boneless pork loin chops (5 ounces each)**
- 2   **tablespoons canola oil**
- 1   **can (10½ ounces) condensed chicken with rice soup, undiluted**
- 1   **medium onion, quartered**
- 1½   **teaspoons dried parsley flakes**

1. In a large resealable plastic bag, combine the flour, mustard, garlic salt and pepper. Add pork, a few pieces at a time, and shake to coat.

2. In a large skillet, brown chops in oil on each side. Transfer to a 3-qt. slow cooker. Top with soup, onion and parsley. Cover and cook on low for 5-6 hours or until meat is tender.

the versatility of pork

Unlike beef, cuts of pork vary little in tenderness. Use dry-heat cooking methods (broiling, grilling, pan-broiling, roasting and stir-frying) when a firm texture is desired. The moist-heat methods of braising or slow-cooking are used when a fork-tender texture is desired.

Saucy Italian Roast

PREP: 10 MIN. • COOK: 8 HOURS • YIELD: 10 SERVINGS

- 1 beef rump roast or bottom round roast
     (3 to 3½ pounds)
- ½ to 1 teaspoon salt
- ½ teaspoon garlic powder
- ¼ teaspoon pepper
- 1 jar (4½ ounces) sliced mushrooms, drained
- 1 medium onion, diced
- 1 jar (14 ounces) spaghetti sauce
- ¼ to ½ cup red wine or beef broth
     Hot cooked pasta

This tender roast is one of my favorite set-and-forget meals. I thicken the juices with a little flour and add ketchup, then serve the sauce and beef slices over pasta.
—**JAN ROAT** RED LODGE, MONTANA

1. Cut roast in half. Combine the salt, garlic powder and pepper; rub over roast. Place in a 5-qt. slow cooker. Top with mushrooms and onion. Combine the spaghetti sauce and wine; pour over meat and vegetables.

2. Cover and cook on low for 8-10 hours or until meat is tender. Slice roast; serve with pasta and pan juices.

Creamy Macaroni And Cheese

What an effortless way to make America's most popular comfort food! This dish turns out cheesy, rich and creamy.
—**JENNIFER BABCOCK** CHICOPEE, MASSACHUSETTS

PREP: 25 MIN. • **COOK:** 2 HOURS
YIELD: 16 SERVINGS (¾ CUP EACH)

- 3 **cups uncooked elbow macaroni**
- 1 **pound process cheese (Velveeta), cubed**
- 2 **cups (8 ounces) shredded Mexican cheese blend**
- 2 **cups (8 ounces) shredded white cheddar cheese**
- 1¾ **cups milk**
- 1 **can (12 ounces) evaporated milk**
- ¾ **cup egg substitute**
- ¾ **cup butter, melted**

1. Cook macaroni according to package directions; drain. Place in a greased 5-qt. slow cooker. Stir in the remaining ingredients.

2. Cover and cook on low for 2-3 hours or until a thermometer reads 160°, stirring once.

Pork Chop Dinner

PREP: 10 MIN. • **BAKE:** 6 HOURS • **YIELD:** 4 SERVINGS

- 6 **to 8 medium carrots (1 pound), coarsely chopped**
- 3 **to 4 medium potatoes, cubed**
- 4 **boneless pork loin chops (¾ inch thick)**
- 1 **large onion, sliced**
- 1 **envelope onion soup mix**
- 2 **cans (10¾ ounces each) condensed cream of mushroom soup, undiluted**

1. Place carrots and potatoes in a 3-qt. slow cooker. Top with pork chops, onion, soup mix and soup. Cover and cook on low for 6-8 hours or until meat and vegetables are tender.

I'm a nurse and work nights, so when I get home in the morning, I put this chicken on to cook. In a few hours, the chicken is moist and tender, and the rich sauce, seasoned with garlic and thyme, is simply delicious.
—**MARY HUMENIUK-SMITH**
PERRY HALL, MARYLAND

Creamy Herbed Chicken

PREP: 5 MIN. • **COOK:** 4 HOURS • **YIELD:** 4 SERVINGS

- 4 **boneless skinless chicken breast halves (4 ounces each)**
- 1 **can (10¾ ounces) condensed cream of chicken soup, undiluted**
- 1 **cup milk**
- 1 **envelope garlic and herb pasta sauce mix**
- 1 **teaspoon dried thyme**
- 1 **teaspoon dried parsley flakes**
  Hot cooked fettuccine

1. Place chicken in a 3-qt. slow cooker. Combine the soup, milk, sauce mix, thyme and parsley; pour over chicken. Cover and cook on low for 4-5 hours or until chicken is tender. Serve with fettuccine.

EDITOR'S NOTE: This recipe was tested with Knorr Garlic Herb Pasta Sauce Mix.

In the winter, big bowls of this soup make a warming supper with a salad and biscuits. It's a simple recipe—just saute the onions early in the day and let the soup simmer until dinnertime.
—**LINDA ADOLPH**
EDMONTON, ALBERTA

Rich French Onion Soup

PREP: 10 MIN. • **COOK:** 5 HOURS • **YIELD:** 10 SERVINGS

- **6 large onions, chopped**
- **½ cup butter**
- **6 cans (10½ ounces each) condensed beef broth, undiluted**
- **1½ teaspoons Worcestershire sauce**
- **3 bay leaves**
- **10 slices French bread, toasted**
  Shredded Parmesan and shredded part-skim mozzarella cheese

1. In a large skillet, saute onions in butter until crisp-tender. Transfer to a 5-qt. slow cooker. Add the broth, Worcestershire sauce and bay leaves.

2. Cover and cook on low for 5-7 hours or until the onions are tender. Discard bay leaves.

3. Ladle soup into ovenproof bowls. Top each with a slice of toast; sprinkle with desired amount of cheese. Place bowls on a baking sheet. Broil for 2-3 minutes or until cheese is lightly golden.

This recipe was given to me many years ago at a New Year's potluck. Since then, it has been a tradition to serve it at our holiday open house. The creamy fondue blend is always a hit!
—GWYNNE FLEENER
COEUR D' ALENE, IDAHO

Parmesan Fondue

PREP/TOTAL TIME: 15 MIN. • **YIELD:** ABOUT 3½ CUPS

- 1½ **to 2 cups milk**
- 2 **packages (8 ounces each) cream cheese, cubed**
- 1½ **cups grated Parmesan cheese**
- ½ **teaspoon garlic salt**
- 1 **loaf (1 pound) French bread, cubed**

1. In a large saucepan, cook and stir the milk and cream cheese over low heat until cheese is melted. Stir in Parmesan cheese and garlic salt; cook and stir until heated through. Keep warm. Serve with bread cubes.

cheese fondue fact

To serve a smooth and delicious cheese fondue, keep in mind that cheese can curdle easily when overheated. Be sure to reduce the heat to low before stirring the cheese into hot liquids. Keep the heat at low while the cheese melts.

Beef in Mushroom Gravy

This is one of the best and easiest meals I've ever made! It has only four ingredients, and they all go into the pot at once. The seasoned soup mix flavors the round steak nicely as it makes its own gravy. The dish tastes wonderful when you serve the meat and gravy over mashed potatoes.

—MARGERY BRYAN MOSES LAKE, WASHINGTON

PREP: 10 MIN. • **COOK:** 7 HOURS • **YIELD:** 6 SERVINGS

- 2 to 2½ pounds boneless beef round steak
- 1 to 2 envelopes onion soup mix
- 1 can (10¾ ounces) condensed cream of mushroom soup, undiluted
- ½ cup water
  Mashed potatoes, optional

1. Cut steak into six serving-size pieces; place in a 3-qt. slow cooker. Combine the soup mix, soup and water; pour over beef. Cover and cook on low for 7-8 hours or until meat is tender. Serve with mashed potatoes if desired.

This rich and flavorful side dish is a real crowd pleaser. It's easy to double, and I always receive compliments when I take it to potlucks.

—SHELIA SCHMITT TOPEKA, KANSAS

Creamy Red Potatoes

PREP: 5 MIN. • **COOK:** 8 HOURS • **YIELD:** 4-6 SERVINGS

- 2 pounds small red potatoes, quartered
- 1 package (8 ounces) cream cheese, softened
- 1 can (10¾ ounces) condensed cream of potato soup, undiluted
- 1 envelope ranch salad dressing mix

1. Place potatoes in a 3-qt. slow cooker. In a small bowl, beat the cream cheese, soup and salad dressing mix until blended. Stir into potatoes. Cover and cook on low for 8 hours or until potatoes are tender.

Slow-Cooked Ribs

Nothing says comfort like a plate full of mouthwatering ribs coated in barbecue sauce. These are especially delicious and tangy.
—**SHARON CRIDER** JUNCTION CITY, KANSAS

PREP: 15 MIN. • **COOK:** 6 HOURS • **YIELD:** 8 SERVINGS

- 4 **pounds boneless country-style pork ribs**
- 1 **cup barbecue sauce**
- 1 **cup Catalina salad dressing**
- ½ **teaspoon minced garlic**
- 2 **tablespoons all-purpose flour**
- ¼ **cup cold water**

1. Cut ribs into serving-size pieces. Place in a 5-qt. slow cooker. Combine barbecue sauce and salad dressing; pour over ribs. Sprinkle with garlic. Cover and cook on low for 6-7 hours or until meat is tender.

2. Remove meat to a serving platter; keep warm. Skim fat from cooking juices; transfer to a small saucepan. Bring liquid to a boil.

3. Combine flour and water until smooth. Gradually stir into the pan. Bring to a boil; cook and stir for 2 minutes or until thickened. Serve with meat.

delectable desserts

Prep time is streamlined with the use of cake mixes and other convenience products, making these decadent dinner finales even sweeter for on-the-go cooks and bakers.

Double Frosted Brownies

PREP: 15 MIN. + CHILLING • **BAKE:** 25 MIN. + COOLING
YIELD: 3 DOZEN

1	package fudge brownie mix (13-inch x 9-inch pan size)
½	cup butter, softened
1½	cups confectioners' sugar
2	tablespoons instant vanilla pudding mix
2	to 3 tablespoons 2% milk
1	can (16 ounces) chocolate fudge frosting

1. Prepare brownie mix according to package directions. Spread the batter into a greased 13-in. x 9-in. baking pan. Bake at 350° for 25-30 minutes or until a toothpick inserted 2 in. from side of pan comes out clean. Cool completely on a wire rack.

2. In a large bowl, beat the butter, sugar and pudding mix until blended. Add enough milk to achieve spreading consistency. Frost brownies. Cover and refrigerate for 30 minutes.

3. Spread with fudge frosting. Cut into bars. Store in the refrigerator.

Just one bite and chocolate lovers will melt over these yummy clusters filled with salted nuts, rice cereal and marshmallows! And they're so pretty, no one can believe how easy they are.

—PAIGE SCOTT
MURFREESBORO,
TENNESSEE

Chocolate Zebra Clusters

PREP/TOTAL TIME: 30 MIN. • **YIELD:** 2½ DOZEN

- 2 **cups (12 ounces) semisweet chocolate chips**
- 12 **ounces white candy coating, coarsely chopped, divided**
- 1¼ **cups salted peanuts**
- 1¼ **cups crisp rice cereal**
- 2¼ **cups miniature marshmallows**
- 1 **teaspoon shortening**

1. Line two baking sheets with waxed paper; set aside. In a microwave, melt chips and 7 oz. white candy coating at 70% power; stir until smooth. Stir in peanuts and cereal. Cool slightly; fold in marshmallows. Drop by rounded tablespoonfuls onto prepared baking sheets.

2. In microwave, melt shortening and remaining candy coating; stir until smooth. Transfer to a pastry or plastic bag; cut a small hole in the corner of bag. Drizzle over clusters. Refrigerate for 5 minutes or until set. Store in an airtight container.

Mocha Cheesecake Bars

PREP: 30 MIN. + CHILLING • **YIELD:** 24 SERVINGS

25 reduced-fat Oreo cookies,
 3 tablespoons fat-free hot fudge ice cream topping
 3 tablespoons butter, melted

FILLING:

 1 envelope unflavored gelatin
 ½ cup cold strong brewed coffee
 2 packages (8 ounces each) reduced-fat cream cheese
 ¾ cup sugar
 1 cup (8 ounces) reduced-fat sour cream
 3 ounces bittersweet chocolate, melted and cooled
24 chocolate-covered coffee beans, optional

1. Place cookies in a food processor. Cover and pulse until fine crumbs form. Add fudge topping and butter; pulse just until blended. Press onto the bottom of a 13-in. x 9-in. dish coated with cooking spray. Refrigerate for 10 minutes.

2. Meanwhile, for filling, in a small saucepan, sprinkle gelatin over coffee; let stand for 1 minute. Heat over low heat, stirring until gelatin is completely dissolved. Remove from the heat; set aside.

3. In a large bowl, beat cream cheese and sugar until smooth. Beat in the sour cream, chocolate and reserved coffee mixture until blended. Pour over crust. Cover and refrigerate for at least 4 hours or until firm.

4. Cut into bars. Garnish with coffee beans if desired. Refrigerate leftovers.

Chocolate Peanut Butter Cookies

PREP: 10 MIN. • **BAKE:** 10 MIN./BATCH • **YIELD:** 4 DOZEN

- 1 package (18¼ ounces) devil's food cake mix
- 2 eggs
- ⅓ cup canola oil
- 1 package (10 ounces) peanut butter chips

1. In a bowl, beat cake mix, eggs and oil (batter will be very stiff). Stir in chips.

2. Roll into 1-in. balls. Place on lightly greased baking sheets; flatten slightly. Bake at 350° for 10 minutes or until a slight indentation remains when lightly touched. Cool for 2 minutes before removing to a wire rack.

storing cookies

Store cooled, baked cookies in an airtight container at room temperature for about 3 days. To freeze cookies for up to 3 months, wrap the cookies in plastic, stack in an airtight container, seal and freeze. Thaw wrapped cookies at room temperature before serving.

Use a packaged cake mix to whip up these quick-to-fix treats in a snap! Their sunny yellow color, big lemon flavor and delightful crunch are sure to bring smiles.

—**JULIA LIVINGSTON** FROSTPROOF, FLORIDA

Lemon Crisp Cookies

PREP/TOTAL TIME: 30 MIN. • **YIELD:** ABOUT 4 DOZEN

- 1 **package (18¼ ounces) lemon cake mix**
- 1 **cup crisp rice cereal**
- ½ **cup butter, melted**
- 1 **egg, lightly beaten**
- 1 **teaspoon grated lemon peel**

1. In a large bowl, combine all the ingredients (dough will be crumbly). Shape into 1-in. balls. Place 2 in. apart on ungreased baking sheets.

2. Bake at 350° for 10-12 minutes or until set. Cool for 1 minute; remove from pan to a wire rack to cool completely.

Candy Bar Croissants

These croissants taste as good as they look. The rich, buttery treats combine convenient refrigerated crescent rolls and chocolate bars.

—**BEVERLY STERLING** GASPORT, NEW YORK

PREP: 15 MIN. • **BAKE:** 15 MIN. + COOLING • **YIELD:** 8 SERVINGS

- 1 **tube (8 ounces) refrigerated crescent rolls**
- 1 **tablespoon butter, softened**
- 2 **plain milk chocolate candy bars (1.55 ounces each), broken into small pieces**
- 1 **egg, lightly beaten**
- 2 **tablespoons sliced almonds**

1. Unroll crescent roll dough; separate into triangles. Brush with butter. Arrange candy bar pieces evenly over triangles; roll up from the wide end.

2. Place point side down on a greased baking sheet; curve ends slightly. Brush with egg and sprinkle with almonds. Bake at 375° for 11-13 minutes or until golden brown. Cool on a wire rack.

Here's a dessert lovely enough for company,
and you can make it a day or two in advance.
—MARGIE SNODGRASS
WILMORE, KENTUCKY

Banana Cream Cheesecake

PREP: 25 MIN. + CHILLING • **YIELD:** 10 SERVINGS

- 1¾ **cups graham cracker crumbs**
- ¼ **cup sugar**
- ½ **cup butter, melted**

FILLING:

- 1 **package (8 ounces) cream cheese, softened**
- ½ **cup sugar**
- 1 **carton (8 ounces) frozen whipped topping, thawed, divided**
- 3 **to 4 medium firm bananas, sliced**
- 1¾ **cups cold milk**
- 1 **package (3.4 ounces) instant banana cream pudding mix**

1. In a small bowl, combine cracker crumbs and sugar; stir in butter. Set aside ½ cup for topping. Press remaining crumb mixture onto the bottom and up the sides of a greased 9-in. springform pan or 9-in. square baking pan. Bake at 350° for 5-7 minutes. Cool on wire rack.

2. In a large bowl, beat cream cheese and sugar until smooth. Fold in 2 cups whipped topping. Arrange half of the banana slices in crust; top with half of the cream cheese mixture. Repeat layers.

3. In a small bowl, whisk milk and pudding mix for 2 minutes. Let stand for 2 minutes or until soft-set; fold in remaining whipped topping. Pour over the cream cheese layer. Sprinkle with reserved crumb mixture. Refrigerate for 1-2 hours or until set.

Raspberry Ribbon Pie

PREP: 20 MIN. + CHILLING • **YIELD:** 6-8 SERVINGS

2	**packages (3 ounces each) cream cheese, softened**
½	**cup confectioners' sugar**
	Dash salt
1	**cup heavy whipping cream, whipped**
	Pastry for deep-dish single-crust pie (9 inches), baked
1	**package (3 ounces) raspberry gelatin**
1¼	**cups boiling water**
1	**tablespoon lemon juice**
1	**package (10 ounces) frozen raspberries in syrup, thawed**

1. In a large bowl, beat the cream cheese, sugar and salt until smooth. Fold in cream. Spread half into pie shell. Chill 30 minutes.

2. Meanwhile, dissolve gelatin in water; add lemon juice and raspberries. Carefully spoon half over cream cheese layer. Chill until set, about 30 minutes.

3. Set aside the remaining gelatin mixture at room temperature. Carefully spread remaining cream cheese mixture over top of pie. Chill for 30 minutes. Top with remaining gelatin. Chill until firm.

Citrus Berry Sherbet

When you serve this delicious, fruity sherbet, no one will guess it is light. It certainly doesn't taste like any low-fat food I've ever eaten!

—**WILMA JONES** MOBILE, ALABAMA

PREP: 25 MIN. + FREEZING • **YIELD:** 1 QUART

- 3 **teaspoons unflavored gelatin**
- 1½ **cups cold orange juice**
- ⅓ **cup sugar**
- 3 **tablespoons lemon juice**
- 1 **tablespoon grated lemon peel**
- 1½ **pounds fresh or frozen strawberries**
- ¾ **cup unsweetened applesauce**

1. In a small saucepan, sprinkle gelatin over orange juice; let stand for 1 minute. Stir in the sugar, lemon juice and peel. Cook over low heat, stirring until gelatin and sugar are completely dissolved. Remove from the heat; cool for 10 minutes.

2. Place the strawberries and applesauce in a blender. Add gelatin mixture; cover and process until smooth. Pour into a shallow freezer container. Cover and freeze for 1 to 1½ hours or until partially set.

3. Transfer to a large bowl; beat on medium speed for 2 minutes. Return to the freezer container; freeze 2-3 hours longer or until firm. Remove from the freezer 10 minutes before serving.

Double Peanut Bars

PREP/TOTAL TIME: 15 MIN. • **YIELD:** 9 SERVINGS

- 1½ **cups Wheaties**
- 1 **cup Multi Grain Cheerios**
- ½ **cup unsalted dry roasted peanuts**
- ½ **cup chopped dried mixed fruit**
- ⅓ **cup packed brown sugar**
- ⅓ **cup honey**
- 3 **tablespoons peanut butter**

1. In a bowl, combine the cereals, peanuts and mixed fruit. In a small saucepan, combine the brown sugar, honey and peanut butter. Cook and stir until the brown sugar and peanut butter are melted and mixture is smooth. Pour over cereal mixture; gently stir to coat evenly.

2. Transfer to an 8-in. square dish coated with cooking spray; gently press down. Cool and cut into bars. Store in the refrigerator.

These sweet no-bake snacks are great energy bars. Any dried fruit works well, but I prefer dried cranberries. Hearty cereals, plus honey, peanuts and peanut butter make the bars popular at my house.

—**KIM ROCKER** LAGRANGE, GEORGIA

The nutty brownie layers in this torte are dressed up with a fluffy frosting that has a rich creamy texture and scrumptious maple taste.

—AMY FLORY
CLEVELAND, GEORGIA

Maple-Mocha Brownie Torte

PREP: 30 MIN. • **BAKE:** 20 MIN. + COOLING • **YIELD:** 12 SERVINGS

- 1 **package brownie mix (13-in. x 9-in. pan size)**
- ½ **cup chopped walnuts**
- 2 **cups heavy whipping cream**
- 2 **teaspoons instant coffee granules**
- ½ **cup packed brown sugar**
- 1½ **teaspoons maple flavoring**
- 1 **teaspoon vanilla extract**
  Chocolate curls or additional walnuts, optional

1. Prepare the batter for brownie mix according to package directions for cake-like brownies. Stir in the chopped walnuts. Pour into two greased 9-in. round baking pans.

2. Bake at 350° for 20-22 minutes or until a toothpick inserted 2 in. from the edge comes out clean. Cool for 10 minutes before removing from pans to wire racks to cool completely.

3. In a large bowl, beat cream and coffee granules until stiff peaks form. Gradually beat in the brown sugar, maple flavoring and vanilla.

4. Spread 1½ cups over one brownie layer; top with second layer. Spread remaining cream mixture over top and sides of torte. Garnish with chocolate curls or walnuts if desired. Store in the refrigerator.

These moist chocolate cupcakes have a fun filling and shiny chocolate frosting that make them different from any others. You may want to make double, because they always disappear in a flash!

—KATHY KITTELL
LENEXA, KANSAS

Cream-Filled Cupcakes

PREP: 20 MIN. • **BAKE:** 15 MIN. + COOLING • **YIELD:** 2 DOZEN

- 1 **package (18¼ ounces) devil's food cake mix**
- 2 **teaspoons hot water**
- ¼ **teaspoon salt**
- 1 **jar (7 ounces) marshmallow creme**
- ½ **cup shortening**
- ⅓ **cup confectioners' sugar**
- ½ **teaspoon vanilla extract**

GANACHE FROSTING:
- 1 **cup (6 ounces) semisweet chocolate chips**
- ¾ **cup heavy whipping cream**

1. Prepare and bake cake batter according to package directions for cupcakes. Cool for 5 minutes before removing from pans to wire racks to cool completely.

2. For filling, in a small bowl, combine water and salt until salt is dissolved. Cool. In a small bowl, beat the marshmallow creme, shortening, confectioners' sugar and vanilla until light and fluffy; add the salt mixture.

3. Cut a small hole in the corner of pastry or plastic bag; insert round pastry tip. Fill the bag with cream filling. Push the tip through the bottom of paper liner to fill each cupcake.

4. Place chocolate in a small bowl. In a small saucepan, bring cream just to a boil. Pour over chocolate; whisk until smooth. Cool, stirring occasionally, to room temperature or until ganache reaches a dipping consistency.

5. Dip cupcake tops into frosting; chill for 20 minutes or until set. Store in the refrigerator.

Chocolate Raspberry Napoleons

PREP: 25 MIN. + CHILLING • **BAKE:** 10 MIN. + COOLING
YIELD: 8 SERVINGS

- 4 **ounces bittersweet chocolate, chopped**
- 1 **cup heavy whipping cream**
- 8 **sheets phyllo dough (14-inches x 9-inches)**
- 6 **tablespoons butter, melted**
- 3 **tablespoons sugar**
- 2 **cups fresh raspberries**
  Confectioners' sugar

1. Place the chocolate in a small bowl. In a small saucepan, bring cream just to a boil. Pour over the chocolate; whisk until smooth. Refrigerate until chilled.

2. Meanwhile, place one sheet of phyllo dough on a work surface (keep remaining dough covered with plastic wrap and a damp towel to prevent it from drying out). Brush with butter; sprinkle with sugar. Repeat layers seven times. Cut into eight rectangles. Place on an ungreased baking sheet.

3. Bake at 350° for 10-12 minutes or until golden brown. Cool on a wire rack.

4. In a small bowl, beat chocolate mixture until soft peaks form, about 15 seconds. Gently split each pastry in half horizontally. Spread 3 tablespoons chocolate mixture over bottom halves; layer with raspberries and remaining chocolate mixture. Replace tops. Sprinkle with confectioners' sugar. Serve immediately.

Strawberry Cake

PREP: 25 MIN. • **BAKE:** 25 MIN. + COOLING
YIELD: 12-16 SERVINGS

- 1 **package (18¼ ounces) white cake mix**
- 1 **package (3 ounces) strawberry gelatin**
- 1 **cup water**
- ½ **cup canola oil**
- 4 **egg whites**
- ½ **cup mashed unsweetened strawberries**
  Whipped cream or frosting for your choice

1. In a large bowl, combine the dry cake mix, gelatin powder, water and oil. Beat on low speed for 1 minute or until moistened; beat on medium for 4 minutes.

2. In a small bowl with clean beaters, beat egg whites on high speed until stiff peaks form. Fold egg whites and mash strawberries into cake batter.

3. Pour into three greased and floured 8-in. round baking pans. Bake at 350° for 25-30 minutes or until a toothpick comes out clean. Cool for 10 minutes before removing from pans to wire racks to cool completely.

4. Frost with whipped cream or frosting. If frosted with whipped cream, store in the refrigerator.

Chocolate Cream Cheese Pie

Nothing finishes off a meal better than a cool and creamy special dessert. Since the pudding in this one needs time to set, I usually start it before starting the rest of the dinner.
—**RHONDA HOGAN** EUGENE, OREGON

PREP/TOTAL TIME: 25 MIN. • **YIELD:** 6 SERVINGS

- 1 package (3 ounces) cream cheese, softened
- 2 tablespoons sugar
- 1¾ cups milk, divided
- 2 cups whipped topping, divided
- 1 graham cracker crust (9 inches)
- 1 package (3.9 ounces) instant chocolate pudding mix
  Miniature semisweet chocolate chips, optional

1. In a small bowl, beat the cream cheese, sugar and 1 tablespoon milk until smooth. Fold in 1 cup whipped topping. Spread evenly into crust.

2. In a small bowl, whisk the pudding mix and remaining milk for 2 minutes. Let stand for 2 minutes or until soft-set. Pour over cream cheese mixture. Chill until set.

3. Just before serving, garnish with remaining whipped topping and chocolate chips if desired.

Pistachio Pudding Parfaits

PREP/TOTAL TIME: 20 MIN. • YIELD: 8 SERVINGS

- 1 **package (8 ounces) cream cheese, softened**
- 1 **cup confectioners' sugar**
- 1½ **cups whipped topping**
- 1 **package (3.4 ounces) instant pistachio pudding mix**
- 10 **pecan shortbread cookies, coarsely crushed**

1. In a small bowl, beat cream cheese and confectioners' sugar. Fold in whipped topping; set aside. Prepare pudding according to package directions; set aside.

2. Spoon 1 tablespoon cookie crumbs into each of eight parfait glasses. Top with half of the pudding and whipped topping mixture. Repeat layers. Top with remaining cookie crumbs. Chill until serving.

Cherry Almond Tart

I use ingredients I have on hand, including canned pie filling and cake mix, to create this dazzling dessert. It's fast to fix, looks elegant and tastes delicious.
—**CONNIE RATERINK** CALEDONIA, MICHIGAN

PREP: 15 MIN. • BAKE: 15 MIN. + COOLING
YIELD: 14-16 SERVINGS

- 1 **package (18¼ ounces) yellow cake mix**
- ⅔ **cup graham cracker crumbs (about 11 squares)**
- ½ **cup butter, softened**
- 1 **egg**
- ½ **cup chopped almonds**
- 1 **package (8 ounces) cream cheese, softened**
- ¼ **cup confectioners' sugar**
- 1 **can (21 ounces) cherry pie filling**
- ½ **cup sliced almonds, toasted**

1. In a large bowl, combine the cake mix, cracker crumbs and butter until crumbly. Beat in egg. Stir in chopped almonds.

2. Press onto the bottom and up the sides of a greased 14-in. pizza pan. Bake at 350° for 11-13 minutes or until lightly browned. Cool completely.

I made these parfaits for my children to take to school on St. Patrick's Day. Everyone loved them! They also can be assembled right before you eat or a few hours beforehand.
—**ROSANNA FOWLER** BEDFORD, INDIANA

3. In a small bowl, beat cream cheese and sugar until smooth. Spread over crust. Top with pie filling. Sprinkle with sliced almonds. Store leftovers in the refrigerator.

Lemon Poppy Seed Cake

PREP: 15 MIN. • **BAKE:** 50 MIN. + COOLING
YIELD: 12-16 SERVINGS

1	package (18¼ ounces) lemon cake mix
1	package (3.4 ounces) instant lemon pudding mix
¾	cup warm water
½	cup canola oil
4	eggs
1	teaspoon lemon extract
1	teaspoon almond extract
⅓	cup poppy seeds
½	cup confectioners' sugar
	Juice of 1 lemon
	Additional confectioners' sugar, optional

1. In a large bowl, combine cake and pudding mix. Add the water, oil, eggs and extracts. Beat for 30 seconds on low speed. Beat for 2 minutes on medium speed. Stir in poppy seeds. Pour into a greased 12-cup fluted tube pan.

2. Bake at 350° for 50-60 minutes or until a toothpick inserted near the center comes out clean. Cool in pan 10 minutes before inverting onto a serving plate.

3. Combine confectioners' sugar and lemon juice; brush over the warm cake. Cool. Dust with additional confectioners' sugar if desired.

> Brownies are an easy way to make something good, and no one seems to tire of them. Served warm with ice cream, these are a favorite!
> **—BARBARA CARLUCCI**
> ORANGE PARK, FLORIDA

Coconut Brownies

PREP: 10 MIN. • **BAKE:** 30 MIN. + COOLING • **YIELD:** 2 DOZEN

- 1 **package fudge brownie mix (13-inch x 9-inch pan size)**
- 1 **cup (8 ounces) sour cream**
- 1 **cup coconut-pecan frosting**
- 2 **eggs**
- ¼ **cup water**
- 1 **cup (6 ounces) semisweet chocolate chips**

1. In a large bowl, combine the brownie mix, sour cream, frosting, eggs and water just until moistened.

2. Pour into a 13-in. x 9-in. baking dish coated with cooking spray. Bake at 350° for 30-35 minutes or until center is set (do not overbake). Sprinkle with chocolate chips; let stand for 5 minutes. Spread the chips over the brownies.

overbaked brownies

There are several reasons why brownies can turn out overbaked. A pan larger than called for in the recipe may have been used, causing the batter to be thin and dry. Or, the oven temperature may have been too high. Also, next time, check the bars 5 minutes sooner than the baking time given in the recipe.

Chocolate Malt Shoppe Pie

I especially like serving this dessert at a cookout or at any event where there are children. It's always a big hit!
—**BETH WANEK** LITTLE CHUTE, WISCONSIN

PREP: 20 MIN. + FREEZING • **YIELD:** 6-8 SERVINGS

- 1½ **cups chocolate wafer crumbs**
- ¼ **cup butter, melted**
- 1 **pint vanilla ice cream, softened**
- ½ **cup crushed malted milk balls**
- 2 **tablespoons milk, divided**
- 3 **tablespoons chocolate malted milk powder**
- 3 **tablespoons marshmallow creme**
- 1 **cup heavy whipping cream**
  Additional heavy whipping cream, whipped, optional
  Additional malted milk balls, optional

1. Combine wafer crumbs and butter; press into an ungreased 9-in. pie pan. Freeze until set. Combine the ice cream, crushed malted milk balls and 1 tablespoon milk; spoon into crust. Freeze for 1 hour.

2. In a large bowl, combine the malted milk powder, marshmallow creme and remaining milk. Add cream; whip until soft peaks form. Spread over ice cream layer. Freeze for several hours or overnight.

3. Just before serving, garnish each serving with additional whipped cream and malted milk balls if desired.

Bring a touch of springtime and lovely lemon flavor to the table in just 10 minutes! Top this dessert with your favorite fresh fruit (I like raspberries) for the perfect mealtime finale.
—**CLAIRE DION**
CANTERBURY, CONNECTICUT

Cake with Lemon Sauce

PREP/TOTAL TIME: 10 MIN. • **YIELD:** 4 SERVINGS

- 1 **package (3 ounces) cream cheese, softened**
- 1¾ **cups cold milk**
- 1 **package (3.4 ounces) instant lemon pudding mix**
- 4 **slices pound cake or angel food cake**
  Fresh raspberries, optional

1. In a small bowl, beat the cream cheese until smooth. Add milk and pudding mix; beat for 2 minutes or until smooth and thickened. Serve with cake. Garnish with raspberries if desired.

Pineapple Rhubarb Pie

PREP: 10 MIN. + STANDING • **BAKE:** 45 MIN. + COOLING
YIELD: 6-8 SERVINGS

3	cups chopped fresh or frozen rhubarb, thawed
2	cans (8 ounces each) crushed pineapple, drained
1½	cups sugar
3	tablespoons quick-cooking tapioca
1	tablespoon lemon juice
½	teaspoon grated lemon peel
1	package (15 ounces) refrigerated pie pastry

1. In a large bowl, combine the rhubarb, pineapple, sugar, tapioca, lemon juice and lemon peel. Let stand for 15 minutes. Line a 9-in. pie plate with bottom pastry. Add the filling.

2. Roll out remaining pastry to fit top of pie; cut slits or make decorative cutouts in pastry. Place over filling; trim, seal and flute edges.

3. Bake at 350° for 45-50 minutes or until crust is golden brown and filling is bubbly. Cool on a wire rack. Refrigerate leftovers.

EDITOR'S NOTE: If using frozen rhubarb, measure rhubarb while still frozen, then thaw completely. Drain in a colander, but do not press liquid out.

Lemon Blueberry Pizza

PREP: 10 MIN. • **BAKE:** 15 MIN. + COOLING • **YIELD:** 8 SERVINGS

- 1 tube (16½ ounces) refrigerated sugar cookie dough
- 1 package (8 ounces) cream cheese, softened
- 2 tablespoons sugar
- ¾ cup (6 ounces) lemon yogurt
- 2 cups fresh blueberries

1. Press cookie dough onto an ungreased 12-in. pizza pan. Bake at 350° for 15-20 minutes or until deep golden brown. Cool on a wire rack.

2. In a small bowl, beat cream cheese and sugar until smooth; stir in yogurt. Spread over crust to within ½ in. of edges. Sprinkle with blueberries. Cut into wedges. Refrigerate leftovers.

Peach Frozen Yogurt

When peaches are in season, we order them by the bushel. This quick and creamy frozen treat has wonderful fresh-fruit flavor. It's a big hit with everyone in my family.
—**STEPHANIE NOHR** CORNELL, WISCONSIN

PREP: 15 MIN. + FREEZING • **YIELD:** 6 SERVINGS

- 2 cups fresh or frozen unsweetened sliced peaches, thawed
- 1 envelope unflavored gelatin
- ¼ cup cold water
- ¼ cup sugar
- 2 cups (16 ounces) vanilla yogurt

1. Place the peaches in a blender; cover and process until pureed. Set aside.

2. In a small saucepan, sprinkle gelatin over cold water; let stand for 1 minute. Stir in sugar. Cook and stir over low heat until gelatin and sugar are dissolved.

3. In a large bowl, combine the yogurt, peach puree and gelatin mixture until blended. Pour into an ungreased 9-in. square dish. Cover and freeze for 3-4 hours or until partially set.

4. Cut into pieces and place in a large bowl; beat on medium speed until smooth. Transfer to a freezer container. Cover and freeze until firm, about 2 hours.

Here's a delightful summertime treat. Cream cheese and lemon yogurt make a tasty topping for this sensational fruit pizza.
—**TASTE OF HOME TEST KITCHEN**

Most of the ingredients in these delicious squares can be found in your pantry. They can be made ahead and frozen for a fast treat anytime.
—TASTE OF HOME TEST KITCHEN

Strawberry Granola Squares

PREP: 5 MIN. • **BAKE:** 25 MIN. + COOLING • **YIELD:** 16 SQUARES

- 1½ **cups granola cereal without raisins**
- ¾ **cup all-purpose flour**
- ⅓ **cup packed brown sugar**
- ½ **teaspoon ground cinnamon**
- 5 **tablespoons cold butter**
- 1 **cup strawberry preserves**

1. In a large bowl, combine the granola, flour, brown sugar and cinnamon; cut in butter until crumbly. Set aside a third of the mixture for topping. Press remaining mixture into a well-greased 9-in. square baking pan. Bake at 375° for 10 minutes.

2. Spread preserves over crust; sprinkle with reserved granola mixture. Bake 15 minutes longer or until filling is bubbly around the edges. Cool on a wire rack. Cut into squares. Store in the refrigerator.

cutting granola bars

Cutting granola bars can be a sticky business. To make it easier, spritz the knife with nonstick cooking spray before starting to cut, repeating as needed.

Strawberry Puff Pastry Dessert

PREP: 30 MIN. • **BAKE:** 15 MIN. + COOLING • **YIELD:** 12 SERVINGS

- 1 **package (17.3 ounces) frozen puff pastry**
- 5 **cups sliced fresh strawberries, divided**
- 6 **ounces white baking chocolate, chopped**
- 1 **package (8 ounces) cream cheese, softened**
- 1 **teaspoon vanilla extract**
- 1 **cup confectioners' sugar**
- ⅓ **cup malted milk powder**
- 2 **cups heavy whipping cream, whipped**
  Strawberry syrup, optional

1. Thaw one puff pastry sheet (save remaining sheet for another use). Unfold pastry; cut lengthwise into three 3-in.-wide strips. Cut each strip into thirds, making nine squares.

2. Place 1 in. apart on ungreased baking sheets. Bake at 400° for 11-13 minutes or until golden brown. Remove to wire racks to cool.

3. Place 2½ cups strawberries in a blender; cover and puree; set aside. In a large microwave-safe bowl, melt white chocolate; stir until smooth. Cool slightly. Add cream cheese and vanilla; beat until smooth. Beat in the confectioners' sugar and malted milk powder until smooth. Stir in the puree. Fold in whipped cream.

4. Split pastry squares in half horizontally. Line an ungreased 13-in. x 9-in. dish with bottom pastry halves, cut side up; spread with 3½ cups strawberry cream. Top with 1 cup of sliced berries. Cover with pastry tops, cut side down.

5. Spread with remaining strawberry cream. Sprinkle with remaining berries. Drizzle with strawberry syrup if desired. Refrigerate leftovers.

This refreshing dessert has a rich shortbread-like crust with a creamy center and a pretty red gelatin top layer. It's easy enough for everyday, but cheery enough to dish up for guests, too.

—LOIS FRAZEE
FERNLEY, NEVADA

Raspberry Squares

PREP: 20 MIN. + CHILLING • **BAKE:** 10 MIN. + COOLING
YIELD: 12-16 SERVINGS

- 1 cup all-purpose flour
- ½ cup finely chopped pecans
- ¼ cup packed brown sugar
- ½ cup butter, melted
- 2 packages (8 ounces each) cream cheese, softened
- ¾ cup sugar
- 1 carton (8 ounces) frozen whipped topping, thawed
- 2 packages (3 ounces each) raspberry gelatin
- 2 cups boiling water
- 2 cups cold water

1. In a large bowl, combine the flour, pecans and brown sugar; stir in the butter until crumbly. Press into an ungreased 13-in. x 9-in. baking dish. Bake at 350° for 10-13 minutes or until lightly browned. Cool on a wire rack.

2. In a large bowl, beat cream cheese and sugar until smooth; fold in whipped topping. Spread over crust. Cover and refrigerate for 1 hour.

3. In a small bowl, dissolve gelatin in boiling water; stir in cold water. Spoon over cream cheese layer. Chill until firm. Cut into squares.

Coffee Ice Cream Pie

PREP: 25 MIN. + FREEZING • **YIELD:** 6-8 SERVINGS

- 1½ **cups Oreo cookie crumbs, divided**
- ¼ **cup butter, melted**
- 2 **pints coffee ice cream, softened**
- 1 **cup miniature marshmallows**
- 1 **cup miniature semisweet chocolate chips**
- 2 **cups whipped topping**
- 2 **tablespoons caramel ice cream topping**
- 2 **tablespoons hot fudge ice cream topping, warmed**
  Additional cream-filled chocolate sandwich cookies, optional

1. In a small bowl, combine 1¼ cups crushed cookies and butter. Press onto the bottom and up the sides of a 9-in. pie plate. In a large bowl, combine the ice cream, marshmallows, chocolate chips and remaining crushed cookies. Spoon into crust. Freeze for 30 minutes.

2. Spread whipped topping over pie. Alternately pipe thin lines of caramel topping and chocolate topping over pie; gently pull a toothpick or sharp knife through lines in one direction.

3. Cover and freeze overnight. May be frozen for up to 2 months. Remove from the freezer 10-15 minutes before cutting. Garnish with cookies if desired.

My family just loves these cupcakes, especially the subtle taste of peanut butter in the frosting. Chocolate frosting is equally delicious on top.
—ALYCE WYMAN
PEMBINA, NORTH DAKOTA

Peanut Butter Cupcakes

PREP: 15 MIN. • **BAKE:** 20 MIN. + COOLING • **YIELD:** 1 ½ DOZEN

- 1 package (18¼ ounces) white cake mix
- 18 miniature peanut butter cups
- 1⅓ cups prepared vanilla frosting
- 2 tablespoons creamy peanut butter

1. Prepare cake mix according to package directions. Spoon about 2 tablespoons of batter into each paper-lined muffin cup. Place a peanut butter cup in each; fill two-thirds full with remaining batter.

2. Bake at 350° for 20-25 minutes or until lightly browned and a toothpick inserted in the cake portion comes out clean. Cool for 10 minutes before removing to wire racks to cool completely.

3. In a small bowl, combine frosting and peanut butter until smooth. Frost cupcakes.

Coconut Rhubarb Dessert

PREP: 25 MIN. • **BAKE:** 25 MIN. • **YIELD:** 12 SERVINGS

- **4 cups sliced fresh or frozen rhubarb**
- **1½ cups sugar**
- **1½ cups water**
- **⅛ teaspoon red food coloring, optional**
- **1 package (18¼ ounces) butter pecan cake mix**
- **1 cup flaked coconut**
- **½ cup chopped pecans**
- **½ cup butter, melted**
- **Vanilla ice cream, optional**

1. In a large saucepan, combine the rhubarb, sugar, water and food coloring if desired. Cook over medium heat for 8-10 minutes or until rhubarb is tender; cool slightly. Transfer to a greased 13-in. x 9-in. baking dish; sprinkle with cake mix. Top with coconut and pecans. Drizzle with butter.

2. Bake at 350° for 25-30 minutes or until a toothpick inserted near the center comes out clean. Serve with ice cream if desired.

Lemon Pie

This refreshing lemon dessert is mixed in minutes and chilled while dinner is being served.
—**JOANNE SCHLABACH** SHREVE, OHIO

PREP/TOTAL TIME: 30 MIN. • **YIELD:** 6 SERVINGS

- **1 can (14 ounces) sweetened condensed milk**
- **½ cup lemon juice**
- **1 carton (8 ounces) frozen whipped topping, thawed**
- **Few drops yellow food coloring, optional**
- **1 graham cracker crust (8 or 9 inches)**

1. In a medium bowl, combine milk and juice. Let stand a few minutes. Stir in whipped topping. Add food coloring if desired. Spoon into crust. Chill until firm.

Vanilla Pudding Dessert

PREP/TOTAL TIME: 30 MIN. • **YIELD:** 12-14 SERVINGS

- 2¾ cups cold milk
- 1 package (5.1 ounces) instant vanilla pudding mix
- 1 can (14 ounces) sweetened condensed milk
- 1 carton (12 ounces) frozen whipped topping, thawed
- 4 cups crushed vanilla wafers (about 120 wafers)
- 3 cups sliced fresh strawberries

1. In a large bowl, whisk the milk and pudding mix for 2 minutes. Let stand for 15 minutes; fold in condensed milk. Set aside 1 tablespoon whipped topping and 2 tablespoons wafer crumbs. Fold remaining whipped topping into pudding.

2. In a 3-qt. serving bowl, layer a third of the strawberries, wafer crumbs and pudding mixture. Repeat layers twice. Sprinkle with reserved wafer crumbs; top with reserved whipped topping. Refrigerate until serving.

Chocolate Chip Snack Cake

Instant pudding mix and cake mix cut the preparation time for this delicious cake that is loaded with chocolate. I often make it for weekend guests and work luncheons.

—**KAREN WALKER** STERLING, VIRGINIA

PREP: 15 MIN. • **BAKE:** 45 MIN. + COOLING
YIELD: 12-15 SERVINGS

- 1 package (18¼ ounces) yellow cake mix
- 1 package (3.4 ounces) instant vanilla pudding mix
- 4 eggs
- 1 cup water
- ½ cup canola oil
- 1 package (12 ounces) miniature semisweet chocolate chips
- 4 ounces German sweet chocolate, grated, divided
  Confectioners' sugar

1. In a large bowl, combine the first five ingredients; beat on low speed for 30 seconds. Beat on medium for 2 minutes. Stir in chocolate chips and half of the grated chocolate.

So easy to prepare, this eye-catching, yummy dessert will go fast—and everyone will want the recipe. To change it up, try peaches, pineapple or bananas instead of strawberries.
—**BETTY CLEMONS** HARTSELLE, ALABAMA

2. Pour into a greased 13-in. x 9-in. baking pan. Bake at 350° for 45-50 minutes or until a toothpick inserted near the center comes out clean.

3. Sprinkle with remaining grated chocolate while slightly warm. Cool completely. Dust with confectioners' sugar.

holidays & parties

Come celebrate the holidays...or host a warm and wonderful get-together for family and friends. These fast and festive recipes make it fun and easy!

Pistachio Pumpkin Bread

PREP: 15 MIN. • **BAKE:** 30 MIN. + COOLING
YIELD: 3 MINI LOAVES (4 SLICES EACH)

- 1 **package (14 ounces) pumpkin quick bread/muffin mix**
- 2 **eggs**
- 1 **cup water**
- 3 **tablespoons canola oil**
- ¼ **to ½ teaspoon rum extract**
- ½ **cup raisins**
- ½ **cup chopped pistachios**

GLAZE:
- ¼ **cup sugar**
- 2 **tablespoons water**
- 1 **tablespoon butter**
- ¼ **teaspoon rum extract**

1. In a large bowl, combine the bread mix, eggs, water, oil and rum extract just until blended. Stir in the raisins and chopped pistachios. Transfer to three greased 5 ¾-in. x 3-in. x 2-in. loaf pans.

2. Bake at 375° for 30-35 minutes or until a toothpick inserted near the center comes out clean. Cool for 5 minutes.

3. Meanwhile, in a small saucepan, combine the sugar, water and butter. Bring to a boil; cook and stir for 3 minutes or until sugar is dissolved. Remove from the heat; stir in extract.

4. Remove loaves from pans to wire racks. With a toothpick, poke holes in the top of each loaf; brush with glaze. Cool completely.

EDITOR'S NOTE: Wrap the breads in colored cellophane, tie with festive ribbon and give as a gifts.

No one will guess these sweet treats with the candy bar center started with store-bought dough. Roll them in colored sugar...or just dip the tops for even faster assembly. Instead of using miniature candy bars, slice regular size Snickers candy bars into 1-inch pieces for the centers.
—TASTE OF HOME TEST KITCHEN

Colorful Candy Bar Cookies

PREP: 35 MIN. • **BAKE:** 10 MIN. • **YIELD:** 2 DOZEN

½ **tube refrigerated sugar cookie dough, softened**
¼ **cup all-purpose flour**
24 **miniature Snickers candy bars**
   Red and green colored sugar

1. In a small bowl, beat cookie dough and flour until combined. Shape 1½ teaspoonfuls of dough around each candy bar. Roll in colored sugar.

2. Place 2 in. apart on parchment paper-lined baking sheets. Bake at 350° for 10-12 minutes or until edges are golden brown. Remove to wire racks.

parchment paper

Parchment paper is a heavy paper that's resistant to grease and moisture. It's excellent for lining baking sheets when making cookies, because it makes cleanup a snap. There is no right or wrong side to parchment paper, so either side can be used. For the best baking results, use a fresh sheet of parchment paper for each pan of cookies.

Pineapple-Orange Cranberry Sauce

This delicious and flavorful side dish comes together in no time at all! It's a quick, versatile and healthy recipe.
—ADRIENNE NICCHIO NORTH MERRICK, NEW YORK

PREP/TOTAL TIME: 5 MIN. • YIELD: 2¾ CUPS

- 1 can (14 ounces) whole-berry cranberry sauce
- 1 can (11 ounces) mandarin oranges, well drained
- 1 can (8 ounces) crushed pineapple, well drained
- ¼ cup chopped pecans, toasted

1. In a small serving bowl, combine the cranberry sauce, oranges and pineapple. Stir in pecans just before serving. Refrigerate leftovers.

Campfire Cobbler

PREP/TOTAL TIME: 30 MIN. • YIELD: 6 SERVINGS

- 1¼ cups biscuit/baking mix
- 1 envelope instant maple and brown sugar oatmeal
- ¼ cup cold butter, cubed
- ⅓ cup milk
- 2 cans (21 ounces each) blueberry pie filling
- ¾ cup unsweetened apple juice
  Vanilla ice cream, optional

1. Prepare grill or campfire for low heat, using 12-16 charcoal briquettes or large wood chips.

2. In a large resealable plastic bag, combine biscuit mix and oatmeal. Add butter; squeeze bag until mixture resembles coarse crumbs. Gradually add milk; knead to form a soft dough. Spread into a greased ovenproof Dutch oven. Combine pie filling and apple juice; pour over dough.

3. Cover Dutch oven. When briquettes or wood chips are covered with white ash, place Dutch oven directly on top of 6-8 of them. Using long-handled tongs, place 6-8 briquettes on pan cover. Cook for 15 minutes or until filling is bubbly.

4. To check for doneness, use the tongs to carefully lift cover. If necessary, cook 5 minutes longer. Serve with ice cream if desired.

At your next campfire, surprise everyone with this wonderful dish for dessert. It is so quick and simple to make—and so good!
—TASTE OF HOME TEST KITCHEN

Old Glory Dessert

PREP: 30 MIN. • **BAKE:** 10 MIN. + COOLING
YIELD: 12-15 SERVINGS

Our Test Kitchen pros took advantage of convenient refrigerated cookie dough to create the crust for this fresh fruit pizza. Easily arranged berries give it a star-spangled and patriotic appeal.
—TASTE OF HOME TEST KITCHEN

- 1 tube (18 ounces) refrigerated sugar cookie dough
- 2 packages (one 8 ounces, one 3 ounces) cream cheese, softened
- ¾ cup confectioners' sugar
- 4½ teaspoons lemon juice
- ½ cup fresh blueberries
- 2 cups quartered fresh strawberries

1. Press cookie dough into a greased 15-in. x 10-in. x 1-in. baking pan. Bake at 350° for 10-12 minutes or until golden brown. Cool on a wire rack.

2. In a large bowl, beat the cream cheese, sugar and lemon juice until smooth. Set aside ¼ cup. Spread remaining cream cheese mixture over crust. Decorate with blueberries and strawberries to resemble a flag.

3. Cut a small hole in a corner of a pastry or plastic bag. Insert star tip #16. Fill with reserved cream cheese mixture. Beginning in one corner, pipe stars in the spaces between the blueberries.

EDITOR'S NOTE: 2 cups of any sugar cookie dough can be substituted for the refrigerated dough.

Bacon-Sausage Quiche Tarts

PREP: 30 MIN. • **BAKE:** 10 MIN. • **YIELD:** 40 APPETIZERS

- 2 **cans (12 ounces each) refrigerated buttermilk biscuits**
- 6 **uncooked breakfast sausage links, chopped**
- 2 **tablespoons chopped onion**
- 2 **tablespoons chopped fresh mushrooms**
- 2 **tablespoons chopped green pepper**
- 1 **package (8 ounces) cream cheese, softened**
- 2 **tablespoons heavy whipping cream**
- 3 **eggs**
- 1½ **cups (6 ounces) finely shredded cheddar cheese, divided**
- 5 **bacon strips, cooked and crumbled**

1. Split each biscuit into two layers; press each into an ungreased miniature muffin cup.

2. In a large skillet, cook the sausage, onion, mushrooms and pepper over medium heat until meat is no longer pink and the vegetables are tender; drain.

3. In a large bowl, beat the cream cheese and cream until smooth. Beat in eggs. Fold in ¾ cup cheddar cheese and the sausage mixture. Spoon 1 tablespoon into each cup. Sprinkle with bacon and remaining cheese. Bake at 375° for 10-15 minutes or until golden brown. Serve warm.

Colorful Peanut Butter Crackers

Ghosts and goblins have you up at night? Don't be afraid to head to the kitchen, because if you're a chocolate lover, you'll want to indulge in this sweet-n-salty midnight snack.
—**RUTH CASSIS**
UNIVERSITY PLACE, WASHINGTON

PREP: 35 MIN. + CHILLING • **YIELD:** 2 DOZEN

4	ounces cream cheese, cubed
½	cup creamy peanut butter
¼	cup honey
48	butter-flavored crackers
2	cups (12 ounces) semisweet chocolate chips
4	teaspoons shortening
¼	cup 2% milk
	Cake decorator holiday shapes

1. In a microwave-safe bowl, heat cream cheese on high for 15 seconds or until very soft. Add peanut butter and honey; stir until smooth. Spread over half of the crackers; top with remaining crackers.

2. In a microwave, melt chocolate chips and shortening; stir until smooth. Heat milk; stir into chocolate mixture.

3. Dip each cracker sandwich in chocolate mixture, allowing excess to drip off. Place on waxed paper-lined baking sheets; decorate as desired. Refrigerate for 45 minutes or until set.

EDITOR'S NOTE: This recipe was tested in a 1,100-watt microwave.

Margarita Chicken

PREP: 10 MIN. + MARINATING • **GRILL:** 10 MIN.
YIELD: 4 SERVINGS

- 1 can (10 ounces) frozen non-alcoholic margarita mix, thawed
- 3 tablespoons lime juice
- 3 garlic cloves, minced
- 4 boneless skinless chicken breast halves (6 ounces each)
- ¼ teaspoon salt
- ¼ teaspoon pepper

1. In a small bowl, combine the margarita mix, lime juice and garlic. Pour 1 cup marinade into a large resealable plastic bag. Add the chicken; seal bag and turn to coat. Refrigerate for 2-4 hours. Cover and refrigerate remaining marinade.

2. Drain and discard marinade. Sprinkle the chicken with salt and pepper. Using long-handled tongs, moisten a paper towel with cooking oil and lightly coat the grill rack.

3. Grill chicken, covered, over medium heat or broil 4 in. from the heat for 5-7 minutes on each side or until a meat thermometer reads 160°, basting frequently with reserved marinade.

Marinated in flavors of garlic and lime, this tangy grilled chicken is ready to go whenever the coals are hot! Serve with roasted corn on the cob and lemonade for summer eating at its most relaxed.
—**KELLY BRUNEMAN** CEDAR PARK, TEXAS

marvelous marinades

Marinades can be used to add flavor to meat and vegetables or to tenderize less-tender cuts of meat. Always marinate in the refrigerator in a glass container or resealable plastic bag. In general, do not reuse marinades. If a marinade is also used as a basting or dipping sauce, reserve a portion before adding the uncooked foods.

Savory Spinach Pie

Even those who aren't morning people will break into smiles when they taste this super spinach pie. Served with cinnamon rolls and seasonal fresh fruit, it's guaranteed to get any day off to a sunny start!

—PAM KRENZKE HILLIARD, OHIO

PREP: 15 MIN. • **BAKE:** 45 MIN. • **YIELD:** 6 SERVINGS

- ¼ **cup chopped onion**
- 2 **tablespoons butter**
- 1 **package (10 ounces) frozen chopped spinach, thawed and well drained**
- ¼ **to ½ teaspoon salt**
- ¼ **teaspoon ground nutmeg**
- 1 **cup (8 ounces) 4% cottage cheese**
- ½ **cup half-and-half cream**
- ¼ **cup grated Parmesan cheese**
- 3 **eggs, lightly beaten**
- 1 **unbaked pastry shell (9 inches)**

1. In a large skillet, saute onion in butter. Remove from the heat; stir in spinach, salt and nutmeg.

2. In a large bowl, combine the cottage cheese, cream, cheese and eggs. Stir in spinach mixture. Pour into pastry shell.

3. Bake at 350° for 45-50 minutes or until a knife inserted near the center comes out clean. Let stand for 5 minutes before cutting.

This is an extremely easy recipe designed to impress your guests. Serve it to them while you're finishing up preparation of the main course and just listen to the raves.

—LISA BOEHM DEEPWATER, MISSOURI

Simple Shrimp Scampi

PREP/TOTAL TIME: 10 MIN. • **YIELD:** 6 SERVINGS

- ¾ **cup butter, cubed**
- 2 **pounds uncooked medium shrimp, peeled and deveined**
- 5 **teaspoons lemon-pepper seasoning**
- 2 **teaspoons garlic powder**
  Lemon wedges, optional

1. In a large skillet over medium heat, melt butter. Add the shrimp, lemon-pepper and garlic powder; cook for 5-8 minutes or until shrimp turn pink. Transfer to individual serving dishes. Serve with lemon wedges if desired.

Southwest Burgers

PREP: 25 MIN. + CHILLING • **GRILL:** 15 MIN. • **YIELD:** 8 SERVINGS

1 **can (15 ounces) black beans, rinsed and drained**
1 **small red onion, finely chopped**
½ **cup frozen corn, thawed**
¼ **cup dry bread crumbs**
1 **can (4 ounces) chopped green chilies**
2 **tablespoons Worcestershire sauce**
1 **teaspoon garlic powder**
½ **teaspoon ground cumin**
¼ **teaspoon pepper**
½ **pound lean ground beef (90% lean)**
½ **pound extra-lean ground turkey**
½ **cup fat-free mayonnaise**
¼ **cup salsa**
8 **slices pepper jack cheese (½ ounce each)**
8 **whole wheat hamburger buns, split**
OPTIONAL TOPPINGS:
   Lettuce leaves, tomato slices and red onion rings

1. In a large bowl, coarsely mash beans. Stir in the onion, corn, bread crumbs, chilies, Worcestershire sauce and seasonings. Crumble beef and turkey over mixture and mix well. Shape into eight patties. Refrigerate for 1 hour. Combine mayonnaise and salsa; refrigerate until serving.

2. Using long-handled tongs, moisten a paper towel with cooking oil and lightly coat the grill rack. Grill burgers, covered, over medium heat or broil 4 in. from the heat for 5-7 minutes on each side or until a meat thermometer reads 165° and juices run clear.

3. Top with cheese; cover and grill 1-2 minutes longer or until cheese is melted. Serve on buns with toppings if desired.

Asparagus Steak Oscar

This recipe combines the delicious taste of fresh asparagus with only the finest of steaks around. Fantastic ingredients make for an elegant meal!
—**CINDY DORSETT** LUBBOCK, TEXAS

PREP/TOTAL TIME: 30 MIN. • **YIELD:** 4 SERVINGS

- 1 **envelope bearnaise sauce**
- 1 **pound fresh asparagus, trimmed**
- ¼ **pound fresh crabmeat**
- 2 **tablespoons butter**
- ½ **teaspoon minced garlic**
- 1 **tablespoon lemon juice**
- 4 **beef tenderloin steaks (1 inch thick and 3 ounces each)**
- ⅛ **teaspoon paprika**

1. Prepare bearnaise sauce according to package directions. Meanwhile, place asparagus in a steamer basket; place in a large saucepan over 1 in. of water. Bring to a boil; cover and steam for 8-10 minutes or until crisp-tender.

2. In a large skillet, saute crab in butter for 3-4 minutes or until heated through. Add garlic; cook 1 minute longer. Stir in lemon juice; keep warm.

3. Grill steaks, covered, over medium heat or broil 4 in. from the heat for 6-8 minutes on each side or until meat reaches desired doneness (for medium-rare, a meat thermometer should read 145°; medium, 160°; well-done, 170°). Top with crab mixture, asparagus and bearnaise sauce. Sprinkle with paprika.

Almond Chocolate Cake

PREP: 15 MIN. • **BAKE:** 65 MIN. + COOLING
YIELD: 12-16 SERVINGS

- 1 **package (18¼ ounces) German chocolate cake mix**
- 1 **package (3.9 ounces) instant chocolate fudge pudding mix**
- 1¼ **cups water**
- ½ **cup canola oil**
- 4 **eggs**
- 3 **teaspoons almond extract**
- 2¾ **cups semisweet chocolate chips, divided**
- 6 **tablespoons refrigerated regular or amaretto-flavored nondairy creamer**
- 1 **tablespoon sliced almonds**

1. In a large bowl, combine the cake, pudding mix, water, oil, eggs and extract; beat until combined. Stir in 2 cups chocolate chips.

2. Pour into a greased and floured 10-in. fluted tube pan. Bake at 350° for 65-70 minutes or until a toothpick inserted near the center comes out clean. Cool for 10 minutes before removing from pan to a wire rack to cool completely.

3. In a small saucepan, combine the creamer and remaining chocolate chips. Cook over low heat until chips are melted; stir until smooth. Cool for 45 minutes. Drizzle over cake. Garnish with almonds.

I came up with this recipe as a way to make one sandwich feed a large group at once. The braid design always impresses the guests at our parties.

—KELLIE MULLEAVY
LAMBERTVILLE, MICHIGAN

Reuben Braids

PREP: 15 MIN. • **BAKE:** 25 MIN.
YIELD: 2 LOAVES (8 SERVINGS EACH)

6	**ounces cooked corned beef brisket, chopped (about 1 cup)**
1½	**cups (6 ounces) shredded Swiss cheese**
¾	**cup sauerkraut, rinsed and well drained**
1	**small onion, chopped**
3	**tablespoons Thousand Island salad dressing**
1	**tablespoon Dijon mustard**
½	**teaspoon dill weed**
2	**packages (8 ounces each) refrigerated crescent rolls**
1	**egg white, lightly beaten**
1	**tablespoon sesame seeds**

1. In a large bowl, combine the first seven ingredients. Unroll one tube of crescent dough onto an ungreased baking sheet; seal seams and perforations.

2. Spread half of the corned beef filling down center of rectangle. On each long side, cut 1-in.-wide strips to within 1 in. of filling. Starting at one end, fold alternating strips at an angle across filling; seal ends. Repeat with the remaining crescent dough and filling. Brush the egg white over the braids; sprinkle with sesame seeds.

3. Bake at 375° for 25-30 minutes or until golden brown. Cool on wire racks for 5 minutes before cutting into slices. Refrigerate leftovers.

Artichoke Spinach Lasagna

PREP: 25 MIN. • **BAKE:** 55 MIN. + STANDING
YIELD: 12 SERVINGS

½ cup chopped onion
1 tablespoon olive oil
4 garlic cloves, minced
1 can (14½ ounces) vegetable or chicken broth
1 teaspoon dried rosemary, crushed
¼ teaspoon ground nutmeg
¼ teaspoon pepper
1 can (14 ounces) water-packed artichoke hearts, rinsed, drained and quartered
1 package (10 ounces) frozen chopped spinach, thawed and squeezed dry
½ cup sliced fresh mushrooms
1 jar (16 ounces) roasted garlic Alfredo or Parmesan and mozzarella pasta sauce
12 no-cook lasagna noodles
3 cups (12 ounces) shredded part-skim mozzarella cheese, divided
1 cup crumbled tomato and basil feta cheese or feta cheese
⅛ teaspoon garlic powder
⅛ teaspoon each dried oregano, parsley flakes and basil

We were served this meatless entree while visiting friends in Maryland. We took the recipe with us when we left and have since added a few more ingredients, which make it even better.

—CAROLE RAGO
ALTOONA, PENNSYLVANIA

lasagna with extra zing

To add a zippier flavor to Artichoke Spinach Lasagna, replace a quarter of the shredded mozzarella cheese with shredded sharp cheddar. It will heighten the flavor.

1. In a large saucepan, saute onion in oil for 2-3 minutes or until tender. Add garlic; cook 1 minute longer. Stir in the broth, rosemary, nutmeg and pepper. Bring to a boil. Add the artichokes, spinach and mushrooms. Reduce heat; cover and simmer for 5 minutes. Stir in pasta sauce.

2. Spread 1 cup sauce mixture into a greased 13-in. x 9-in. baking dish. Top with three noodles and ¾ cup mozzarella cheese. Repeat layers three times. Top with remaining sauce mixture and mozzarella cheese. Sprinkle with feta cheese, garlic powder, oregano, parsley and basil.

3. Cover and bake at 350° for 40 minutes. Uncover; bake 15 minutes longer or until noodles are tender. Let stand for 10 minutes before cutting.

Pumpkin Cream Cheese Pie

After spending an afternoon in the chilly October air at our town's pumpkin-rolling contest, my family, including my grandchildren, head over to my house for a fun pumpkin-themed meal, including this luscious dessert.
—**DIANE SELICH** VASSAR, MICHIGAN

PREP: 10 MIN. • **BAKE:** 70 MIN. • **YIELD:** 6-8 SERVINGS

- 1 **package (8 ounces) cream cheese, softened**
- 3 **tablespoons confectioners' sugar**
- ½ **teaspoon vanilla extract**
- 1 **unbaked pastry shell (9 inches)**

FILLING:
- 1⅔ **cups heavy whipping cream**
- 1½ **cups canned pumpkin**
- 2 **eggs, lightly beaten**
- ¾ **cup sugar**
- 1¾ **teaspoons pumpkin pie spice**

1. In a small bowl, beat the cream cheese, confectioners' sugar and vanilla until smooth. Spread into pastry shell.

2. In another small bowl, whisk filling ingredients until smooth. Pour over cream cheese layer. Cover edges loosely with foil.

3. Bake at 350° for 70-80 minutes or until a knife inserted near the center comes out clean. Cool on a wire rack. Store in the refrigerator.

Mint Sandwich Cookies

PREP: 40 MIN. • **BAKE:** 10 MIN. + COOLING • **YIELD:** 40 COOKIES

- 1 tube (18 ounces) refrigerated sugar cookie dough, softened
- ¼ cup all-purpose flour
- ⅛ teaspoon peppermint extract
  Coarse sugar
- 40 chocolate-covered thin mints

1. In a large bowl, beat the cookie dough, flour and extract until blended. Roll into ½-in. balls.

2. Place 2 in. apart on greased baking sheets. Coat the bottom of a glass with cooking spray, then dip in coarse sugar. Flatten balls with prepared glass to ¼-in. thickness, dipping in additional sugar as needed.

3. Bake at 350° for 7-9 minutes or until set. Carefully remove one cookie from baking sheet. Immediately turn cookie over and place a mint on the bottom of the cookie; top with another cookie, pressing lightly. Repeat with remaining cookies and mints. Cool on wire racks.

EDITOR'S NOTE: This recipe was tested with Necco chocolate-covered thin mints.

Cherries over Creamy Fluff

This sweet, no-bake dish is a definite keeper. The recipe has been in our family for more than 40 years. We've always enjoyed cherry pie filling, but use whatever kind you like. Blueberry tastes wonderful, too. And it couldn't be easier!
—**BARB COOAN** BIRCHWOOD, WISCONSIN

PREP: 20 MIN. + CHILLING • **YIELD:** 7-8 SERVINGS

- 1 package (8 ounces) cream cheese, softened
- ½ cup sugar
- 1 teaspoon vanilla extract
- 2 cups heavy whipping cream, whipped
- 2 cups miniature marshmallows
- 1 can (21 ounces) cherry pie filling

1. In a large bowl, beat the cream cheese, sugar and vanilla until fluffy. Fold in whipped cream and marshmallows. Cover and refrigerate for at least 30 minutes.

2. Spoon the cream cheese mixture into dessert bowls. Top with pie filling.

S'more Ice Cream Pie

Our pretty s'more pie will make you glad you're not camping! Boys and girls will adore the hot toasty marshmallows atop the rocky road ice cream.
—TASTE OF HOME TEST KITCHEN

PREP: 20 MIN. + FREEZING • **YIELD:** 4 SERVINGS

- ⅔ cup graham cracker crumbs
- 2 tablespoons sugar
- 3 tablespoons butter, melted
- 2½ cups rocky road ice cream, softened
- ⅔ cup marshmallow creme
- ¾ cup miniature marshmallows

1. In a small bowl, combine cracker crumbs and sugar; stir in butter. Press onto the bottom and up the sides of a 7-in. pie plate coated with cooking spray. Bake at 325° for 7-9 minutes or until lightly browned. Cool on a wire rack.

2. Carefully spread ice cream into crust; freeze until firm. Spread marshmallow creme over ice cream. Top with marshmallows; gently press into creme. Cover and freeze for 4 hours or overnight.

3. Just before serving, broil 6 in. from the heat for 1-2 minutes or until marshmallows are golden brown.

Coconut Pistachio Pie

PREP: 20 MIN. + CHILLING • **YIELD:** 8 SERVINGS

- 2½ cups flaked coconut, lightly toasted
- ⅓ cup butter, melted
- 2 cups cold 2% milk
- 2 packages (3.4 ounces each) instant pistachio pudding mix
- 1 cup whipped topping
- 2 tablespoons chopped pistachios, optional

1. In a small bowl, combine coconut and butter. Press onto the bottom and up the sides of a greased 9-in. pie plate. Refrigerate for at least 30 minutes or until firm.

2. In a small bowl, whisk milk and pudding mixes for 2 minutes. Let stand for 2 minutes or until soft-set. Spread 1½ cups over crust.

3. Fold whipped topping into remaining pudding; spread over pie. Sprinkle with pistachios if desired. Cover and refrigerate for at least 2 hours.

Lightly toasted coconut in the crust pairs so well with the pale green pistachio pudding in this quick and pretty pie. You can make it ahead, when convenient, then chill until serving.
—TASTE OF HOME TEST KITCHEN

Dark Chocolate Fondue

PREP/TOTAL TIME: 20 MIN. • **YIELD:** 2 CUPS

- 2 **tablespoons all-purpose flour**
- 1½ **cups 2% milk**
- 2 **dark chocolate candy bars (1.55 ounces each), chopped**
- 3 **ounces milk chocolate, chopped**
- 2 **tablespoons light corn syrup**
  Cubed angel food cake and assorted fresh fruit

1. In a small saucepan, combine flour and milk until smooth. Bring to a boil over medium-high heat; cook and stir for 1 minute or until thickened. Reduce heat to low. Stir in chocolate and corn syrup. Cook and stir until melted.

2. Transfer to a small fondue pot and keep warm. Serve with cake cubes and fruit.

TASTY TIP: Dark Chocolate Fondue also makes a delectable way to dress up chunks of pineapple, slices of banana or scoops of fat-free frozen yogurt.

Green Beans Supreme

PREP/TOTAL TIME: 25 MIN. • **YIELD:** 12-16 SERVINGS

- 4 packages (16 ounces each) frozen cut green beans
- ¼ cup finely chopped onion
- ¼ cup butter, cubed
- 2 tablespoons all-purpose flour
- 1 teaspoon salt
- 1 teaspoon paprika
- 1 teaspoon Worcestershire sauce
- ½ teaspoon ground mustard
- 2 cups evaporated milk
- 8 ounces process cheese (Velveeta), shredded

TOPPING:
- ¼ cup dry bread crumbs
- 2 teaspoons butter, melted

1. Cook green beans according to package directions. Meanwhile, in a Dutch oven, saute onion in butter until tender. Remove from the heat; whisk in the flour, salt, paprika, Worcestershire sauce and mustard until blended.

2. Gradually stir in milk. Bring to a boil; cook and stir for 2 minutes or until thickened and bubbly. Remove from the heat; stir in cheese.

3. Drain beans; gently fold into cheese sauce. Transfer to a large serving bowl. Toss bread crumbs and butter; sprinkle over beans.

leftover evaporated milk

When you have leftover evaporated milk, a great way to avoid wasting it is to pour it in ice cube trays. Once frozen, the cubes store nicely in a resealable freezer bag. Just pop out what you need and thaw. Be sure to use new ice cube trays, or the milk may absorb odors from previous use.

Here's a nice alternative to plain green bean casserole. I prepare a well-seasoned cheese sauce that lends a little zip to the familiar side dish.

—HEATHER CAMPBELL
LAWRENCE, KANSAS

Shrimp Gazpacho

This refreshing, cold, tomato-based soup features shrimp, cucumber and avocados. Serve it as an appetizer or as a meal by itself.

—TASTE OF HOME TEST KITCHEN

PREP: 10 MIN. + CHILLING
YIELD: 12 SERVINGS (ABOUT 3 QUARTS)

- 6 cups spicy hot V8 juice
- 2 cups cold water
- 1 pound cooked medium shrimp, peeled and deveined
- 2 medium tomatoes, seeded and diced
- 1 medium cucumber, seeded and diced
- 2 medium ripe avocados, diced
- ½ cup lime juice
- ½ cup minced fresh cilantro
- ½ teaspoon salt
- ¼ to ½ teaspoon hot pepper sauce

1. In a large bowl, combine all ingredients. Cover and refrigerate for 1 hour. Serve cold.

EDITOR'S NOTE: This recipe is best served the same day it's made.

Everyone thinks I've gone to a lot of trouble when making this refreshing summer drink, but it's so easy! I also like to make my own pretty ice cubes by adding ½ cup lemon juice and a mint sprig to 4 cups water.

—**BONNIE HAWKINS** ELKHORN, WISCONSIN

Lemony Cooler

PREP: 15 MIN. + CHILLING • **YIELD:** 8 SERVINGS (2 QUARTS)

- 3 cups white grape juice
- ½ cup sugar
- ½ cup lemon juice
- 1 bottle (1 liter) club soda, chilled
  Ice cubes
  Assorted fresh fruit, optional

1. In a pitcher, combine the grape juice, sugar and lemon juice; stir until sugar is dissolved. Refrigerate until chilled.

2. Just before serving, stir in club soda. Serve over ice. Garnish with fresh fruit if desired.

Sweet apples and spicy curry combine in this rich soup, which is perfect for fall. A small serving is all you need to satisfy.
—**JANE SHAPTON** IRVINE, CALIFORNIA

Curried Pumpkin Apple Soup

PREP: 15 MIN. • **COOK:** 25 MIN.
YIELD: 8 SERVINGS (2 QUARTS)

- **2 medium Golden Delicious apples, peeled and coarsely chopped**
- **1 medium onion, chopped**
- **1 medium leek (white portion only), sliced**
- **2 tablespoons butter**
- **3 garlic cloves, minced**
- **2 to 3 teaspoons curry powder**
- **1 can (15 ounces) solid-pack pumpkin**
- **4 cups chicken broth**
- **1 cup heavy whipping cream**
- **Salt to taste**

1. In a large saucepan, saute the apples, onion and leek in butter until tender. Add garlic and curry; cook 1 minute longer. Add pumpkin and broth; bring to a boil. Reduce heat; cover and simmer for 20 minutes. Stir in cream; heat through (do not boil).

2. Remove from the heat; cool slightly. In a blender, process soup in batches until smooth. Season with salt.

Asparagus Omelet

PREP: 40 MIN. • **COOK:** 20 MIN. • **YIELD:** 4 OMELETS

 1   **envelope hollandaise sauce mix**
 1   **cup milk**
 ¼   **cup butter, softened**
 8   **bacon strips, diced**
 ½   **pound fresh mushrooms, sliced**
 1   **pound asparagus, trimmed and cut into 1-inch pieces**
 3   **tablespoons water**
12   **eggs, lightly beaten**
 1   **cup (4 ounces) shredded part-skim mozzarella cheese**

1. In a large saucepan, prepare the hollandaise sauce mix with milk and butter according to package directions; keep warm.

2. In a large skillet, cook bacon over medium heat until crisp; remove to paper towels. In the drippings, saute mushrooms until tender; set aside.

3. Place asparagus and water in a microwave-safe bowl. Cover and microwave on high for 4-5 minutes or until crisp-tender; drain and keep warm.

4. Coat a 10-in. skillet with cooking spray and place over medium heat; add ¾ cup beaten eggs (3 eggs) to skillet (mixture should set immediately at edges).

5. As eggs set, push cooked edges toward the center, letting uncooked portion flow underneath. When the eggs are set, sprinkle a fourth of the asparagus, ¼ cup cheese and a fourth of the mushrooms on one side and sprinkle with cheese; fold other side over filling. Invert omelet onto a plate to serve. Repeat for remaining omelets. Top with hollandaise sauce and bacon.

Simple Lemon Fruit Dip

My husband's a construction worker, and this is a great treat to put in his lunch with whatever fresh fruit he wants. It keeps all week long in the fridge.
—**MEGAN WILKINSON** MORGAN, UTAH

PREP/TOTAL TIME: 5 MIN. • **YIELD:** 1⅔ CUPS

- 1 **cup cold milk**
- 1 **package (3.4 ounces) instant lemon pudding mix**
- 1 **cup (8 ounces) sour cream**
  Assorted fresh fruit

1. In a small bowl, whisk milk and pudding mix for 2 minutes (mixture will be thick). Whisk in sour cream. Chill until serving. Serve with fruit.

Cinnamon Apple Crumble Pie

Here's a dessert any busy hostess will love! It goes together in minutes, yet looks and tastes like it took much more time.
—**CAROLYN RUCH** NEW LONDON, WISCONSIN

PREP: 15 MIN. • **BAKE:** 50 MIN. + COOLING
YIELD: 6-8 SERVINGS

- 1 **can (21 ounces) apple pie filling**
- 1 **unbaked pastry shell (9 inches)**
- ½ **teaspoon ground cinnamon**
- 4 **tablespoons butter, divided**
- 1½ **to 2 cups crushed pecan shortbread cookies**

1. Pour pie filling into pastry shell. Sprinkle with cinnamon and dot with 1 tablespoon butter. Melt remaining butter. Place cookie crumbs in a small bowl; stir in butter until coarse crumbs form. Sprinkle over filling. Cover edges of pastry loosely with foil.

2. Bake at 450° for 10 minutes. Reduce heat to 350°; remove foil and bake for 40-45 minutes or until crust is golden brown and filling is bubbly. Cool on a wire rack for at least 2 hours.

This tasty, golden brown turkey breast is just four ingredients away! And with its low sodium, fat and cholesterol levels, you can feel good about eating it. It's simply delicious.

—**AUDREY PETTERSON**
MAIDSTONE, SASKATCHEWAN

Cranberry-Glazed Turkey Breast

PREP: 20 MIN. • **BAKE:** 1½ HOURS + STANDING
YIELD: 12 SERVINGS

- 1¼ cups jellied cranberry sauce
- ⅔ cup thawed unsweetened apple juice concentrate
- 2 tablespoons butter
- 1 bone-in turkey breast (5 to 6 pounds)

1. In a small saucepan, bring the cranberry sauce, apple juice concentrate and butter to a boil. Remove from the heat; cool.

2. Carefully loosen skin of turkey breast. Set aside ½ cup sauce for basting and ¾ cup for serving. Spoon remaining sauce onto the turkey, rubbing mixture under and over the skin.

3. Place turkey on a rack in a shallow roasting pan. Bake, uncovered, at 325° for 1½ to 2 hours or until a meat thermometer reads 170°, basting occasionally with reserved sauce. Cover and let stand for 10 minutes before carving. Warm reserved ¾ cup sauce; serve with turkey.

safety first!

When handling raw poultry, it's important to place it on a plastic cutting board rather than wood for easier cleaning. To avoid contamination with other foods, always wash your hands and anything that has come in contact with the uncooked poultry (such as knives, cutting boards, countertops) with hot soapy water.

Zippy Steak Chili

PREP: 15 MIN. • **COOK:** 6 HOURS • **YIELD:** 5 SERVINGS

- 1 **pound beef top sirloin steak, cut into ½-inch cubes**
- ½ **cup chopped onion**
- 2 **tablespoons canola oil**
- 2 **tablespoons chili powder**
- 1 **teaspoon garlic powder**
- 1 **teaspoon ground cumin**
- 1 **teaspoon dried oregano**
- 1 **teaspoon pepper**
- 2 **cans (10 ounces each) diced tomatoes and green chilies, undrained**
- 1 **can (15½ ounces) chili starter**
  Shredded cheddar cheese, chopped onion and sour cream, optional

1. In a large skillet, cook steak and onion in oil over medium heat until meat is no longer pink. Sprinkle with seasonings.

Looking for a thick, chunky chili with a little extra-special kick for football Sunday? Try this recipe. It was given to me by a co-worker originally from Texas.
—DENISE HABIB
POOLESVILLE, MARYLAND

2. In a 5-qt. slow cooker, combine tomatoes and chili starter. Stir in beef mixture. Cover and cook on low for 6-8 hours or until meat is tender. Serve with cheese, onion and sour cream if desired.

EDITOR'S NOTE: This recipe was tested with Bush's Traditional Chili Starter.

Fresh Berry Pie

PREP: 10 MIN. + CHILLING • **COOK:** 10 MIN. + COOLING
YIELD: 6-8 SERVINGS

1½ **cups sugar**
¼ **cup cornstarch**
Pinch salt
1½ **cups cold water**
1 **package (3 ounces) strawberry or raspberry gelatin**
1 **quart fresh strawberries or raspberries**
1 **pastry shell (9 inches), baked**
Whipped cream and fresh mint, optional

1. In a saucepan, combine the sugar, cornstarch, salt and water until smooth; bring to a boil over medium-high heat. Cook and stir for 2 minutes. Remove from the heat; stir in dry gelatin until dissolved. Cool until mixture begins to partially set.

Our family and friends helped make the wedding of our daughter, Hannah, to now-husband Robert a truly beautiful day. Folks pitched in with the music, flowers, buffet and more. This pie was one of the many wonderful desserts.
—BARBARA ROSSI
WALLA WALLA, WASHINGTON

2. Remove stems from strawberries. Arrange berries, tip end up, in pastry shell; spoon gelatin mixture over fruit. Refrigerate until set, about 2 hours. Garnish with whipped cream and mint if desired.

TIP: Bake pastry shells several days ahead if desired. Store cooled shells in air-tight containers.

Valentine Napoleons

PREP/TOTAL TIME: 30 MIN. • YIELD: 12 SERVINGS

- 1 **package (17.3 ounces) frozen puff pastry, thawed**
- 1 **cup cold milk**
- 1 **package (3.4 ounces) instant vanilla pudding mix**
- 1 **cup heavy whipping cream**
- ¼ **cup confectioners' sugar**
- 1¼ **cups sliced fresh strawberries**
  Additional confectioners' sugar

1. On a lightly floured surface, roll out each pastry sheet to ⅛-in. thickness. Using a 3½-in. heart-shaped cookie cutter, cut out 12 hearts. Place on ungreased baking sheets. Bake at 400° for 8-11 minutes or until golden brown. Remove to wire racks to cool.

2. In a large bowl, whisk milk and pudding mix for 2 minutes (mixture will be thick).

3. In another large bowl, beat cream until it begins to thicken. Beat in confectioners' sugar until soft peaks form. Fold into pudding.

4. Split puff pastry hearts in half. Place bottom halves on serving plates. Spoon ¼ cup filling over each; top with strawberries and pastry tops. Sprinkle with confectioners' sugar.

These pastries are quick to fix, thanks to convenient puff pastry. I fill the hearts with a pudding-and-cream mixture and strawberries.
—**KATHLEEN TAUGHER**
EAST TROY, WISCONSIN

Tastes Like Eggnog Cake

My holiday eggnog cake uses a convenient boxed mix and comes out perfect every time! It always gets compliments, and most people think that I spend hours in the kitchen working on it. My husband's colleagues at work ask for it every Christmas.
—**LISA BARRETT** DURANGO, COLORADO

PREP: 30 MIN. • BAKE: 25 MIN. + COOLING
YIELD: 12-15 SERVINGS

- 1 **package (18¼ ounces) yellow cake mix**
- 1 **teaspoon ground nutmeg**
- ¼ **teaspoon ground ginger**

FROSTING:
- 1½ **cups heavy whipping cream**
- 3 **tablespoons confectioners' sugar**
- 1 **teaspoon rum extract**

1. Prepare cake batter according to package directions, adding nutmeg and ginger to dry ingredients. Pour into a greased 13-in. x 9-in. baking pan.

2. Bake at 350° for 25-30 minutes or until a toothpick inserted near the center comes out clean. Cool on a wire rack.

3. For frosting, in a small bowl, beat cream and confectioners' sugar until stiff peaks form. Fold in extract. Spread over cake. Store in the refrigerator.

A quick-bread mix is the secret behind this speedy and versatile spice cake. It's moist, flecked with bits of apple, and fabulous for dessert or as a breakfast coffee cake.

—MARILYN TERMAN
COLUMBUS, OHIO

Iced Apple Snack Cake

PREP: 15 MIN. • **BAKE:** 35 MIN. + COOLING
YIELD: 12-15 SERVINGS

½ cup butter, softened
½ cup packed brown sugar
3 eggs
1 teaspoon vanilla extract
1 package (15.4 ounces) nut quick bread mix
1 teaspoon ground cinnamon
2 medium tart apples, peeled and finely chopped
½ cup raisins
ICING:
¾ cup confectioners' sugar
¼ teaspoon ground cinnamon
2 tablespoons butter, melted
¼ teaspoon vanilla extract
3 to 5 tablespoons 2% milk

1. In a large bowl, cream butter and brown sugar until light and fluffy. Beat in eggs and vanilla. Add quick-bread mix and cinnamon and mix well. Fold in apples and raisins.

2. Transfer to a greased 13-in. x 9-in. baking dish. Bake at 350° for 35-40 minutes or until a toothpick inserted near the center comes out clean. Cool on a wire rack.

3. In a small bowl, combine the confectioners' sugar, cinnamon, butter, vanilla and enough milk to achieve desired consistency. Drizzle over cake.

Holiday Pinwheel Cookies

PREP: 20 MIN. + CHILLING • **BAKE:** 10 MIN./BATCH
YIELD: 2¼ DOZEN

- 1   **tube (16½ ounces) refrigerated sugar cookie dough**
- ½   **cup all-purpose flour**
- 3   **tablespoons red colored sugar**
- 3   **tablespoons green colored sugar**

1. Let cookie dough stand at room temperature for 5-10 minutes to soften. In a small bowl, beat cookie dough and flour until combined. Divide dough in half.

2. On a lightly floured surface, roll one portion into a 12-in. x 7-in. rectangle. Sprinkle with red sugar. Tightly roll up jelly-roll style, starting with a short side; wrap in plastic wrap. Repeat with remaining dough and green sugar. Refrigerate 2 hours or until firm.

3. Unwrap and cut into ½-in. slices. Place 2 in. apart on ungreased baking sheets. Bake at 350° for 8-10 minutes or until edges begin to brown. Cool for 1 minute before removing from pans to wire racks. Store in an airtight container.

Little helpers will have a blast helping to create these adorable pinwheels. They're an absolute cinch to make!
—**KAREN MOORE** JACKSONVILLE, FLORIDA

cookie floss

To keep their round shape when slicing refrigerator cookies, use dental floss. Slide a piece (about 1 foot long) under the roll of dough, crisscross the ends above the dough and pull until you've cut right through.

general index

This index lists each recipe by major ingredients and mixes or convenience items used.

apples & applesauce
ABC Muffins, 92
Apple Cinnamon Turnovers, 45
Apple Granola Dessert, 170
Apple-Nut Blue Cheese Tartlets, 21
Apple Pinwheels, 90
Apple Spice Waffles, 33
Cinnamon Apple Crumble Pie, 235
Curried Pumpkin Apple Soup, 233
Iced Apple Snack Cake, 240

apricots
Apricot & White Chocolate Coffee Cake, 83
Chicken, Pear & Gorgonzola Tarts, 8

artichokes
Antipasto Potato Bake, 55
Artichoke Crescent Appetizers, 22
Artichoke Ham Puffs, 139
Artichoke Spinach Lasagna, 226
Greek Pizza, 123
Hot Spinach Artichoke Dip, 13

asparagus
Asparagus Brunch Pockets, 24
Asparagus Omelet, 234
Asparagus Snack Squares, 18
Asparagus Steak Oscar, 223
Early-Bird Asparagus Supreme, 66

avocado & guacamole
Chili Cheese Dip, 14
Guacamole Appetizer Squares, 23

Salsa Spaghetti Squash, 138
Shrimp Gazpacho, 232

bacon & bacon bits
Asparagus Omelet, 234
Autumn Beans, 72
Bacon-Sausage Quiche Tarts, 218
Breakfast Bundles, 35
Breakfast Pizza, 50
Cheesy Wild Rice Soup, 107
Corn and Squash Soup, 110
Guacamole Appetizer Squares, 23
Scrambled Egg Poppers, 34
Spanish Hominy, 59
Spinach Bacon Tartlets, 26
Zesty Potato Cheese Soup, 108

baking chips & english toffee bits
Almond Chocolate Cake, 224
Apricot & White Chocolate Coffee Cake, 83
Chocolate Chip Pancakes, 37
Chocolate Chip Snack Cake, 211
Chocolate Peanut Butter Cookies, 189
Chocolate Pudding Cake, 171
Chocolate Zebra Clusters, 187
Coconut Brownies, 201
Coffee Ice Cream Pie, 208
Colorful Peanut Butter Crackers, 219
Corny Chocolate Crunch, 16
Hazelnut Crescent Rolls, 88

bananas
Banana Cream Cheesecake, 191
Banana Nut Bread, 80

barley
Ground Beef and Barley Soup, 109

beans
Autumn Beans, 72
Broccoli Bean Bake, 61
Chili Tots, 149
Hot Chili Cheese Dip, 172
Hot Dog Bean Soup, 105
Pepperoni Pizza Chili, 105

Polenta Chili Casserole, 156
Salsa Spaghetti Squash, 138
Southwest Burgers, 222
Taco-Filled Peppers, 132
Taco Pizza, 153
Texas Black Bean Soup, 175
Zesty Tacos, 165

beef (also see ground beef)
Asian Beef Noodles, 129
Asparagus Steak Oscar, 223
Barbecue Beef Kabobs, 162
Beef Fillets with Grilled Vegetables, 160
Beef in Mushroom Gravy, 182
Burgundy Steak, 159
Corned Beef Hash and Eggs, 44
Ginger Sirloin Strips, 133
Glazed Beef Tournedos, 141
Italian Pot Roast, 122
Mushroom 'n' Steak Stroganoff, 168
Reuben Braids, 225
Roast Beef and Gravy, 172
Saucy Italian Roast, 177
Savory Italian Beef Sandwiches, 175
Savory Steak Salad, 152
Sirloin in Wine Sauce, 137
Southwest Burgers, 222
Steak with Orange-Thyme Sauce, 128
Sweet and Savory Brisket, 169
Zippy Steak Chili, 237

beets
And the Beets Go On, 74

PAGE 88

biscuits: frozen, refrigerated & biscuit/baking mix

Apple Cinnamon Turnovers, 45
Apple Spice Waffles, 33
Apricot & White Chocolate Coffee Cake, 83
Bacon-Sausage Quiche Tarts, 218
Breakfast Biscuits 'n' Eggs, 49
Campfire Cobbler, 216
Cheeseburger Biscuit Bake, 130
Chicken a la King, 134
Chocolate Chip Pancakes, 37
Easy Chicken Potpie, 148
Easy Orange Rolls, 89
French Onion Drop Biscuits, 87
Lemon Pull-Apart Coffee Cake, 86
Pepperoni Pizza Muffins, 91
Sour Cream Pan Biscuits, 80
Teddy Bear Biscuits, 94

blackberries

Breakfast Crepes with Berries, 37

blueberries

Baked Blueberry Pancake, 39
Campfire Cobbler, 216
Lemon Blueberry Pizza, 204
Old Glory Dessert, 217

bread: store-bought

Chicken French Bread Pizza, 24
Chicken Salad in Baskets, 18
Feta Pitas, 11
Italian Sausage Strata, 48
Overnight Raisin French Toast, 51
Parmesan Fondue, 181
Peaches & Cream French Toast, 32
Rich French Onion Soup, 180

bread dough: dinner rolls & breadsticks
(also see bread, store-bought)

Braided Pizza Loaf, 121
Caramel Sweet Rolls, 87
Cherry Danish, 92
Oat Cinnamon Rolls, 97

Pepperoni Pizza Twists, 28
Pesto Breadsticks, 97
Scrambled Egg Poppers, 34
Speedy Cinnamon Rolls, 91
Three-Meat Stromboli, 81

broccoli

Beef Broccoli Supper, 150
Broccoli Bean Bake, 61
Broccoli Cheese Soup, 111
Broccoli Rice Casserole, 75
Fresh Broccoli Salad, 58
Mac 'n' Cheese Soup, 112
Slow-Cooked Ham 'n' Broccoli, 173
Turkey and Gravy Baskets, 150

cakes, cake mix, brownies & brownie mix

ABC Muffins, 92
Almond Chocolate Cake, 224
Banana Nut Bread, 80
Cherry Almond Tart, 199
Chocolate Chip Snack Cake, 211
Chocolate Peanut Butter Cookies, 189
Chocolate Pudding Cake, 171
Coconut Brownies, 201
Coconut Rhubarb Dessert, 210
Cream-Filled Cupcakes, 195
Double Frosted Brownies, 186
Lemon Crisp Cookies, 190
Lemon Poppy Seed Bread, 93
Lemon Poppy Seed Cake, 200
Maple-Mocha Brownie Torte, 194
Peanut Butter Cupcakes, 209
Rippled Coffee Cake, 99
Strawberry Cake, 197
Tastes Like Eggnog Cake, 239

candy & candy coating
(also see chocolate)

Candy Bar Croissants, 190
Chocolate-Orange Scones, 85
Chocolate Zebra Clusters, 187
Colorful Candy Bar Cookies, 215
Corny Chocolate Crunch, 16

PAGE 45

Crunchy Candy Clusters, 170
Dark Chocolate Fondue, 230

carrots

Carrots with Sugar Snap Peas, 70
Skillet Ranch Vegetables, 67

cereal

Apple Granola Dessert, 170
Barbecue Muncher Mix, 25
Breakfast Bundles, 35
Chocolate Zebra Clusters, 187
Corny Chocolate Crunch, 16
Crunchy Candy Clusters, 170
Double Peanut Bars, 193
Lemon Crisp Cookies, 190
Ranch Potato Casserole, 57
Strawberry Granola Squares, 205

cheese
(also see cream cheese)

Apple-Nut Blue Cheese Tartlets, 21
Brie in Puff Pastry, 21
Cheesy Onion Roll-Ups, 9
Cheesy Shell Lasagna, 161
Cheesy Wild Rice Soup, 107
Chili Cheese Dip, 14
Creamy Macaroni and Cheese, 178
Feta Pitas, 11
Goat Cheese, Pear & Onion Pizza, 22
Gouda Bites, 25
Green Beans Supreme, 231
Hot Spinach Artichoke Dip, 13
Layered Shrimp Dip, 28
No-Bones Chicken Wing Dip, 9
Parmesan Fondue, 181
Savory Mediterranean Orzo, 54

PAGE 224

cherries

Cherries over Creamy Fluff, 228
Cherry Almond Tart, 199
Cherry Danish, 92
Chocolate-Cherry Cream Crepes, 45

chicken

Barbecue Chicken Burritos, 140
Chicken a la King, 134
Chicken & Corn Bread Bake, 157
Chicken Enchilada Bake, 147
Chicken Fettuccine Alfredo
  with Veggies, 127
Chicken French Bread Pizza, 24
Chicken, Pear & Gorgonzola Tarts, 8
Chicken Salad Cups, 10
Chicken Salad in Baskets, 18
Chicken Taco Cups, 15
Chicken Tortellini Soup, 116
Chicken Wild Rice Chowder, 103
Creamy Herbed Chicken, 179
Creamy Italian Chicken, 174
Crescent Chicken Bundles, 135
Crispy Taco Wings, 20
Easy Chicken Potpie, 148
Grilled Chicken with Peaches, 120
Margarita Chicken, 220
No-Bones Chicken Wing Dip, 9
Raspberry Glazed Wings, 12

Saucy Chicken Strips, 136
Simple Chicken Soup, 102
Southwest Chicken and Rice, 165
Wild Rice Chicken Dinner, 158

chocolate

Almond Chocolate Cake, 224
Apricot & White Chocolate
  Coffee Cake, 83
Chocolate Chip Pancakes, 37
Chocolate Chip Snack Cake, 211
Chocolate Malt Shoppe Pie, 202
Chocolate-Orange Scones, 85
Chocolate Pudding Cake, 171
Chocolate Raspberry Napoleons, 196
Coconut Brownies, 201
Colorful Peanut Butter Crackers, 219
Cream-Filled Cupcakes, 195
Dark Chocolate Fondue, 230
Double Chocolate Fondue, 26
Mint Sandwich Cookies, 228
Mocha Cheesecake Bars, 188
Strawberry Puff Pastry Dessert, 206

coconut

Coconut Brownies, 201
Coconut Pistachio Pie, 229
Coconut Rhubarb Dessert, 210

coleslaw mix

Southern Coleslaw, 64
Spicy Shrimp Wraps, 125

cookies & cookie dough

Breakfast Bundles, 35
Cinnamon Apple Crumble Pie, 235
Coffee Ice Cream Pie, 208
Colorful Candy Bar Cookies, 215
Colorful Peanut Butter Crackers, 219
Holiday Pinwheel Cookies, 241
Lemon Blueberry Pizza, 204
Mint Sandwich Cookies, 228
Mocha Cheesecake Bars, 188
Old Glory Dessert, 217
Pistachio Pudding Parfaits, 199
Vanilla Pudding Dessert, 211

corn, corn bread & cornmeal

Bratwurst Hash, 149
Chicken & Corn Bread Bake, 157
Corn & Bean Bake, 62
Corn and Squash Soup, 110
Country Fish Chowder, 115
Creamy Pumpkin Polenta, 63
Mexican Corn Bread, 82
Pantry-Shelf Salmon Chowder, 111
Polenta Chili Casserole, 156
Ramen Corn Chowder, 106
Shoepeg Corn Supreme, 66
Squash Dressing, 68

cottage cheese

Savory Spinach Pie, 221

cranberries & cranberry sauce

And the Beets Go On, 74
Cranberry Cream Cheese Muffins, 98
Cranberry-Glazed Turkey Breast, 236
Cranberry Sweet-and-Sour Pork, 146
Ginger Sirloin Strips, 133
Oat Cinnamon Rolls, 97
Pineapple-Orange Cranberry Sauce, 216
Savory Steak Salad, 152

cream cheese

Artichoke Crescent Appetizers, 22
Cake with Lemon Sauce, 202

PAGE 208

Cheesy Onion Roll-Ups, 9
Cherries over Creamy Fluff, 228
Cherry Almond Tart, 199
Chocolate Cream Cheese Pie, 198
Crab Spread, 17
Cranberry Cream Cheese Muffins, 98
Crescent Chicken Bundles, 135
Fold-Over Tortilla Bake, 144
Horseradish Ham Cubes, 20
Hot Chili Cheese Dip, 172
Layered Shrimp Dip, 28
Mocha Cheesecake Bars, 188
No-Bones Chicken Wing Dip, 9
Old Glory Dessert, 217
Parmesan Fondue, 181
Pistachio Pudding Parfaits, 199
Pumpkin Cream Cheese Pie, 227
Raspberry Ribbon Pie, 192
Raspberry Squares, 207
Strawberry Puff Pastry Dessert, 206

PAGE 117

crepes
Breakfast Crepes with Berries, 37
Chocolate-Cherry Cream Crepes, 45

crescent rolls
Apple Pinwheels, 90
Artichoke Crescent Appetizers, 22
Asparagus Brunch Pockets, 24
Asparagus Snack Squares, 18
Brunch Pizza, 47
Candy Bar Croissants, 190
Crescent Chicken Bundles, 135
Garlic Poppy Seed Spirals, 82
Gouda Bites, 25
Guacamole Appetizer Squares, 23
Hazelnut Crescent Rolls, 88
Reuben Braids, 225
Scrambled Egg Brunch Bread, 42
Speedy Sausage Squares, 40
Spicy Egg Bake, 46
Taco Twists, 126
Zucchini Pie, 50

croutons
Squash Bake, 76
Tangy Caesar Salad, 77

eggs & egg substitute
Asparagus Omelet, 234
Breakfast Bake, 34
Breakfast Biscuits 'n' Eggs, 49
Breakfast Burritos, 36
Breakfast Pizza, 50
Brunch Enchiladas, 49
Brunch Pizza, 47
Corned Beef Hash and Eggs, 44
Italian Sausage Strata, 48
Overnight Raisin French Toast, 51
Peaches & Cream French Toast, 32
Scrambled Egg Brunch Bread, 42
Scrambled Egg Poppers, 34
Speedy Sausage Squares, 40
Spicy Egg Bake, 46
Sunrise Frittata, 39
Tex-Mex Quiche, 38
Wake-Up Wonton Cups, 43
Zucchini Pie, 50

fish & seafood
Asian Shrimp Soup, 117
Colorful Crab Stir-Fry, 124
Country Fish Chowder, 115
Crab 'n' Penne Casserole, 154
Crab Spread, 17
Layered Shrimp Dip, 28
Pantry-Shelf Salmon Chowder, 111
Pesto Halibut, 139
Shrimp Gazpacho, 232
Simple Shrimp Scampi, 221
Spicy Shrimp Wraps, 125
Tuna in the Straw Casserole, 145

frosting
Coconut Brownies, 201
Double Frosted Brownies, 186
Peanut Butter Cupcakes, 209

fruit
(also see specific kinds)
Fruit Pancake Roll-Ups, 33
Marshmallow Fruit Dip, 16
Simple Lemon Fruit Dip, 235

gelatin
Citrus Berry Sherbet, 193
Fresh Berry Pie, 238
Mocha Cheesecake Bars, 188
Peach Frozen Yogurt, 204
Raspberry Ribbon Pie, 192
Raspberry Squares, 207
Strawberry Cake, 197

gravy
Turkey and Gravy Baskets, 150

green beans
Corn & Bean Bake, 62
Dressed-Up French Green Beans, 57
Green Beans Amandine, 60
Green Beans Supreme, 231
Meat Loaf Dinner, 161
Tortellini Soup, 109
Wild Rice Chicken Dinner, 158

PAGE 150

ground beef

Beef Broccoli Supper, 150
Braided Pizza Loaf, 121
Cheeseburger Biscuit Bake, 130
Cheesy Shell Lasagna, 161
Chili Tots, 149
Church Supper Hot Dish, 164
Fold-Over Tortilla Bake, 144
Ground Beef and Barley Soup, 109
Ground Beef Noodle Soup, 102
Hearty Wild Rice Soup, 104
Meat Loaf Dinner, 161
Party Meatballs, 11
Pepperoni Pizza Chili, 105
Southwest Burgers, 222
Stovetop Beef 'n' Shells, 157
Taco-Filled Peppers, 132
Taco Pizza, 153
Taco Twists, 126
Tortellini Soup, 109
Zesty Tacos, 165

ham

Artichoke Ham Puffs, 139
Breakfast Biscuits 'n' Eggs, 49
Ham 'n' Noodle Hot Dish, 151
Horseradish Ham Cubes, 20
Mac 'n' Cheese Soup, 112
Scrambled Egg Brunch Bread, 42
Slow-Cooked Ham 'n' Broccoli, 173
Sunrise Frittata, 39
Turkey Cordon Bleu Pasta, 140

hominy

Spanish Hominy, 59

hot dogs

Hot Dog Bean Soup, 105

hot roll mix
(also see sweet rolls)

Herb Focaccia Bread, 84
Italian Cloverleaf Rolls, 88
Rum Sweet Rolls, 96

ice cream &
ice cream topping

Chocolate Malt Shoppe Pie, 202
Coffee Ice Cream Pie, 208
Mocha Cheesecake Bars, 188
S'more Ice Cream Pie, 229

lemons & limes

Cake with Lemon Sauce, 202
Citrus Berry Sherbet, 193
Lemon Blueberry Pizza, 204
Lemon Crisp Cookies, 190
Lemon Pie, 210
Lemon Poppy Seed Bread, 93
Lemon Poppy Seed Cake, 200
Lemon Pull-Apart Coffee Cake, 86
Lemony Cooler, 232
Margarita Chicken, 220
Simple Lemon Fruit Dip, 235

marshmallows

Cherries over Creamy Fluff, 228
Chocolate Zebra Clusters, 187
Coffee Ice Cream Pie, 208
Cream-Filled Cupcakes, 195
Crunchy Candy Clusters, 170
Marshmallow Fruit Dip, 16
S'more Ice Cream Pie, 229
Speedy Sweet Potatoes, 69

meatballs

Party Meatballs, 11

muffin mix

Mexican Corn Bread, 82
Pistachio Pumpkin Bread, 214
Squash Dressing, 68

mushrooms

Asparagus Omelet, 234
Cheesy Shell Lasagna, 161
Chicken a la King, 134
Creamy Italian Chicken, 174
Italian Sausage Strata, 48
Mixed Veggies, 72
Mushroom 'n' Steak Stroganoff, 168
Pizza Pork Chops, 134
Saucy Chicken Strips, 136
Saucy Italian Roast, 177
Sirloin in Wine Sauce, 137
Stuffing Baskets, 74
Tuna in the Straw Casserole, 145
Turkey Cordon Bleu Pasta, 140

nuts &
peanut butter

Apple-Nut Blue Cheese Tartlets, 21
Banana Nut Bread, 80
Barbecue Muncher Mix, 25
Chocolate Peanut Butter Cookies, 189
Chocolate Zebra Clusters, 187
Coconut Pistachio Pie, 229
Colorful Peanut Butter Crackers, 219
Crunchy Candy Clusters, 170
Double Peanut Bars, 193
Peanut Butter Cupcakes, 209
Pistachio Pumpkin Bread, 214

PAGE 145

oats & oatmeal

Campfire Cobbler, 216
Oat Cinnamon Rolls, 97

onions

Cheesy Onion Roll-Ups, 9
Goat Cheese, Pear & Onion Pizza, 22
French Onion Bread, 95
French Onion Drop Biscuits, 87
Rich French Onion Soup, 180
Sweet Onion Pie, 40

oranges & orange juice

Chocolate-Orange Scones, 85
Citrus Berry Sherbet, 193
Pineapple-Orange Cranberry Sauce, 216
Steak with Orange-Thyme Sauce, 128

pancakes & pancake mix
(also see waffles)

Baked Blueberry Pancake, 39
Chocolate Chip Pancakes, 37
Chocolate-Orange Scones, 85
Fruit Pancake Roll-Ups, 33

pasta, pasta mix & noodles

Artichoke Spinach Lasagna, 226
Asian Beef Noodles, 129
Asian Shrimp Soup, 117
Burgundy Steak, 159
Cheesy Shell Lasagna, 161
Chicken Fettuccine Alfredo
   with Veggies, 127
Chicken Tortellini Soup, 116
Church Supper Hot Dish, 164
Colorful Pasta Salad, 66
Crab 'n' Penne Casserole, 154
Creamy Macaroni and Cheese, 178
Ground Beef Noodle Soup, 102
Ham 'n' Noodle Hot Dish, 151
Mac 'n' Cheese Soup, 112
Mushroom 'n' Steak Stroganoff, 168

PAGE 39

Ramen Corn Chowder, 106
Roasted Pepper Tortellini, 131
Savory Mediterranean Orzo, 54
Saucy Italian Roast, 177
Stovetop Beef 'n' Shells, 157
Tortellini Soup, 109
Turkey Cordon Bleu Pasta, 140

peaches & pears

Chicken, Pear & Gorgonzola Tarts, 8
Goat Cheese, Pear & Onion Pizza, 22
Grilled Chicken with Peaches, 120
Peach Frozen Yogurt, 204
Peaches & Cream French Toast, 32
Peachy Ginger Pork, 121

peas

Ham 'n' Noodle Hot Dish, 151
Mixed Veggies, 72

pepperoni & salami

Pepperoni Pizza Chili, 105
Pepperoni Pizza Muffins, 91
Pepperoni Pizza Twists, 28
Pizza Pork Chops, 134
Three-Meat Stromboli, 81

peppers

Taco-Filled Peppers, 132

pesto: prepared & dry mix

Greek Pizza, 123
Italian Party Appetizers, 29
Pesto Breadsticks, 97
Pesto Halibut, 139

phyllo dough & shells

Apple-Nut Blue Cheese Tartlets, 21
Chicken, Pear & Gorgonzola Tarts, 8
Chocolate Raspberry Napoleons, 196
Spinach Bacon Tartlets, 26

pie crust: cookie, crumb & pastry

Chicken Salad Cups, 10
Chocolate Cream Cheese Pie, 198
Cinnamon Apple Crumble Pie, 235
Fresh Berry Pie, 238
Lemon Pie, 210
Pineapple Rhubarb Pie, 203
Pumpkin Cream Cheese Pie, 227
Raspberry Ribbon Pie, 192
Savory Spinach Pie, 221
Sweet Onion Pie, 40
Tex-Mex Quiche, 38

pie filling

Campfire Cobbler, 216
Cherries over Creamy Fluff, 228
Cherry Almond Tart, 199
Cherry Danish, 92
Chocolate-Cherry Cream Crepes, 45
Cinnamon Apple Crumble Pie, 235
Fruit Pancake Roll-Ups, 33

pineapple

Pineapple-Orange Cranberry Sauce, 216
Pineapple Rhubarb Pie, 203

PAGE 203

PAGE 227

pizza crust: pre-made & refrigerated

Breakfast Pizza, 50
Goat Cheese, Pear & Onion Pizza, 22
Greek Pizza, 123
Taco Pizza, 153

pizza sauce

Pepperoni Pizza Chili, 105
Pepperoni Pizza Twists, 28
Roasted Pepper Tortellini, 131

popcorn

Corny Chocolate Crunch, 16

pork (also see bacon & bacon bits; ham; pepperoni & salami; sausage)

Cranberry Sweet-and-Sour Pork, 146
Crispy Baked Wontons, 27
Great Pork Chop Bake, 163
Old-Fashioned Pork Chops, 176
Peachy Ginger Pork, 121
Pizza Pork Chops, 134
Pork Chop Dinner, 178
Pork Chops and Chilies Casserole, 155
Savory Stuffed Pork Chops, 131
Slow-Cooked Ribs, 183

potatoes, mashed potatoes & frozen hash browns (also see sweet potatoes)

Antipasto Potato Bake, 55
Bratwurst Hash, 149
Breakfast Bake, 34
Broccoli Cheese Soup, 111
Brunch Pizza, 47
Chili Tots, 149
Church Supper Hot Dish, 164
Corned Beef Hash and Eggs, 44
Country Fish Chowder, 115
Creamy Pumpkin Soup, 114
Creamy Red Potatoes, 182
Great Pork Chop Bake, 163
Meat Loaf Dinner, 161
Nacho Hash Brown Casserole, 77
Ranch Potato Casserole, 57
Sausage Hash Brown Bake, 41
Sunrise Frittata, 39
Tuna in the Straw Casserole, 145

pretzels

Barbecue Muncher Mix, 25

pudding & pudding mix

Almond Chocolate Cake, 224
Banana Cream Cheesecake, 191
Cake with Lemon Sauce, 202
Chocolate Chip Snack Cake, 211
Chocolate Cream Cheese Pie, 198
Chocolate Pudding Cake, 171
Coconut Pistachio Pie, 229
Double Frosted Brownies, 186
Lemon Poppy Seed Bread, 93
Lemon Poppy Seed Cake, 200
Pistachio Pudding Parfaits, 199
Simple Lemon Fruit Dip, 235
Valentine Napoleons, 239
Vanilla Pudding Dessert, 211

puff pastry & cream puff shells

Artichoke Ham Puffs, 139

Brie in Puff Pastry, 21
Strawberry Puff Pastry Dessert, 206
Turkey and Gravy Baskets, 150
Valentine Napoleons, 239

pumpkin

Creamy Pumpkin Polenta, 63
Creamy Pumpkin Soup, 114
Curried Pumpkin Apple Soup, 233
Pistachio Pumpkin Bread, 214
Pretty Pumpkin Wontons, 12
Pumpkin Cream Cheese Pie, 227

quiche

Bacon-Sausage Quiche Tarts, 218
Savory Spinach Pie, 221
Sweet Onion Pie, 40
Tex-Mex Quiche, 38

quick bread mix

Cranberry Cream Cheese Muffins, 98
Iced Apple Snack Cake, 240
Pistachio Pumpkin Bread, 214

raspberries

Breakfast Crepes with Berries, 37
Chocolate Raspberry Napoleons, 196
Fresh Berry Pie, 238
Fruit Pancake Roll-Ups, 33
Raspberry Glazed Wings, 12
Raspberry Ribbon Pie, 192
Raspberry Squares, 207

PAGE 218

rhubarb

Coconut Rhubarb Dessert, 210
Pineapple Rhubarb Pie, 203

rice & rice mix

Beef Broccoli Supper, 150
Broccoli Rice Casserole, 75
Cheesy Wild Rice Soup, 107
Chicken Wild Rice Chowder, 103
Colorful Rice Medley, 64
Easy Spanish Rice, 60
Hearty Wild Rice Soup, 104
Instant Fried Rice, 69
Pork Chops and Chilies Casserole, 155
Slow-Cooked Ham 'n' Broccoli, 173
Southwest Chicken and Rice, 165
Wild Rice Chicken Dinner, 158

ricotta cheese

Pretty Pumpkin Wontons, 12

roasted red peppers & pimientos

Antipasto Potato Bake, 55
Artichoke Crescent Appetizers, 22
Bratwurst Hash, 149
Broccoli Bean Bake, 61
Roasted Pepper Tortellini, 131
Roasted Red Pepper Soup, 113
Savory Mediterranean Orzo, 54
Sunrise Frittata, 39
Wild Rice Chicken Dinner, 158

salad dressing, prepared dip & salad dressing mix

Barbecue Beef Kabobs, 162
Beef Fillets with Grilled Vegetables, 160
Chili Cheese Dip, 14
Colorful Pasta Salad, 66
Creamy Italian Chicken, 174
Creamy Red Potatoes, 182
French Onion Drop Biscuits, 87
Fresh Broccoli Salad, 58
No-Bones Chicken Wing Dip, 9
Ranch Potato Casserole, 57

Sausage Hash Brown Bake, 41
Savory Steak Salad, 152
Skillet Ranch Vegetables, 67
Slow-Cooked Ribs, 183
Southern Coleslaw, 64
Tangy Caesar Salad, 77
Zesty Tacos, 165

salsa & picante sauce

Breakfast Burritos, 36
Chicken Taco Cups, 15
Easy Spanish Rice, 60
Hot Chili Cheese Dip, 172
Layered Shrimp Dip, 28
Salsa Spaghetti Squash, 138
Spicy Egg Bake, 46
Spicy Shrimp Wraps, 125
Sunrise Frittata, 39
Taco-Filled Peppers, 132
Taco Pizza, 153
Taco Twists, 126

sauce: bottled, canned, dry mix & jarred (also see pesto; pizza sauce; salsa & picante sauce; spaghetti sauce; tomato sauce)

Artichoke Spinach Lasagna, 226
Asparagus Omelet, 234
Asparagus Steak Oscar, 223
Baked Vegetable Medley, 73
Barbecue Beef Kabobs, 162
Barbecue Chicken Burritos, 140
Barbecue Muncher Mix, 25
Broccoli Rice Casserole, 75
Brunch Enchiladas, 49
Chicken Enchilada Bake, 147
Chicken Fettuccine Alfredo
   with Veggies, 127
Crab 'n' Penne Casserole, 154
Cranberry Sweet-and-Sour Pork, 146
Creamy Herbed Chicken, 179
Fold-Over Tortilla Bake, 144
Glazed Beef Tournedos, 141
Ground Beef Noodle Soup, 102
Layered Shrimp Dip, 28
No-Bones Chicken Wing Dip, 9

Party Meatballs, 11
Slow-Cooked Ham 'n' Broccoli, 173
Slow-Cooked Ribs, 183
Turkey Stir-Fry, 137
Zippy Steak Chili, 237

sauerkraut

Reuben Braids, 225

sausage (also see pepperoni & salami)

Bacon-Sausage Quiche Tarts, 218
Bratwurst Hash, 149
Breakfast Burritos, 36
Brunch Pizza, 47
Italian Sausage Strata, 48
Roasted Pepper Tortellini, 131
Sausage Hash Brown Bake, 41
Skillet Sausage Stuffing, 56
Speedy Sausage Squares, 40

seasoning mix

Brunch Enchiladas, 49
Chicken Taco Cups, 15
Crispy Taco Wings, 20
Guacamole Appetizer Squares, 23
Instant Fried Rice, 69
Spicy Shrimp Wraps, 125
Taco-Filled Peppers, 132
Taco Pizza, 153
Zesty Tacos, 165

PAGE 147

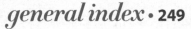

PAGE 77

Shoepeg Corn Supreme, 66
Simple Chicken Soup, 102
Sirloin in Wine Sauce, 137
Slow-Cooked Ham 'n' Broccoli, 173
Squash Bake, 76
Squash Dressing, 68
Squash Stuffing Casserole, 71
Tortellini Soup, 109
Tuna in the Straw Casserole, 145
Turkey Cordon Bleu Pasta, 140
Wild Rice Chicken Dinner, 158
Zesty Potato Cheese Soup, 108

soup mix

Beef in Mushroom Gravy, 182
Early-Bird Asparagus Supreme, 66
French Onion Bread, 95
Italian Pot Roast, 122
Mushroom 'n' Steak Stroganoff, 168
Party Meatballs, 11
Pork Chop Dinner, 178
Roast Beef and Gravy, 172
Saucy Chicken Strips, 136
Savory Italian Beef Sandwiches, 175
Speedy Vegetable Soup, 114
Sweet and Savory Brisket, 169

spaghetti sauce

Cheesy Shell Lasagna, 161
Pizza Pork Chops, 134
Saucy Italian Roast, 177

spinach

Artichoke Spinach Lasagna, 226
Creamy Spinach Casserole, 58
Hot Spinach Artichoke Dip, 13
Makeover Garlic Spinach Balls, 14
Savory Mediterranean Orzo, 54
Savory Spinach Pie, 221
Savory Stuffed Pork Chops, 131
Spinach Bacon Tartlets, 26

strawberries & strawberry jam

Citrus Berry Sherbet, 193
Fresh Berry Pie, 238
Fruit Pancake Roll-Ups, 33

soup: condensed
(also see soup mix)

Baked Vegetable Medley, 73
Beef Broccoli Supper, 150
Beef in Mushroom Gravy, 182
Broccoli Cheese Soup, 111
Broccoli Rice Casserole, 75
Brunch Enchiladas, 49
Burgundy Steak, 159
Cheesy Wild Rice Soup, 107
Chicken & Corn Bread Bake, 157
Church Supper Hot Dish, 164
Corn & Bean Bake, 62
Creamy Herbed Chicken, 179
Creamy Italian Chicken, 174
Creamy Red Potatoes, 182
Creamy Spinach Casserole, 58
Easy Chicken Potpie, 148
Great Pork Chop Bake, 163
Ground Beef and Barley Soup, 109
Hearty Wild Rice Soup, 104
Hot Dog Bean Soup, 105
Italian Pot Roast, 122
Mac 'n' Cheese Soup, 112
Mushroom 'n' Steak Stroganoff, 168
Nacho Hash Brown Casserole, 77
Old-Fashioned Pork Chops, 176
Pantry-Shelf Salmon Chowder, 111
Pepperoni Pizza Muffins, 91
Pork Chop Dinner, 178
Pork Chops and Chilies Casserole, 155
Rich French Onion Soup, 180
Roast Beef and Gravy, 172
Sausage Hash Brown Bake, 41

Old Glory Dessert, 217
Strawberry Cake, 197
Strawberry Granola Squares, 205
Strawberry Puff Pastry Dessert, 206
Valentine Napoleons, 239
Vanilla Pudding Dessert, 211

stuffing cubes & stuffing mix

Chicken & Corn Bread Bake, 157
Creamy Spinach Casserole, 58
Crescent Chicken Bundles, 135
Makeover Garlic Spinach Balls, 14
Savory Stuffed Pork Chops, 131
Skillet Sausage Stuffing, 56
Squash Bake, 76
Squash Stuffing Casserole, 71
Stuffing Baskets, 74

sweet potatoes

Speedy Sweet Potatoes, 69

PAGE 193

sweet rolls
(also see hot roll mix)

Apple Pinwheels, 90
Caramel Sweet Rolls, 87
Cherry Danish, 92
Easy Orange Rolls, 89
Oat Cinnamon Rolls, 97

Rum Sweet Rolls, 96
Speedy Cinnamon Rolls, 91

tomatoes & sun-dried tomatoes

Cheesy Shell Lasagna, 161
Creamy Tomato Basil Soup, 106
Feta Pitas, 11
Fold-Over Tortilla Bake, 144
Guacamole Appetizer Squares, 23
Ground Beef and Barley Soup, 109
Italian Party Appetizers, 29
Pepperoni Pizza Chili, 105
Spanish Hominy, 59
Stovetop Beef 'n' Shells, 157
Texas Black Bean Soup, 175
Zesty Tacos, 165
Zippy Steak Chili, 237

tomato sauce

Braided Pizza Loaf, 121
Cheeseburger Biscuit Bake, 130
Chili Tots, 149
Pepperoni Pizza Chili, 105
Spanish Hominy, 59
Stovetop Beef 'n' Shells, 157

tortillas & taco shells

Barbecue Chicken Burritos, 140
Breakfast Burritos, 36
Brunch Enchiladas, 49
Cheesy Onion Roll-Ups, 9
Chicken Enchilada Bake, 147
Fold-Over Tortilla Bake, 144
Spicy Shrimp Wraps, 125
Zesty Tacos, 165

turkey

Cranberry-Glazed Turkey Breast, 236
Crispy Baked Wontons, 27
Southwest Burgers, 222
Spinach Bacon Tartlets, 26
Turkey and Gravy Baskets, 150
Turkey Cordon Bleu Pasta, 140
Turkey Stir-Fry, 137

vegetables: frozen & fresh
(also see specific kinds)

Baked Vegetable Medley, 73
Barbecue Beef Kabobs, 162
Beef Fillets with Grilled Vegetables, 160
Chicken Fettuccine Alfredo
   with Veggies, 127
Chicken Tortellini Soup, 116
Colorful Crab Stir-Fry, 124
Colorful Pasta Salad, 66
Crab Spread, 17
Easy Chicken Potpie, 148
Hot Spinach Artichoke Dip, 13
Mixed Veggies, 72
Polenta Chili Casserole, 156
Simple Chicken Soup, 102
Skillet Ranch Vegetables, 67
Speedy Vegetable Soup, 114
Tuna in the Straw Casserole, 145
Turkey Stir-Fry, 137

waffles

Apple Spice Waffles, 33

whipped topping

Banana Cream Cheesecake, 191
Chocolate Cream Cheese Pie, 198
Coconut Pistachio Pie, 229
Coffee Ice Cream Pie, 208
Lemon Pie, 210
Marshmallow Fruit Dip, 16
Pistachio Pudding Parfaits, 199

Raspberry Squares, 207
Vanilla Pudding Dessert, 211

winter squash

Corn and Squash Soup, 110
Salsa Spaghetti Squash, 138

wontons

Chicken Taco Cups, 15
Crispy Baked Wontons, 27
Pretty Pumpkin Wontons, 12
Wake-Up Wonton Cups, 43

yellow squash
(also see zucchini)

Crab 'n' Penne Casserole, 154
Savory Mediterranean Orzo, 54
Skillet Ranch Vegetables, 67
Squash Bake, 76
Squash Dressing, 68
Squash Stuffing Casserole, 71

yogurt

Breakfast Crepes with Berries, 37
Lemon Blueberry Pizza, 204
Marshmallow Fruit Dip, 16
Peach Frozen Yogurt, 204

zucchini

Crab 'n' Penne Casserole, 154
Skillet Ranch Vegetables, 67
Tortellini Soup, 109
Zucchini Pie, 50

PAGE 110

alphabetical index

A

ABC Muffins, 92
Almond Chocolate Cake, 224
And the Beets Go On, 74
Antipasto Potato Bake, 55
Apple Cinnamon Turnovers, 45
Apple Granola Dessert, 170
Apple Pinwheels, 90
Apple Spice Waffles, 33
Apple-Nut Blue Cheese Tartlets, 21
Apricot & White Chocolate Coffee Cake, 83
Artichoke Crescent Appetizers, 22
Artichoke Ham Puffs, 139
Artichoke Spinach Lasagna, 226
Asian Beef Noodles, 129
Asian Shrimp Soup, 117
Asparagus Brunch Pockets, 24
Asparagus Omelet, 234
Asparagus Snack Squares, 18
Asparagus Steak Oscar, 223
Autumn Beans, 72

B

Bacon-Sausage Quiche Tarts, 218
Baked Blueberry Pancake, 39
Baked Vegetable Medley, 73
Banana Cream Cheesecake, 191
Banana Nut Bread, 80
Barbecue Beef Kabobs, 162
Barbecue Chicken Burritos, 140
Barbecue Muncher Mix, 25
Beef Broccoli Supper, 150
Beef Fillets with Grilled Vegetables, 160
Beef in Mushroom Gravy, 182
Braided Pizza Loaf, 121
Bratwurst Hash, 149
Breakfast Bake, 34
Breakfast Biscuits 'n' Eggs, 49
Breakfast Bundles, 35
Breakfast Burritos, 36
Breakfast Crepes with Berries, 37
Breakfast Pizza, 50
Brie in Puff Pastry, 21
Broccoli Bean Bake, 61
Broccoli Cheese Soup, 111
Broccoli Rice Casserole, 75
Brunch Enchiladas, 49
Brunch Pizza, 47
Burgundy Steak, 159

C

Cake with Lemon Sauce, 202
Campfire Cobbler, 216
Candy Bar Croissants, 190
Caramel Sweet Rolls, 87
Carrots with Sugar Snap Peas, 70
Cheeseburger Biscuit Bake, 130
Cheesy Onion Roll-Ups, 9
Cheesy Shell Lasagna, 161
Cheesy Wild Rice Soup, 107
Cherries over Creamy Fluff, 228
Cherry Almond Tart, 199
Cherry Danish, 92
Chicken & Corn Bread Bake, 157
Chicken a la King, 134
Chicken Enchilada Bake, 147
Chicken Fettuccine Alfredo
    with Veggies, 127
Chicken French Bread Pizza, 24
Chicken Salad Cups, 10
Chicken Salad in Baskets, 18
Chicken Taco Cups, 15
Chicken Tortellini Soup, 116
Chicken Wild Rice Chowder, 103

PAGE 103

Chicken, Pear & Gorgonzola Tarts, 8
Chili Cheese Dip, 14
Chili Tots, 149
Chocolate-Cherry Cream Crepes, 45
Chocolate Chip Pancakes, 37
Chocolate Chip Snack Cake, 211
Chocolate Cream Cheese Pie, 198
Chocolate Malt Shoppe Pie, 202
Chocolate-Orange Scones, 85
Chocolate Peanut Butter Cookies, 189
Chocolate Pudding Cake, 171
Chocolate Raspberry Napoleons, 196
Chocolate Zebra Clusters, 187
Church Supper Hot Dish, 164
Cinnamon Apple Crumble Pie, 235
Citrus Berry Sherbet, 193
Coconut Brownies, 201
Coconut Pistachio Pie, 229
Coconut Rhubarb Dessert, 210
Coffee Ice Cream Pie, 208

PAGE 24

PAGE 215

Colorful Candy Bar Cookies, 215
Colorful Crab Stir-Fry, 124
Colorful Pasta Salad, 66
Colorful Peanut Butter Crackers, 219
Colorful Rice Medley, 64
Corn & Bean Bake, 62
Corn and Squash Soup, 110
Corned Beef Hash and Eggs, 44
Corny Chocolate Crunch, 16
Country Fish Chowder, 115
Crab 'n' Penne Casserole, 154
Crab Spread, 17
Cranberry Cream Cheese Muffins, 98
Cranberry Sweet-and-Sour Pork, 146
Cranberry-Glazed Turkey Breast, 236
Cream-Filled Cupcakes, 195
Creamy Herbed Chicken, 179
Creamy Italian Chicken, 174
Creamy Macaroni and Cheese, 178
Creamy Pumpkin Polenta, 63
Creamy Pumpkin Soup, 114
Creamy Red Potatoes, 182
Creamy Spinach Casserole, 58
Creamy Tomato Basil Soup, 106
Crescent Chicken Bundles, 135
Crispy Baked Wontons, 27
Crispy Taco Wings, 20
Crunchy Candy Clusters, 170
Curried Pumpkin Apple Soup, 233

D

Dark Chocolate Fondue, 230

Double Chocolate Fondue, 26
Double Frosted Brownies, 186
Double Peanut Bars, 193
Dressed-Up French Green Beans, 57

E

Early-Bird Asparagus Supreme, 66
Easy Chicken Potpie, 148
Easy Orange Rolls, 89
Easy Spanish Rice, 60

F

Feta Pitas, 11
Fold-Over Tortilla Bake, 144
French Onion Bread, 95
French Onion Drop Biscuits, 87
Fresh Berry Pie, 238
Fresh Broccoli Salad, 58
Fruit Pancake Roll-Ups, 33

G

Garlic Poppy Seed Spirals, 82
Ginger Sirloin Strips, 133
Glazed Beef Tournedos, 141
Goat Cheese, Pear & Onion Pizza, 22
Gouda Bites, 25
Great Pork Chop Bake, 163
Greek Pizza, 123
Green Beans Amandine, 60

Green Beans Supreme, 231
Grilled Chicken with Peaches, 120
Ground Beef and Barley Soup, 109
Ground Beef Noodle Soup, 102
Guacamole Appetizer Squares, 23

H

Ham 'n' Noodle Hot Dish, 151
Hazelnut Crescent Rolls, 88
Hearty Wild Rice Soup, 104
Herb Focaccia Bread, 84
Holiday Pinwheel Cookies, 241
Horseradish Ham Cubes, 20
Hot Chili Cheese Dip, 172
Hot Dog Bean Soup, 105
Hot Spinach Artichoke Dip, 13

I

Iced Apple Snack Cake, 240
Instant Fried Rice, 69
Italian Cloverleaf Rolls, 88
Italian Party Appetizers, 29
Italian Pot Roast, 122
Italian Sausage Strata, 48

L

Layered Shrimp Dip, 28
Lemon Blueberry Pizza, 204
Lemon Crisp Cookies, 190

PAGE 60

PAGE 214

Lemon Pie, 210
Lemon Poppy Seed Bread, 93
Lemon Poppy Seed Cake, 200
Lemon Pull-Apart Coffee Cake, 86
Lemony Cooler, 232

M

Mac 'n' Cheese Soup, 112
Makeover Garlic Spinach Balls, 14
Maple-Mocha Brownie Torte, 194
Margarita Chicken, 220
Marshmallow Fruit Dip, 16
Meat Loaf Dinner, 161
Mexican Corn Bread, 82
Mint Sandwich Cookies, 228
Mixed Veggies, 72
Mocha Cheesecake Bars, 188
Mushroom 'n' Steak Stroganoff, 168

N

Nacho Hash Brown Casserole, 77
No-Bones Chicken Wing Dip, 9

O

Oat Cinnamon Rolls, 97
Old Glory Dessert, 217
Old-Fashioned Pork Chops, 176
Overnight Raisin French Toast, 51

P

Pantry Chili, 111
Parmesan Fondue, 181
Party Meatballs, 11
Peach Frozen Yogurt, 204
Peaches & Cream French Toast, 32
Peachy Ginger Pork, 121
Peanut Butter Cupcakes, 209
Pepperoni Pizza Chili, 105
Pepperoni Pizza Muffins, 91
Pepperoni Pizza Twists, 28
Pesto Breadsticks, 97
Pesto Halibut, 139
Pineapple-Orange Cranberry Sauce, 216
Pineapple Rhubarb Pie, 203
Pistachio Pudding Parfaits, 199

Pistachio Pumpkin Bread, 214
Pizza Pork Chops, 134
Polenta Chili Casserole, 156
Pork Chop Dinner, 178
Pork Chops and Chilies Casserole, 155
Pretty Pumpkin Wontons, 12
Pumpkin Cream Cheese Pie, 227

PAGE 139

PAGE 106

Shoepeg Corn Supreme, 66
Shrimp Gazpacho, 232
Simple Chicken Soup, 102
Simple Lemon Fruit Dip, 235
Simple Shrimp Scampi, 221
Sirloin in Wine Sauce, 137
Skillet Ranch Vegetables, 67
Skillet Sausage Stuffing, 56
Slow-Cooked Ham 'n' Broccoli, 173
Slow-Cooked Ribs, 183
S'more Ice Cream Pie, 229
Sour Cream Pan Biscuits, 80
Southern Coleslaw, 64
Southwest Burgers, 222
Southwest Chicken and Rice, 165
Spanish Hominy, 59
Speedy Cinnamon Rolls, 91
Speedy Sausage Squares, 40
Speedy Sweet Potatoes, 69
Speedy Vegetable Soup, 114
Spicy Egg Bake, 46
Spicy Shrimp Wraps, 125
Spinach Bacon Tartlets, 26
Squash Bake, 76
Squash Dressing, 68
Squash Stuffing Casserole, 71
Steak with Orange-Thyme Sauce, 128
Stovetop Beef 'n' Shells, 157
Strawberry Cake, 197
Strawberry Granola Squares, 205
Strawberry Puff Pastry Dessert, 206
Stuffing Baskets, 74
Sunrise Frittata, 39
Sweet and Savory Brisket, 169
Sweet Onion Pie, 40

R

Ramen Corn Chowder, 106
Ranch Potato Casserole, 57
Raspberry Glazed Wings, 12
Raspberry Ribbon Pie, 192
Raspberry Squares, 207
Reuben Braids, 225
Rich French Onion Soup, 180
Rippled Coffee Cake, 99
Roast Beef and Gravy, 172
Roasted Pepper Tortellini, 131
Roasted Red Pepper Soup, 113
Rum Sweet Rolls, 96

S

Salsa Spaghetti Squash, 138
Saucy Chicken Strips, 136
Saucy Italian Roast, 177
Sausage Hash Brown Bake, 41
Savory Italian Beef Sandwiches, 175
Savory Mediterranean Orzo, 54
Savory Spinach Pie, 221
Savory Steak Salad, 152
Savory Stuffed Pork Chops, 131
Scrambled Egg Brunch Bread, 42
Scrambled Egg Poppers, 34

T

Taco-Filled Peppers, 132
Taco Pizza, 153
Taco Twists, 126
Tangy Caesar Salad, 77
Tastes Like Eggnog Cake, 239
Teddy Bear Biscuits, 94
Texas Black Bean Soup, 175
Tex-Mex Quiche, 38
Three-Meat Stromboli, 81
Tortellini Soup, 109
Tuna in the Straw Casserole, 145
Turkey and Gravy Baskets, 150
Turkey Cordon Bleu Pasta, 140
Turkey Stir-Fry, 137

V

Valentine Napoleons, 239
Vanilla Pudding Dessert, 211
Wake-Up Wonton Cups, 43
Wild Rice Chicken Dinner, 158

Z

Zesty Potato Cheese Soup, 108
Zesty Tacos, 165
Zippy Steak Chili, 237
Zucchini Pie, 50

PAGE 40

COOKING TERMS

Here's a quick reference for some of the cooking terms used in Taste of Home recipes:

BASTE—To moisten food with melted butter, pan drippings, marinades or other liquid to add more flavor and juiciness.

BEAT—A rapid movement to combine ingredients using a fork, spoon, wire whisk or electric mixer.

BLEND—To combine ingredients until just mixed.

BOIL—To heat liquids until bubbles form that cannot be "stirred down." In the case of water, the temperature will reach 212°.

BONE—To remove all meat from the bone before cooking.

CREAM—To beat ingredients together to a smooth consistency, usually in the case of butter and sugar for baking.

DASH—A small amount of seasoning, less than 1/8 teaspoon. If using a shaker, a dash would comprise a quick flip of the container.

DREDGE—To coat foods with flour or other dry ingredients. Most often done with pot roasts and stew meat before browning.

FOLD—To incorporate several ingredients by careful and gentle turning with a spatula. Used generally with beaten egg whites or whipped cream when mixing into the rest of the ingredients to keep the batter light.

JULIENNE—To cut foods into long thin strips much like matchsticks. Used most often for salads and stir-fry dishes.

MINCE—To cut into very fine pieces. Used often for garlic or fresh herbs.

PARBOIL—To cook partially, usually used in the case of chicken, sausages and vegetables.

PARTIALLY SET—Describes the consistency of gelatin after it has been chilled for a small amount of time. Mixture should resemble the consistency of egg whites.

PUREE—To process foods to a smooth mixture. Can be prepared in an electric blender, food processor, food mill or sieve.

SAUTE—To fry quickly in a small amount of fat, stirring almost constantly. Most often done with onions, mushrooms and other chopped vegetables.

SCORE—To cut slits partway through the outer surface of foods. Often used with ham or flank steak.

STIR-FRY—To cook meats and/or vegetables with a constant stirring motion in a small amount of oil in a wok or skillet over high heat.